JESUS
OF NAZARETH

Jesus of Nazareth

PART TWO

Holy Week
From the Entrance into Jerusalem
to the Resurrection

by

Joseph Ratzinger
Pope Benedict XVI

English translation provided by the
Vatican Secretariat of State

IGNATIUS PRESS   SAN FRANCISCO

Original German edition:
Jesus von Nazareth:
Zweiter Teil:
Vom Einzug in Jerusalem
bis zur Auferstehung
© 2011 by Libreria Editrice Vaticana, Vatican City
All rights reserved

Translated by Philip J. Whitmore

Front cover art (left):
Christ's Passion: Descent from the Cross
and
Front cover art (right):
Christ's Appearance Behind Locked Doors
The Maestà Altarpiece
Painted 1308–1311 for the Cathedral of Siena
by Duccio di Buoninsegna
Museo dell'Opera Metropolitana, Siena, Italy
©Scala/Art Resource, New York

Photograph of Pope Benedict XVI by Stefano Spaziani

Cover design by Roxanne Mei Lum

© 2011 by Libreria Editrice Vaticana, Vatican City
Published in the United States © 2011 Ignatius Press, San Francisco
All rights reserved
ISBN 978-1-58617-500-9 (HB)
Library of Congress Control Number 2010937202
Printed in the United States of America ∞

CONTENTS

v

The following abbreviations are used for books of the Bible:

Acts	Acts of the Apostles	Jas	James
		Jer	Jeremiah
Amos	Amos	Jn	John
Bar	Baruch	1 Jn	1 John
1 Chron	1 Chronicles	2 Jn	2 John
2 Chron	2 Chronicles	3 Jn	3 John
Col	Colossians	Job	Job
1 Cor	1 Corinthians	Joel	Joel
2 Cor	2 Corinthians	Jon	Jonah
Dan	Daniel	Josh	Joshua
Deut	Deuteronomy	Jud	Judith
Eccles	Ecclesiastes	Jude	Jude
Eph	Ephesians	Judg	Judges
Esther	Esther	1 Kings	1 Kings
Ex	Exodus	2 Kings	2 Kings
Ezek	Ezekiel	Lam	Lamentations
Ezra	Ezra	Lev	Leviticus
Gal	Galatians	Lk	Luke
Gen	Genesis	1 Mac	1 Maccabees
Hab	Habakkuk	2 Mac	2 Maccabees
Hag	Haggai	Mal	Malachi
Heb	Hebrews	Mic	Micah
Hos	Hosea	Mk	Mark
Is	Isaiah	Mt	Matthew

Nahum	Nahum	1 Sam	1 Samuel
Neh	Nehemiah	2 Sam	2 Samuel
Num	Numbers	Sir	Sirach
Obad	Obadiah		(Ecclesiasticus)
1 Pet	1 Peter	Song	Song of Solomon
2 Pet	2 Peter	1 Thess	1 Thessalonians
Phil	Phillipians	2 Thess	2 Thessalonians
Philem	Philemon	1 Tim	1 Timothy
Prov	Proverbs	2 Tim	2 Timothy
Ps	Psalms	Tit	Titus
Rev	Revelation	Tob	Tobit
	(Apocalypse)	Wis	Wisdom
Rom	Romans	Zech	Zechariah
Ruth	Ruth	Zeph	Zephaniah

The following abbreviations are also used:

CCSL: Corpus Christianorum, Series Latina. Turnhout, 1953–. This is a collection of critical editions of all the Latin texts from the first eight centuries of the Christian era. By February 2010, 194 volumes had been published.

PG: Patrologia Graeca, ed. Jacques-Paul Migne, 161 vols., Paris, 1857–1866. This is a collection of ancient Christian sources in Greek.

PL: Patrologia Latina, ed. Jacques-Paul Migne, 217 vols., Paris, 1844–1855. This is a collection of ancient Christian sources in Latin.

TDNT: Theological Dictionary of the New Testament, ed. G. Kittel and G. Friedrich, 10 vols., Grand Rapids: Eerdmans, 1964–1976.

Publisher's Note

The Revised Standard Version (RSV) is the preferred translation for scriptural quotations within the text. In some instances, however, in order to reflect as clearly as possible the verbal associations emphasized by the author, it has been necessary to translate directly from the original biblical text.

At last I am able to present to the public Part Two of my book on Jesus of Nazareth. In view of the predictable variety of reactions to Part One, it has been a source of great encouragement to me that such leading exegetes as Martin Hengel (who sadly has since passed away), Peter Stuhlmacher, and Franz Mussner have strongly confirmed me in my desire to continue my work and to complete the task I had begun. While not agreeing with every detail of my book, they regarded it, in terms of both content and method, as an important contribution that should be brought to fruition.

A further joy for me is the fact that in the meantime this book has, so to speak, acquired an ecumenical companion in the comprehensive volume of the Protestant theologian Joachim Ringleben, *Jesus* (2008). Anyone who reads both books will see, on the one hand, the great difference in approach and in underlying theological presuppositions through which the contrasting confessional backgrounds of the two authors are concretely expressed. Yet, at the same time, a profound unity emerges in the essential understanding of the person of Jesus and his message. Despite the differing theological viewpoints, it is the same faith that is at work, and it is the same Lord Jesus who is encountered. It is my hope that these two books, both in their differences and in their essential common ground, can offer an ecumenical witness that, at the present time and in its own way, can serve the fundamental common task of Christians.

I also note with gratitude that discussion of the methodology and hermeneutics of exegesis, and of exegesis as a historical and theological discipline, is becoming more lively despite a certain resistance to some recent developments. I consider especially important the book by Marius Reiser *Bibelkritik und Auslegung der Heiligen Schrift* (2007), which brings together a series of previously published essays, forms them into a whole, and offers important guidelines for new exegetical approaches, without abandoning those aspects of the historical-critical method that are of continuing value.

One thing is clear to me: in two hundred years of exegetical work, historical-critical exegesis has already yielded its essential fruit. If scholarly exegesis is not to exhaust itself in constantly new hypotheses, becoming theologically irrelevant, it must take a methodological step forward and see itself once again as a theological discipline, without abandoning its historical character. It must learn that the positivistic hermeneutic on which it has been based does not constitute the only valid and definitively evolved rational approach; rather, it constitutes a specific and historically conditioned form of rationality that is both open to correction and completion and in need of it. It must recognize that a properly developed faith-hermeneutic is appropriate to the text and can be combined with a historical hermeneutic, aware of its limits, so as to form a methodological whole.

Naturally, this combination of two quite different types of hermeneutic is an art that needs to be constantly remastered. But it can be achieved, and as a result the great insights of patristic exegesis will be able to yield their fruit once more in a new context, as Reiser's book demonstrates. I would not presume to claim that this combination of the two hermeneutics is already fully accomplished in my book. But I hope to have taken a significant step in that direction. Fundamentally this is a matter of finally putting into practice the methodological principles formulated for exegesis by the Second Vatican Council (in *Dei Verbum* 12), a task that unfortunately has scarcely been attempted thus far.

Perhaps it would be helpful at this point to clarify once more the guiding intention of my book.

I need hardly say that I did not set out to write a "Life of Jesus". Excellent studies are already available concerning chronological and topographical questions to do with the life of Jesus. I refer especially to *Jesus of Nazareth: Message and History* by Joachim Gnilka (translated by Siegfried S. Schatzmann; Peabody, Mass., 1997) and to the exhaustive study by John P. Meier, *A Marginal Jew* (4 vols., New York, 1991, 1994, 2001, 2009).

A Catholic theologian has labeled my book, together with Romano Guardini's masterpiece, *The Lord*, as an example of "Christology from above", not without issuing a warning about the dangers inherent in such an approach. The truth is that I have not attempted to write a Christology. In the German-speaking world there is already a whole series of important Christologies by authors ranging from Wolfhart Pannenberg through Walter Kasper to Christoph Schönborn, to which the magnum opus of Karl-Heinz Menke, *Jesus ist Gott der Sohn* (2008), may now be added.

Closer to my intention is the comparison with the theological treatise on the mysteries of the life of Jesus, presented in its classic form by Saint Thomas Aquinas in his *Summa Theologiae* (*S. Th.* III, qq. 27–59). While my book has many points of contact with this treatise, it is nevertheless situated in a different historical and spiritual context, and in that sense it also has a different inner objective that determines the structure of the text in essential ways.

In the foreword to Part One, I stated that my concern was to present "the figure and the message of Jesus". Perhaps it would have been good to assign these two words—figure and message—as a subtitle to the book, in order to clarify its underlying intention. Exaggerating a little, one could say that I set out to discover the real Jesus, on the basis of whom something like a "Christology from below" would then become possible. The quest for the "historical Jesus", as conducted in mainstream critical exegesis in accordance with its hermeneutical presuppositions, lacks sufficient content to exert any significant historical impact. It is focused too much on the past for it to make possible a personal relationship with Jesus. In the combination of the two hermeneutics of which I spoke earlier, I have attempted to develop a way of observing and listening to the Jesus of the Gospels that can indeed lead to personal encounter and that, through collective listening with Jesus' disciples across the ages, can indeed attain sure knowledge of the real historical figure of Jesus.

This task was even more difficult in Part Two than in Part One, because only in this second volume do we encounter the decisive sayings and events of Jesus' life. I have tried to maintain a distance from any controversies over particular points and to consider only the essential words and deeds of Jesus—guided by the hermeneutic of faith, but at the same time adopting a responsible attitude toward historical reason, which is a necessary component of that faith.

Even if there will always be details that remain open for discussion, I still hope that I have been granted an insight into the figure of our Lord that can be helpful to all readers who seek to encounter Jesus and to believe in him.

On the basis of the underlying intention of the book as here expounded—to understand the figure of Jesus, his words and his actions—it is clear that the infancy narratives would not fall directly within the scope of the present book. I will try, however, to keep the promise that I made in Part One (p. xxiv) and to prepare a small monograph on this subject, if I am given the strength.

Rome, on the Feast of Saint Mark
25 April 2010

JOSEPH RATZINGER, BENEDICT XVI

CHAPTER ONE

The Entrance into Jerusalem and the Cleansing of the Temple

1. The Entrance into Jerusalem

Saint John's Gospel speaks of three Passover feasts celebrated by Jesus in the course of his public ministry: the first, which is linked to the cleansing of the Temple (2:13–25), the Passover of the multiplication of the loaves (6:4), and finally the Passover of his death and Resurrection (for example, 12:1, 13:1), which became "his" great Passover, the basis for the Christian celebration of Easter, the Christian Passover. The Synoptics contain just *one* Passover feast—that of the Cross and Resurrection; indeed, in Saint Luke's Gospel, Jesus' path is presented as a single pilgrim ascent from Galilee to Jerusalem.

To begin with, it is an "ascent" in a geographical sense: the Sea of Galilee is situated about 690 feet below sea level, whereas Jerusalem is on average 2500 feet above. The Synoptics each contain three prophecies of Jesus' Passion as steps in this ascent, steps that at the same time point to the inner ascent that is accomplished in the outward climb: going up to the Temple as the place where God wished "his name [to] dwell", in the words of the Book of Deuteronomy (12:11, 14:23).

The ultimate goal of Jesus' "ascent" is his self-offering on the Cross, which supplants the old sacrifices; it is the ascent that the Letter to the Hebrews describes as going up, not to a sanctuary made by human hands, but to heaven itself, into the presence of God (9:24). This ascent into God's presence leads via the Cross—it is the ascent toward "loving to the end" (cf. Jn 13:1), which is the real mountain of God.

The immediate goal of Jesus' pilgrim journey is, of course, Jerusalem, the Holy City with its Temple, and the "Passover of the Jews", as John calls it (2:13). Jesus had set out with the Twelve, but they were gradually joined by an ever-increasing crowd of pilgrims. Matthew and Mark tell us that as he was leaving Jericho there was already "a great multitude" following Jesus (Mt 20:29; Mk 10:46).

An incident occurring on this final stretch of the journey increases the expectation of the one who is to come and focuses the wayfarers' attention upon Jesus in an altogether new way. Along the path sits a blind beggar, Bartimaeus. Having discovered that Jesus is among the pilgrims, he cries out incessantly: "Jesus, Son of David, have mercy on me!" (Mk 10:47). People try to calm him down, but it is useless, and finally Jesus calls him over. To his plea, "Master, let me receive my sight", Jesus replies, "Go your way; your faith has made you well."

Bartimaeus could see again, "and he followed [Jesus] on the way" (Mk 10:48–52). Now that he could see, he became a fellow pilgrim on the way to Jerusalem. The Davidic theme and the accompanying Messianic hope now spread to the crowd: Was it possible that this Jesus, with whom they were walking, might actually be the new David for whom they were waiting? As he made his entrance into the Holy City, had the hour come when he would reestablish the Davidic kingdom?

The preparations that Jesus makes with his disciples reinforce this hope. Jesus comes from Bethphage and Bethany to the Mount of Olives, the place from which the Messiah was expected to enter. He sends two disciples ahead of him, telling them that they will find a tethered donkey, a young animal on which no one has yet sat. They are to untie it and bring it to him. Should anyone ask by what authority they do so, they are to say: "The Lord has need of it" (Mk 11:3; Lk 19:31). The disciples find the donkey. As anticipated, they are asked by what right they act; they give the response they were told to give—and they are allowed to carry out their mission. So Jesus rides on a borrowed donkey into the city and, soon afterward, has the animal returned to its owner.

To today's reader, this may all seem fairly harmless, but for the Jewish contemporaries of Jesus it is full of mysterious allusions. The theme of the kingdom and its promises is ever-present. Jesus claims the right of kings, known throughout antiquity, to requisition modes of transport (cf. Pesch, *Markusevangelium* II, p. 180). The use of an

3

animal on which no one had yet sat is a further pointer to the right of kings. Most striking, though, are the Old Testament allusions that give a deeper meaning to the whole episode.

The first recalls Genesis 49:10–11—Jacob's blessing, in which Judah is promised the scepter, the ruler's staff, which is not to depart from between his feet "until he comes to whom it belongs; and to him shall be the obedience of the peoples". Of him it is said that he binds his donkey to the vine (49:11). The tethered donkey, then, indicates the one who is to come, "to [whom] shall be the obedience of the peoples".

Even more important is Zechariah 9:9, the text that Matthew and John quote explicitly for an understanding of "Palm Sunday": "Tell the daughter of Zion, Behold, your king is coming to you, humble, and mounted on a donkey, and on a colt, the foal of a donkey" (Mt 21:5; cf. Zech 9:9; Jn 12:15). The meaning of these prophetic words for the understanding of the figure of Jesus we have already considered at some length in our exegesis of the beatitude concerning the meek (cf. Part One, pp. 80–84). He is a king who destroys the weapons of war, a king of peace and a king of simplicity, a king of the poor. And finally we saw that he reigns over a kingdom that stretches from sea to sea, embracing the whole world (cf. ibid., pp. 81–82); we were reminded of the new world-encompassing kingdom of Jesus that extends from sea to sea in the communities of the breaking of bread in communion with Jesus Christ, as the kingdom of his peace (cf. ibid., p. 84). None of this could be seen at the time, but in retrospect those things that could be indicated only from afar, hidden in the prophetic vision, are revealed.

For now let us note this: Jesus is indeed making a royal claim. He wants his path and his action to be understood in terms of Old Testament promises that are fulfilled in his person. The Old Testament speaks of him—and vice versa: he acts and lives within the word of God, not according to projects and wishes of his own. His claim is based on obedience to the mission received from his Father. His path is a path into the heart of God's word. At the same time, through this anchoring of the text in Zechariah 9:9, a "Zealot" exegesis of the kingdom is excluded: Jesus is not building on violence; he is not instigating a military revolt against Rome. His power is of another kind: it is in God's poverty, God's peace, that he identifies the only power that can redeem.

Let us return to the narrative. The donkey is brought to Jesus, and now something unexpected happens: the disciples lay their garments on the donkey. While Matthew (21:7) and Mark (11:7) simply say: "and he sat upon it", Luke writes: "They set Jesus upon it" (19:35). This is the expression that is used in the First Book of Kings in the account of Solomon's installation on the throne of his father, David. There we read that King David commanded Zadok the priest, Nathan the prophet, and Benaiah: "Take with you the servants of your lord, and cause Solomon my son to ride on my own mule, and bring him down to Gihon; and let Zadok the priest and Nathan the prophet there anoint him king over Israel" (1 Kings 1:33–34).

The spreading out of garments likewise belongs to the tradition of Israelite kingship (cf. 2 Kings 9:13). What the disciples do is a gesture of enthronement in the tradition of the Davidic kingship, and it points to the Messianic hope that grew out of the Davidic tradition. The pilgrims who came to Jerusalem with Jesus are caught up in the disciples' enthusiasm. They now spread their garments on the street along which Jesus passes. They pluck branches from the trees and cry out verses from Psalm 118, words of blessing from Israel's pilgrim liturgy, which on their lips become a Messianic proclamation: "Hosanna! Blessed is he who comes in the name of the Lord! Blessed is the kingdom of our father David that is coming! Hosanna in the highest!" (Mk 11:9–10; cf. Ps 118:26).

This acclamation is recounted by all four evangelists, albeit with some variation in detail. There is no need here to go into the differences, important though they are for "tradition criticism" and for the theological vision of the individual evangelists. Let us try merely to understand the essential outlines, especially since the Christian liturgy has adopted this greeting, interpreting it in the light of the Church's Easter faith.

First comes the exclamation "Hosanna!" Originally this was a word of urgent supplication, meaning something like: Come to our aid! The priests would repeat it in a monotone on the seventh day of the Feast of Tabernacles, while processing seven times around the altar of sacrifice, as an urgent prayer for rain. But as the Feast of Tabernacles gradually changed from a feast of petition into one of

6

praise, so too the cry for help turned more and more into a shout of jubilation (cf. Lohse, *TDNT* IX, p. 682).

By the time of Jesus, the word had also acquired Messianic overtones. In the Hosanna acclamation, then, we find an expression of the complex emotions of the pilgrims accompanying Jesus and of his disciples: joyful praise of God at the moment of the processional entry, hope that the hour of the Messiah had arrived, and at the same time a prayer that the Davidic kingship and hence God's kingship over Israel would be reestablished.

As mentioned above, this passage from Psalm 118: "Blessed is he who enters in the name of the LORD!" had originally formed part of Israel's pilgrim liturgy used for greeting pilgrims as they entered the city or the Temple. This emerges clearly from the second part of the verse: "We bless you from the house of the LORD." It was a blessing that the priests addressed and, as it were, bestowed upon the pilgrims as they arrived. But in the meantime the phrase "who enters in the name of the LORD" had acquired Messianic significance. It had become a designation of the one promised by God. So from being a pilgrim blessing, it became praise of Jesus, a greeting to him as the one who comes in the name of the Lord, the one awaited and proclaimed by all the promises.

It may be that this strikingly Davidic note, found only in Saint Mark's text, conveys most accurately the pilgrims' actual expectations at that moment. Luke, on the other hand, writing for Gentile Christians, completely omits the Hosanna and the reference to David, and in its place he gives an exclamation reminiscent of Christmas: "Peace in heaven and glory in the highest!" (19:38; cf. 2:14). All three Synoptic Gospels, as well as Saint John, make it very clear that the scene of Messianic homage to Jesus was played out on his entry into the city and that those taking part were not the inhabitants of Jerusalem, but the crowds who accompanied Jesus and entered the Holy City with him.

This point is made most clearly in Matthew's account through the passage immediately following the Hosanna to Jesus, Son of David: "When he entered Jerusalem, all the city was stirred, saying: Who is this? And the crowds said: This is the prophet Jesus from Nazareth of Galilee" (Mt 21:10–11). The parallel with the story of the wise men from the East is unmistakable. On that occasion, too, the people in the city of Jerusalem knew nothing of the new-born king of the Jews; the news about him caused Jerusalem to be "troubled" (Mt 2:3). Now the people were "quaking": the word that Matthew uses, *eseísthē* (*seíō*), describes the vibration caused by an earthquake.

People had heard of the prophet from Nazareth, but he did not appear to have any importance for Jerusalem, and the people there did not know him. The crowd that paid homage to Jesus at the gateway to the city was not the same crowd that later demanded his crucifixion. In this two-stage account of the failure to recognize Jesus—through a combination of indifference and fear—we see something of the city's tragedy of which Jesus spoke a number of times, most poignantly in his eschatological discourse.

Matthew's account has another important text concerning the reception given to Jesus in the Holy City. After the cleansing of the Temple, the children in the Temple repeat the words of homage: "Hosanna to the Son of David!" (21:15). Jesus defends the children's joyful acclamation against the criticism of "the chief priests and the scribes" by quoting Psalm 8: "Out of the mouths of babies and infants you have brought perfect praise" (v. 2). We will return later to this scene in our discussion of the cleansing of the Temple. For now let us try to understand what Jesus meant by the reference to Psalm 8, with which he opened up a much broader salvation-historical perspective.

His meaning becomes clear if we recall the story recounted by all three Synoptic evangelists, in which children were brought to Jesus "that he might touch them". Despite the resistance of the disciples, who wanted to protect him from this imposition, Jesus calls the children to himself, lays his hands on them, and blesses them. He explains this gesture with the words: "Let the children come to me; do not hinder them; for to such belongs the kingdom of God. Truly, I say to you, whoever does not receive the kingdom of God like a child shall not enter it" (Mk 10:13–16). The children serve Jesus as an example of the littleness before God that is necessary in order to pass through the "eye of a needle", the image that he used immediately afterward in the story of the rich young man (Mk 10:17–27).

In the previous chapter we find the scene where Jesus responds to the disciples' dispute over rank by placing a child in their midst, taking it into his arms and saying:

9

"Whoever receives one such child in my name receives me" (Mk 9:33–37). Jesus identifies himself with the child—he himself has become small. As Son he does nothing of himself, but he acts wholly from the Father and for the Father.

The passage that follows a few verses later can also be understood on this basis. Here Jesus speaks no longer of children, but of "little ones", and the term "little ones" designates believers, the company of the disciples of Jesus Christ (cf. Mk 9:42). In the faith they have found this true littleness that leads mankind into its truth.

This brings us back to the children's Hosanna: in the light of Psalm 8, the praise of these children appears as an anticipation of the great outpouring of praise that his "little ones" will sing to him far beyond the present hour.

The early Church, then, was right to read this scene as an anticipation of what she does in her liturgy. Even in the earliest post-Easter liturgical text that we possess— the *Didachē* (ca. 100)—before the distribution of the holy gifts the Hosanna appears, together with the Maranatha: "Let his grace draw near, and let this present world pass away. Hosanna to the God of David. Whoever is holy, let him approach; whoever is not, let him repent. Maranatha. Amen" (10, 6).

The *Benedictus* also entered the liturgy at a very early stage. For the infant Church, "Palm Sunday" was not a thing of the past. Just as the Lord entered the Holy City that day on a donkey, so too the Church saw him coming again and again in the humble form of bread and wine.

The Church greets the Lord in the Holy Eucharist as the one who is coming now, the one who has entered into her midst. At the same time, she greets him as the one who continues to come, the one who leads us toward his coming. As pilgrims, we go up to him; as a pilgrim, he comes to us and takes us up with him in his "ascent" to the Cross and Resurrection, to the definitive Jerusalem that is already growing in the midst of this world in the communion that unites us with his body.

2. *The Cleansing of the Temple*

Mark tells us that after the welcome he received, Jesus went into the Temple, saw everything that was there, and as it was already late he returned to Bethany, where he was staying that week. On the following day, he went into the Temple again and began to drive out those who were selling and those who were buying: "He overturned the tables of the money-changers and the seats of those who sold pigeons" (11:15).

He justified this action using a quotation from Isaiah that he combined with a passage from Jeremiah: "'My house shall be called a house of prayer for all the nations[.]' But you have made it a den of robbers" (Mk 11:17; cf. Is 56:7; Jer 7:11). What was Jesus doing? What did he want to say?

In the exegetical literature there are three principal lines of interpretation that we must briefly consider.

First, there is the thesis that the cleansing of the Temple constituted an attack, not on the Temple as such, but only on its misuse. After all, the traders were licensed by the Jewish authorities, who made a large profit from their activities. To this extent the trading of the moneychangers and cattle-merchants was legitimate according to the rules in force at the time; indeed, it made sense to exchange the widely circulated Roman coins (considered idolatrous, since they bore the emperor's image) for Temple currency in the spacious Court of the Gentiles and to sell animals for sacrifice in the same place. Yet this mixture of Temple and business did not correspond to the purpose for which the Court of the Gentiles was intended in terms of the Temple's overall layout.

In acting as he did, Jesus was attacking the existing practice that had been set up by the Temple aristocracy, but he was not violating the Law and the Prophets—on the contrary: he was implementing the true law, Israel's divine law, in opposition to a custom that had become deeply corrupt and had become "law". Only this can explain the failure to intervene on the part of either the Temple police or the Roman cohort that stood ready in the castle Antonia. The Temple authorities merely asked Jesus by what authority he acted in this way.

This supports the thesis that Vittorio Messori in particular has argued at length, namely, that in cleansing the Temple, Jesus was acting in accordance with the Law and opposing the Temple's misuse. Were we simply to conclude that Jesus "appears as a mere reformer defending Jewish precepts on holiness" (as Eduard Schweizer says, quoted in Pesch, *Markusevangelium* II, p. 200), we would fail to do justice to the significance of the incident. Jesus' words show that his claim goes deeper, since by acting in this way he was seeking to fulfill the Law and the Prophets.

Now we come to a second, conflicting exegesis—the political, revolutionary interpretation of the incident. Even at the time of the Enlightenment, attempts were made to portray Jesus as a political agitator. But the two-volume work by Robert Eisler, *Iesous basileus ou basileusas* (Heidelberg, 1929/1930), was the first to argue consistently from the whole of the New Testament corpus that "Jesus was a political revolutionist of apocalyptic stamp, who attempted an uprising in Jerusalem and was taken captive and put to death by the Romans" (Hengel, *Was Jesus a Revolutionist?* p. 4). The book created quite a stir, but given the particular circumstances of the 1930s, it had little lasting impact at the time.

Not until the 1960s did an intellectual and political climate emerge in which this vision could acquire explosive force. Now it was Samuel George Frederick Brandon, in his book *Jesus and the Zealots* (New York, 1967), who made the exegesis of Jesus as a political revolutionary seem academically plausible. He locates Jesus in the line of the Zealot movement, which looked to the priest Phinehas, Aaron's grandson, for its biblical foundation. Phinehas had run his spear through an Israelite who had become involved with an idolatrous woman. He was considered a model for those who were "zealous" for the Law, for the worship of God alone (cf. Num 25).

The Zealot movement traced its historical origins to the initiative of Mattathias, father of the Maccabee brothers, who expressed in these words his opposition to the attempt to absorb Israel into the uniform Hellenistic culture, thereby robbing it of its religious identity: "We will not obey the king's words by turning aside from our religion to the right hand or to the left" (1 Mac 2:22). This declaration led to an uprising against the Hellenistic tyranny. Mattathias put his words into action: he killed the man who, according to the instructions of the Hellenistic authorities, wanted to sacrifice publicly to the gods. "When Mattathias saw it, he burned with zeal ... he ran and killed him upon the altar.... Thus he burned with zeal for the law" (1 Mac 2:24–26). From that moment, the slogan "zeal" (in Greek, *zēlos*) became the byword for readiness to stand up for Israel's faith with force, to defend Israel's law and freedom by treading the path of violence.

According to the thesis of Eisler and Brandon—which led to a great wave of political theologies and theologies of revolution in the 1960s—Jesus belongs within this line of the "*zēlos*" of the Zealots. The cleansing of the Temple serves as the central proof of this thesis, since it was unambiguously an act of violence that could not have been achieved without violence, even though the evangelists did their best to conceal this. Moreover, the fact that the people hailed Jesus as Son of David and harbinger of the Davidic kingdom is construed as a political statement, and the crucifixion of Jesus by the Romans for claiming to be "King of the Jews" is seen as definitive proof that he was a revolutionary—a Zealot—and that he was executed as such.

Since that time, there has been a noticeable reduction in the wave of theologies of revolution that attempt to justify violence as a means of building a better world—the "kingdom"—by interpreting Jesus as a "Zealot". The cruel consequences of religiously motivated violence are only too evident to us all. Violence does not build up the kingdom of God, the kingdom of humanity. On the contrary, it is a favorite instrument of the Antichrist, however idealistic its religious motivation may be. It serves, not humanity, but inhumanity.

But what about Jesus? Was he a Zealot? Was the cleansing of the Temple a summons to political revolution? Jesus' whole ministry and his message—from the temptations in the desert, his baptism in the Jordan, the Sermon on the Mount, right up to the parable of the Last Judgment (Mt 25) and his response to Peter's confession—point in a radically different direction, as we saw in Part One of this book.

No; violent revolution, killing others in God's name, was not his way. His "zeal" for the kingdom of God took quite a different form. We do not know exactly what the pilgrims had in mind when they spoke, while "enthroning" Jesus, of the "coming kingdom of our father David". But what Jesus himself thought and intended he made very clear by his gestures and by the prophetic words that formed the context for his actions.

At the time of David, the donkey had been a sign of kingship, and so Zechariah, basing himself on this tradition, depicts the new king of peace riding into the Holy

City on a donkey. But even in Zechariah's day, and still more by the time of Jesus, it was the horse that had come to signify the might of the mighty, while the donkey had become the animal of the poor, and so it served to express an entirely different image of kingship.

It is true that Zechariah proclaims a kingdom that extends "from sea to sea". Yet precisely in this way he distances himself from any national frame of reference and points toward a new universality, in which the world finds God's peace and is united, beyond borders of any kind, in worship of the one God. In the kingdom of which he speaks, the weapons of war are destroyed. What for him remains a mysterious vision—the precise shape of which cannot be clearly discerned by the contemplation of the one coming from afar—slowly becomes clear in the course of Jesus' ministry; only after the Resurrection, though, as the Gospel is brought to the Gentiles, does it gradually take on a definite shape. Yet even at the time of the entrance into Jerusalem, the connection with late prophecy in which Jesus situated his action gave to his gesture a direction that was radically opposed to the "Zealot" interpretation.

In the prophecy of Zechariah, Jesus found not only the image of the king of peace arriving on a donkey, but also the vision of the slain shepherd, who saves by his death, as well as the image of the Pierced One on whom all eyes will gaze. The other broad frame of reference within which Jesus located his ministry was the vision of the Suffering Servant who, in serving, offers up his life for the multitude and thus brings salvation (cf. Is 52:13—53:12).

This late prophecy is the interpretative key with which Jesus unlocks the Old Testament. After Easter, he himself would become the key to a new reading of the Law and the Prophets.

Let us now consider the interpretation that Jesus himself gives to the act of cleansing the Temple. We begin with Mark's account, which, apart from one or two details, is very similar to Matthew's and Luke's. After the cleansing of the Temple, so Mark tells us, "[Jesus] taught". The essential content of this "teaching" is succinctly expressed in these words of Jesus: "Is it not written: 'My house shall be called a house of prayer for all the nations'? But you have made it a den of robbers" (Mk 11:17). In this synthesis of Jesus' "teaching" on the Temple—as we saw earlier—two different prophecies are combined.

The first is the universalist vision of the Prophet Isaiah (56:7) of a future in which all peoples come together in the house of God to worship the Lord as the one God. In the layout of the Temple, the vast Court of the Gentiles in which this whole episode takes place is the open space to which the whole world is invited, in order to pray there to the one God. Jesus' action underlines this profound openness of expectation which animated Israel's faith. Even if Jesus consciously limits his own ministry to Israel, he still embodies the universalist tendency to open Israel in such a way that all can recognize in its God the one God common to the whole world. In answer to the question of what Jesus actually brought to mankind, we argued in Part One of this book that he brought God to the nations (p. 44). According to his own testimony, this fundamental purpose is what lies behind the cleansing of the Temple: to remove whatever obstacles there may be to the common recognition and worship of God—and thereby to open up a space for common worship.

A similar conclusion may be drawn from a brief scene recounted by John concerning "Palm Sunday". We must of course remember that in John's account, the Temple cleansing took place during Jesus' *first* Passover, at the beginning of his ministry. The Synoptics, on the other hand—as we have already seen—contain only *one* Passover, and so the cleansing of the Temple perforce takes place in the very last days of Jesus' ministry. While the majority of exegetes assumed until recently that John's chronology is "theological" and not historically exact, today it is becoming clearer that there are good reasons to consider John's account chronologically accurate as well—here, as elsewhere, he shows himself to be very well informed concerning times, places, and sequences of events, notwithstanding the profoundly theological character of the material. Yet there is no need for us to enter into what is ultimately a secondary discussion. Let us simply examine this brief episode, which, although it does not coincide chronologically in John's account with the cleansing of the Temple, nevertheless sheds further light on its inner meaning.

The evangelist tells us that among the pilgrims there were also some Greeks, "who went up to worship at the feast" (Jn 12:20). These Greeks approached "Philip, who was from Bethsaida in Galilee," with the request: "Sir, we wish to see Jesus" (12:21). In the man with the Greek name from half-Gentile Galilee, they evidently saw a mediator who could give them access to Jesus. We may detect a distant echo in these words spoken by Greeks, "Sir, we wish to see Jesus", of Saint Paul's vision of the Macedonian who said to him: "Come over to Macedonia and help us" (Acts 16:9). The Gospel goes on to say that Philip discussed the matter with Andrew and that the two of them together brought the request to Jesus. Jesus replied—as so often in John's Gospel—in a mysterious way that was puzzling at the time: "The hour has come for the Son of man to be glorified. Truly, truly, I say to you, unless a grain of wheat falls into the earth and dies, it remains alone; but if it dies, it bears much fruit" (12:23–24). When asked by a group of Greek pilgrims for an opportunity to meet him, Jesus responds with a prophecy of the Passion, in which he points to his imminent death as "glorification"—glorification that is manifested in great fruitfulness. What does this mean?

It is not some brief, external encounter between Jesus and the Greeks that matters. There is to be another, far deeper encounter. The Greeks will indeed "see" him: through the Cross he comes toward them. He comes as the grain of wheat that has died, and he will bear fruit among them. They will see his "glory": in the crucified Jesus they will find the true God, the one they were seeking in their myths and their philosophy. The universality of which Isaiah's prophecy speaks (56:7) is brought into the light of the Cross: from the Cross, the one God becomes visible to the nations; in the Son they will recognize the Father, that is to say, the one God, who revealed himself in the burning bush.

Let us now return to the cleansing of the Temple. Here Isaiah's universalist promise is combined with this prophecy from Jeremiah (7:11): "You have made my house into a den of robbers." We will return briefly to Jeremiah's battle over the Temple in our exegesis of Jesus' eschatological discourse, but let us anticipate the essential argument here. Jeremiah is an impassioned advocate of the unity of worship and life in the context of divine justice. He fights against a politicization of the faith that would see God's constant protection of the Temple as something guaranteed, for the sake of maintaining the cult. But God does not protect a Temple that has been turned into a "den of robbers".

In the combination of worship and trade, which Jesus denounces, he evidently sees the situation of Jeremiah's time repeating itself. In this sense, his words and actions constitute a warning that could be understood, together with his reference to the destruction of this Temple, as an echo of Jeremiah. But neither Jeremiah nor Jesus is responsible for destroying the Temple: both, through their passion, indicate who and what it is that truly destroys the Temple.

This exegesis of the cleansing of the Temple emerges even more clearly in a saying of Jesus that only John quotes in this context but that Matthew and Mark attribute, in somewhat distorted form, to the false witnesses at Jesus' trial. There is no doubt that this saying originated on the lips of Jesus, and it is equally clear that it belongs in the context of the cleansing of the Temple.

In Mark's Gospel, the false witness accuses Jesus of saying: "I will destroy this temple that is made with hands, and in three days I will build another, not made with hands" (Mk 14:58). The "witness" probably comes quite close to Jesus' actual words, but he is mistaken in one crucial point: it is not Jesus who destroys the Temple—it is those who turn it into a den of robbers who abandon it to destruction, just as in Jeremiah's day.

In John's Gospel, Jesus' actual words are rendered thus: "Destroy this temple, and in three days I will raise it up" (2:19). This was how Jesus responded to the Jewish officials' demand for a sign to demonstrate his authority for acting as he did in the cleansing of the Temple. His "sign" is the Cross and Resurrection. The Cross and Resurrection give him authority as the one who ushers in true worship. Jesus justifies himself through his Passion—the sign of Jonah that he gives to Israel and to the world.

Yet this saying has an even deeper significance. As John rightly says, the disciples understood it in its full depth only after the Resurrection, in their memory—in the collective memory of the community of disciples enlightened by the Holy Spirit, that is, the Church.

The rejection and crucifixion of Jesus means at the same time the end of this Temple. The era of the Temple is over. A new worship is being introduced, in a Temple not built by human hands. This Temple is his body, the

Risen One, who gathers the peoples and unites them in the sacrament of his body and blood. He himself is the new Temple of humanity. The crucifixion of Jesus is at the same time the destruction of the old Temple. With his Resurrection, a new way of worshipping God begins, no longer on this or that mountain, but "in spirit and truth" (Jn 4:23).

So what can we say on the subject of Jesus' "*zēlos*"? John provides a most helpful saying, specifically in the context of the cleansing of the Temple, that answers this question precisely and thoroughly. He tells us that, at the time of the cleansing of the Temple, the disciples remembered that it is written: "Zeal for your house will consume me" (2:17). This is taken from the great "Passion Psalm" 69. Living according to God's word leads to the psalmist's isolation; for him it becomes an additional source of suffering imposed upon him by the enemies who surround him. "Save me, O God! For the waters have come up to my neck.... It is for your sake that I have borne reproach.... Zeal for your house has consumed me ..." (Ps 69:1, 7, 9).

In the just man exposed to suffering, the memory of the disciples recognized Jesus: zeal for God's house leads him to the Passion, to the Cross. This is the fundamental transformation that Jesus brought to the theme of zeal—*zēlos*. The "zeal" that would serve God through violence he transformed into the zeal of the Cross. Thus he definitively established the criterion for true zeal—the zeal of self-giving love. This zeal must become the Christian's goal; it contains the authoritative answer to the question about Jesus' relation to the Zealot movement.

This exegesis is further confirmed by two brief episodes with which Matthew concludes the account of the cleansing of the Temple.

"The blind and the lame came to him in the temple, and he healed them" (21:14). In contrast to the cattle-trading and money-changing, Jesus brings his healing goodness. This is the true cleansing of the Temple. Jesus does not come as a destroyer. He does not come bearing the sword of the revolutionary. He comes with the gift of healing. He turns toward those who, because of their afflictions, have been driven to the margins of life and society. He reveals God as the one who loves and his power as the power of love.

All this is further illustrated by the fact that the children repeat the Hosanna acclamation that the great had denied him (Mt 21:15). From these "little ones", praise will always come to him (cf. Ps 8:2)—from those able to see with pure and undivided hearts, from those who are open to his goodness.

These two brief episodes, then, announce the coming of the new Temple, the Temple that Jesus came on earth to build.

CHAPTER TWO

Jesus' Eschatological Discourse

In Saint Matthew's Gospel, after the "woes" with which
Jesus denounced the scribes and Pharisees—that is to say,
in the context of the discourses given after his entrance
into Jerusalem—there is a mysterious saying of Jesus that
Luke also quotes (albeit at an earlier point, during the
journey toward the Holy City): "O Jerusalem, Jerusalem, killing the prophets and stoning those who are sent
to you! How often would I have gathered your children
together as a hen gathers her brood under her wings,
and you would not! Behold, your house is forsaken and
desolate ..." (Mt 23:37–38; Lk 13:34–35). This passage
clearly reveals Jesus' profound love for Jerusalem and his
impassioned efforts to elicit from the Holy City a positive
response to the message he must proclaim, the message
with which he takes his place in the long line of God's
messengers from earlier salvation history.

The image of the protective, solicitous mother bird
comes from the Old Testament: God "found [Jacob] in a

desert land ... he encircled him, he cared for him, he kept him as the apple of his eye. Like an eagle that stirs up its nest, that flutters over its young, spreading out its wings, catching them, bearing them on its pinions" (Deut 32:10–11). One is reminded of the beautiful passage from Psalm 36:7: "How precious is your mercy, O God! The children of men take refuge in the shadow of your wings."

Here Jesus expresses his own ministry and his summons to discipleship in terms of the powerful goodness of God himself, who protects Jerusalem with outstretched wings (Is 31:5). Yet this same goodness invites the free consent of the chicks, which they refuse: "and you would not!" (Mt 23:37).

The misfortune to which this refusal leads is described by Jesus mysteriously yet unmistakably in a saying couched in the language of ancient prophecy. Jeremiah records the words spoken by God concerning the abuses in the Temple: "I have forsaken my house; I have abandoned my heritage" (12:7). Jesus says exactly the same thing: "Your house is forsaken" (Mt 23:38). God is withdrawing. The Temple is no longer the place where he sets down his name. It will be left empty; henceforth it is merely "your house".

There is a remarkable parallel to this saying of Jesus in the writings of Flavius Josephus, the historian of the Jewish War. Tacitus likewise took up the same idea in his own historical writing (cf. *Hist.* 5, 13). Flavius Josephus reports strange happenings in the final years before the outbreak of the Jewish War, all of which, in different and unsettling

ways, heralded the end of the Temple. The historian tells
of seven such signs altogether. Here I shall limit my comments to the one that bears a strange resemblance to the
somber words of Jesus quoted above.

The event took place at Pentecost in A.D. 66 "At
the Feast of Pentecost, when the priests had gone into
the inner court of the Temple at night to perform the
usual ceremonies, they declared that they were aware,
first of a violent movement and a loud crash, then of
a concerted cry: 'Let us go hence'" (*The Jewish War*,
p. 361). Whatever exactly may have happened, one thing
is clear: in the final years before the dramatic events of
the year 70, the Temple was enveloped in a mysterious
premonition that its end was approaching. "Your house
will be deserted." Using the first person plural that is
characteristic of divine utterances in the Bible (cf. Gen
1:26, for example), God himself is announcing ("Let us
go hence!") that he is to depart from the Temple, to leave
it "empty". A historic change of incalculable significance
was in the air.

After this saying about the deserted house—which prophesies, not yet directly the destruction of the Temple, but
rather its inner demise, the loss of its meaning as a place of
encounter between God and man—Matthew's text continues with Jesus' great eschatological discourse, which
takes as its central themes the destruction of the Temple,
the destruction of Jerusalem, the Last Judgment, and the
end of the world. This discourse, found in all three Synoptic Gospels with certain variations, could perhaps be

described as the most difficult text in the whole of the Gospels.

This is due in some measure to the difficulty of the content. The text refers partly to historical events that have taken place in the meantime, but mainly to a future that lies altogether beyond time and reality as we know it: indeed, it brings them to an end. A future is proclaimed that exceeds our categories yet can only be represented using models drawn from our experience, and they are inevitably inadequate for the purpose. This explains why Jesus, speaking as he always does in continuity with the Law and the Prophets, presents this material using a tissue of scriptural allusions, within which he locates the new element of his mission, the mission of the Son of Man.

While this vision of things to come is expressed largely through images drawn from tradition, intended to point us toward realities that defy description, the difficulty of the content is compounded by all the problems arising from the text's redaction history: the very fact that Jesus' words here are intended as continuations of tradition rather than literal descriptions of things to come meant that the redactors of the material could take these continuations a stage further, in the light of their particular situations and their audience's capacity to understand, while taking care to remain true to the essential content of Jesus' message.

It cannot be the task of this book to enter into the text's many detailed problems of redaction criticism and history of transmission. I shall limit myself to exploring three

aspects of Jesus' eschatological discourse in which the
underlying intentions of its composition become clear.

1. *The End of the Temple*

Before returning to the words of Jesus, we must cast a
glance at the historical events of the year 70. The Jewish
War had begun in the year 66, with the expulsion of the
procurator Gessius Florus and the successful resistance to
the Roman counterattack. This was not merely a war of
Jews against Romans: in broader terms, it was a civil war
between rival Jewish factions and their ringleaders. This was
what accounted for the full horror of the fight for Jerusalem.

Eusebius of Caesarea (d. ca. 339) and—from a different
perspective—Epiphanius of Salamis (d. 403) tell us that
even before the beginning of the siege of Jerusalem, the
Christians had fled to the city of Pella beyond the Jordan.
According to Eusebius, they decided to flee after a command to do so had been communicated to "those who
were worthy" by a revelation (*Hist. Eccl.* III/5). Epiphanius, on the other hand, writes: "Christ had told them to
abandon Jerusalem and go elsewhere, because it would
be besieged" (*Haer.* 29, 8). In fact we find an instruction
to flee in Jesus' eschatological discourse: "But when you
see the desolating sacrilege set up where it ought not to
be .... then let those who are in Judea flee to the moun-
tains ..." (Mk 13:14).

It cannot be determined which event or reality it was
that the Christians identified as the sign of the "abomination that makes desolate", precipitating their departure,

but there was no shortage of possible candidates—incidents in the course of the Jewish War that could be interpreted as this sign foretold by Jesus. The expression itself is taken from the Book of Daniel (9:27, 11:31, 12:11), where it referred to the Hellenistic desecration of the Temple. This symbolic description, drawn from Israel's history, is open to a variety of interpretations as a prophecy of things to come. So Eusebius' text is thoroughly plausible, in the sense that certain highly regarded members of the early Christian community could have recognized in some particular event, "by a revelation", the sign that had been foretold, and they could have interpreted it as an instruction to begin their flight.

Alexander Mittelstaedt points out that in the summer of 66, the former high priest Annas II was chosen, together with Joseph ben Gorion, as director of military operations for the war—the same Annas who a few years earlier, in A.D. 62, had decreed the death of James, "brother of the Lord" and leader of the Jewish Christian community (*Lukas als Historiker*, p. 68). The appointment of Annas could easily have been interpreted by the Jewish Christians as a sign for them to leave. Admittedly, this is only one hypothesis among many. The flight of the Jewish Christians nevertheless reinforces with great clarity the Christians' rejection of the "Zealot" reading of the message of the Bible and of Jesus himself: their hope is of an altogether different kind.

Let us return to the Jewish War. Vespasian, who had been put in charge of the operation by Nero, suspended all military action when the emperor's death was announced in the year 68. Soon afterward, on 1 July 69, Vespasian himself was proclaimed the new emperor. So he assigned the task of conquering Jerusalem to his son Titus.

According to Flavius Josephus, Titus must have arrived at the gates of the Holy City just at the time of the Passover feast, on the fourteenth day of the month Nisan, and therefore on the fortieth anniversary of Jesus' crucifixion. Thousands of pilgrims were pouring into Jerusalem. John of Gischala, one of the rival leaders of the rebellion, smuggled armed fighters, disguised as pilgrims, into the Temple, where they began to massacre the followers of his opponent, Eleazar ben Simon, and so once again the sanctuary was defiled with innocent blood (cf. Mittelstaedt, *Lukas als Historiker* p. 72). Yet this was only a foretaste of the unconscionable cruelties that ensued as the fanaticism of one side and the mounting anger of the other spiraled into ever-increasing brutality.

There is no need here to consider the details of the conquest and destruction of city and Temple. Yet it may be useful to reproduce the text with which Mittelstaedt summarizes the cruel unfolding of the drama: "The end of the Temple took place in three stages: first the suspension of the regular sacrifice, by which the sanctuary was reduced to a fortress, then it was set on fire, again in three stages ... and finally the ruins were demolished after the fall of the city. The decisive destruction ... took place through fire; the subsequent demolition is just a postscript ... those who survived and did not then fall victim to famine or plague could anticipate the circus, the mine, or slavery" (pp. 84–85).

The death toll given by Flavius Josephus is 1,100,000 (*The Jewish War*, p. 371). Orosius (*Hist. Adv. Pag.* VII, 9, 7) and likewise Tacitus (*Hist.* V, 13) speak of 600,000 dead. Mittelstaedt says these figures are exaggerated, and it would be more realistic to assume about 80,000 dead (p. 83). Anyone who reads all the written accounts, with their tales of murder, massacre, looting, arson, hunger, desecration of corpses, and environmental destruction (everywhere within an eleven-mile radius was deforested and laid waste), can understand Jesus' comment, based on a passage from the Book of Daniel (12:1): "For in those days there will be such tribulation as has not been from the beginning of the creation which God created until now, and never will be" (Mk 13:19).

In Daniel's text, this prophecy of doom is followed by a promise: "But at that time your people shall be delivered, every one whose name shall be found written in the book" (12:1). Similarly in Jesus' discourse, horror does not have the last word: the days are shortened and the elect are saved. God grants to evil and to evildoers a large measure of freedom—too large, we might think. Even so, history does not slip through his fingers.

In the midst of this whole drama, which is unfortunately all too typical of countless tragedies throughout history, a key event in salvation history took place, marking a turning point with far-reaching consequences for the entire history of religions and of the human race: on 5 August in the year 70, "the daily sacrifice in the Temple had to be abandoned because of famine and scarcity of material" (Mittelstaedt, *Lukas als Historiker*, p. 78).

It is true that after the destruction of the Temple by Nebuchadnezzar in 587 B.C., the burnt offerings were suspended for around seventy years. Then for a second time, between 166 and 164 B.C. under the Hellenistic ruler Antiochus IV, the Temple was profaned and the sacrificial cult of the one God was replaced by sacrifices to Zeus. But on both occasions the Temple was restored and the worship prescribed by the Torah was resumed.

The destruction that took place in the year 70 was definitive. Attempts to restore the Temple under Emperor Hadrian through the revolt of Bar Kochba (A.D. 132–135), and later under Julian (361), were unsuccessful. The revolt of Bar Kochba actually led Hadrian to prohibit the Jewish people from entering the area in and around Jerusalem. In the place of the Holy City, the emperor built a new one, known henceforth as Aelia Capitolina, where the cult of Jupiter Capitolinus was celebrated. "Emperor Constantine in the fourth century was the first to allow the Jews, once a year, on the anniversary of the destruction of Jerusalem, to visit the City in order to grieve at the wall of the Temple" (Gnilka, *Nazarener*, p. 72).

For Judaism, the end of the sacrifice, the destruction of the Temple, must have come as a tremendous shock. Temple and sacrifice lie at the very heart of the Torah. Now there was no longer any atonement in the world, no longer anything that could serve as a counterweight to its further contamination by evil. What is more: God, who had set down his name in the Temple, and thus in a mysterious way dwelt within it, had now lost his dwelling place on earth. What had become of the Covenant? What had become of the promise?

One thing is clear: the Bible—the Old Testament—had to be read anew. The Judaism of the Sadducees, which was entirely bound to the Temple, did not survive this catastrophe; Qumran—which despite its opposition to the Herodian Temple, lived in expectation of a renewed Temple—also disappeared from history. There are two possible responses to this situation, two ways of reading the Old Testament anew after the year 70: the reading in the light of Christ, based on the Prophets, and the rabbinical reading.

Among the Jewish schools of thought prevailing at the time of Jesus, the only one to survive was Pharisaism, which acquired a new center in the rabbinic school of Jamnia and there developed its own particular way of reading and interpreting the Old Testament after the loss of the Temple, centered on the Torah. Only then did it become possible to speak of "Judaism" in the strict sense as a way of viewing the canon of Scripture as revelation and reading it anew in the physical absence of Temple worship. That worship no longer existed. In this sense, Israel's faith also took on a new guise after the year 70.

After centuries of antagonism, we now see it as our task to bring these two ways of rereading the biblical texts— the Christian way and the Jewish way—into dialogue

33

with one another, if we are to understand God's will and his word aright.

Saint Gregory Nazianzen (d. ca. 390), contemplating with hindsight the destruction of the Temple of Jerusalem, divided up the world's religious history into a series of phases. He speaks of the patience of God, who does not impose upon man anything too hard to understand: God acts like a good schoolteacher or a doctor. He slowly puts an end to certain customs, allows others to continue, and thus leads man forward. "A departure from time-honored, customary ways is, after all, not easy. Am I making my point? The first change cut away idols but allowed sacrifices to remain; the second stripped away sacrifices but did not forbid circumcision. Then, when men had been reconciled to the withdrawal, they agreed to let go what had been left them as a concession" (*Oration* 31, "On the Holy Spirit", par. 25). From the perspective of this Church Father, even the sacrifices prescribed by the Torah appear as something merely allowed to remain—as a stage along the path to true worship of God, something temporary that had to be surpassed and was, indeed, surpassed by Christ.

At this point the decisive question that presents itself is: How did Jesus himself see this? And how did Christians understand him? The extent to which particular details of the eschatological discourse are attributable to Jesus himself we need not consider here. That he foretold the demise of the Temple—its theological demise, that is, from the standpoint of salvation history—is beyond doubt. As evidence for this, besides the eschatological discourse, there is above all the passage about the deserted house with which we began (Mt 23:37–38; Lk 13:34–35) and the words of the false witnesses at Jesus' trial (Mt 26:61; 27:40; Mk 14:58; 15:29; Acts 6:14)—words that reappear as a taunt at the foot of the Cross and which the Fourth Gospel places earlier, in their correct form, on the lips of Jesus himself (Jn 2:19).

Inasmuch as it belonged to the Father, Jesus loved the Temple (cf. Lk 2:49) and taught there gladly. He defended it as a house of prayer for all peoples and tried to prepare it for that function. Yet he knew that the age of this Temple was over and that something new was to come, linked to his death and Resurrection.

Through attentive listening and reading, the early Church had to grapple with these somewhat mysterious and fragmentary sayings of Jesus—his references to the Temple and above all to the Cross and Resurrection—piecing them together until finally it was possible to recognize the full picture that Jesus wished to convey. This was no easy task, but it was begun on the day of Pentecost, and we may say that all the essential elements of the new synthesis had already been worked out in Paul's theology before the outward demise of the Temple.

Regarding the relationship of the earliest community to the Temple, the Acts of the Apostles has this to say: "Day by day, attending the temple together and breaking bread in their homes, they partook of food with glad and generous hearts" (2:46). So two key locations are named for the life of the infant Church: for preaching and prayer they meet in the Temple, which they still regard and accept as the house of God's word and the house of prayer; on the other hand, the breaking of bread—the new "cultic" center of the lives of the faithful—is celebrated in their houses as places of assembly and communion in the name of the risen Lord.

Even if up to this point there has been no explicit distancing from the sacrifices of the Law, an essential distinction has nevertheless been drawn. The place of the sacrifices has now been taken by the "breaking of bread". Yet concealed beneath this simple phrase is a reference to the legacy of the Last Supper, to fellowship in the Lord's body—to his death and Resurrection.

As for the new theological synthesis that sees in the death and Resurrection of Jesus the end of the Temple's place in salvation history, even before its outward destruction, there are two names that stand out: Stephen and Paul.

Within the original Jerusalem community, Stephen belongs to the group of "Hellenists", Greek-speaking Jewish Christians whose new understanding of the Law paved the way for Pauline Christianity. The great discourse with which Stephen seeks to present his new vision of salvation history, as recounted in the Acts of the Apostles, breaks off at the key point. His opponents' anger has already reached fever pitch and is unleashed in the stoning of the messenger. The real point at issue, though, is clearly indicated in the formulation of the charge brought before the Sanhedrin:

"We have heard him say that this Jesus of Nazareth will destroy this place [that is, the Temple], and will change the customs which Moses delivered to us" (Acts 6:14). It is all to do with Jesus' prophecy concerning the demise of the Temple of stone and concerning the new and entirely different Temple, words that Stephen makes his own and openly declares in the course of his testimony.

Even if we cannot reconstruct Saint Stephen's theological vision in detail, its nucleus is clear: the era of the stone Temple and its sacrificial worship is past. For God himself said: "Heaven is my throne, and earth my footstool. What house will you build for me ... or what is the place of my rest? Did not my hand make all these things?" (Acts 7:49–50; cf. Is 66:1–2).

Stephen is familiar with the Prophets' critique of the former cult. For him the era of Temple sacrifices and with it the era of the Temple itself came to an end with Jesus; now the Prophets' words can come into their own. Something new has begun, in which the cult's original meaning is brought to fulfillment.

The life and the message of Saint Stephen remain as a fragment that is cut short by his stoning, although at the same time this is what brings his message and his life to their completion: in his passion he becomes one with Christ. Both his trial and his death resemble the Passion of Jesus. Like the crucified Lord, he too prays as he dies: "Lord, do not hold this sin against them!" (Acts 7:60). The task of fully expounding this theological vision in order to build up the Church of the Gentiles fell to another: to Paul,

37

who as Saul had consented to the killing of Stephen (cf. Acts 8:1).

It is not the task of this book to delineate the principal elements of Pauline theology, not even those concerned with worship and the Temple. Our concern is simply the early Church's conviction that long before its outward destruction, the era of the Temple in salvation history had come to an end—as Jesus had declared with his references to the "deserted house" and the new Temple.

Saint Paul's enormous efforts to build up the Church of the Gentiles by developing a form of Christianity "free from the Law" had nothing to do with the Temple. His quarrel with the various currents within Jewish Christianity revolved around the basic "customs" through which Jewish identity was expressed: circumcision, the Sabbath, food laws, purity regulations. While the question over the necessity of these "customs" for salvation gave rise to some fierce battles among Christians, too, leading ultimately to Paul's arrest in Jerusalem, strangely there is not a hint to be found anywhere of a dispute over the Temple and the necessity of its sacrifices, even though, according to the Acts of the Apostles, "a great many of the priests were obedient to the faith" (6:7).

Still, Paul did not simply ignore the question. On the contrary, the belief that all sacrifices are fulfilled in the Cross of Jesus Christ, that in him the underlying intention of all sacrifices is accomplished, namely expiation, that Jesus in this way has taken the place of the Temple, that he himself is the new Temple: all of this lies at the very heart of Paul's teaching.

A brief indication must suffice. The most important text is found in the Letter to the Romans (3:23–25): "Since all have sinned and fall short of the glory of God, they are justified by his grace as a gift, through the redemption which is in Christ Jesus, whom God put forward as an expiation by his blood, to be received by faith. This was to show God's righteousness, because in his divine forbearance he had passed over former sins."

The Greek word that is here translated as "expiation" is *hilastērion*, of which the Hebrew equivalent is *kappōret*. This word designated the covering of the Ark of the Covenant. This is the place over which YHWH appears in a cloud, the place of the mysterious presence of God. This holy place is sprinkled with the blood of the bull killed as a sin-offering on the Day of Atonement—the *Yom ha-Kippurim* (cf. Lev 16), "whose life is offered up to God in place of the life forfeited by sinful men" (Wilckens, *Theologie des Neuen Testaments* II/1, p. 235). The thinking here is that the blood of the victim, into which all human sins are absorbed, actually touches the Divinity and is thereby cleansed—and in the process, human beings, represented by the blood, are also purified through this contact with God: an astonishing idea both in its grandeur and its incompleteness, an idea that could not remain the last word in the history of religions or the last word in the faith history of Israel.

When Paul applies the word *hilastērion* to Jesus, designating him as the seal of the Ark of the Covenant and thus as the locus of the presence of the living God, the entire Old Testament theology of worship (and with it all the theologies of worship in the history of religions) is "preserved and surpassed" [*aufgehoben*] and raised to a completely new level. Jesus himself is the presence of the living God. God and man, God and the world, touch one another in him. The meaning of the ritual of the Day of Atonement is accomplished in him. In his self-offering on the Cross, Jesus, as it were, brings all the sin of the world deep within the love of God and wipes it away. Accepting the Cross, entering into fellowship with Christ, means entering the realm of transformation and expiation.

All this is hard for us to understand today; we will return to it in greater detail when we consider the Last Supper and Jesus' death on the Cross, and we will try to understand it. Here our intention is simply to demonstrate that Paul has already completely absorbed the Temple and its sacrificial theology into his Christology. For Paul, the Temple with its worship is "demolished" with Christ's crucifixion; its place is now taken by the living Ark of the Covenant—the crucified and risen Christ. If with Ulrich Wilckens we may accept that Romans 3:25 is a "Jewish-Christian faith-formula" (*Theologie des Neuen Testaments* I/3, p. 182), then we see how quickly this insight matured within Christianity—from the beginning it was known that the risen Lord is the new Temple, the real meeting place between God and man. Wilckens can therefore rightly say: "From the beginning, Christians simply did not take part in Temple worship.... The destruction of the Temple in A.D. 70 did not therefore constitute a religious problem for Christians" (*Theologie des Neuen Testaments* II/1, p. 31).

Thus it also becomes clear that the great theological vision of the Letter to the Hebrews merely expounds in greater detail what in essence Paul had already said and what Paul in turn had found already substantially contained within the earlier ecclesial tradition. Later, we shall see that, in its own way, the high-priestly prayer of Jesus offers a similar reinterpretation of the event of the Day of Atonement and hence of the heart of Old Testament redemption theology, seeing it fulfilled in the Cross.

2. *The Times of the Gentiles*

A superficial reading or hearing of Jesus' eschatological discourse would give the impression that Jesus linked the end of Jerusalem chronologically to the end of the world, especially when we read in Matthew: "Immediately after the tribulation of those days the sun will be darkened ...; then will appear the sign of the Son of man in heaven ..." (24:29–30). This direct chronological connection between the end of Jerusalem and the end of the whole world seems to be further confirmed when we come across these words a few verses later: "Truly, I say to you, this generation will not pass away till all these things take place ..." (24:34).

On first glance, it seems that Luke was the only one to downplay this connection. In his account we read: "They will fall by the edge of the sword, and be led captive among all nations; and Jerusalem will be trodden down by the Gentiles, until the times of the

Gentiles are fulfilled" (21:24). Between the destruction of Jerusalem and the end of the world, "the times of the Gentiles" are here inserted. Luke has been accused of thereby shifting the temporal axis of the Gospels and of Jesus' original message, recasting the end of time as the intermediate time and, thus, inventing the time of the Church as a new phase of salvation history. But if we look closely, we find that these "times of the Gentiles" are also foretold, in different terms and at a different point, in the versions of Jesus' discourse recounted by Matthew and Mark.

Matthew quotes the following saying of Jesus: "And this gospel of the kingdom will be preached throughout the whole world, as a testimony to all nations; and then the end will come" (24:14). And in Mark we read: "The gospel must first be preached to all nations" (13:10).

We see at once how much care is needed when making connections within this discourse of Jesus; the text is woven together from individual strands of tradition that do not present a straightforward linear argument but that must, as it were, be read in the light of one another. In the third section of this chapter ("Prophecy and Apocalyptic"), we will look in more detail at this redactional question, which is of great significance for a correct understanding of the text.

From the content, it is clear that all three Synoptic Gospels recognize a time of the Gentiles: the end of time can come only when the Gospel has been brought to all peoples. The time of the Gentiles—the time of the Church made up of all the peoples of the world—is not

an invention of Saint Luke: it is the common patrimony
of all the Gospels.

At this point we encounter once again the connection
between the Gospel tradition and the basic elements of
Pauline theology. If Jesus says in the eschatological discourse that the Gospel must first be proclaimed to the Gentiles and only then can the end come, we find exactly the
same thing in Paul's Letter to the Romans: "A hardening
has come upon part of Israel, until the full number of the
Gentiles come in, and so all Israel will be saved" (11:25–26).
The full number of the Gentiles and all Israel: in this formula we see the universalism of the divine salvific will. For
our purposes, though, the important point is that Paul, too,
recognizes an age of the Gentiles, which is the present and
which must be fulfilled if God's plan is to attain its goal.

The fact that the early Church was unable to assess
the chronological duration of these *kairoí* ("times") of the
Gentiles and that it was generally assumed they would
be fairly short is ultimately a secondary consideration.
The essential point is that these times were both asserted
and foretold and that, above all else and prior to any cal-
culation of their duration, they had to be understood
and were understood by the disciples in terms of a mission: to accomplish now what had been proclaimed and
demanded—by bringing the Gospel to all peoples.

The restlessness with which Paul journeyed to the
nations, so as to bring the message to all and, if possible, to fulfill the mission within his own lifetime—this
restlessness can only be explained if one is aware of the

historical and eschatological significance of his exclamation: "Necessity is laid upon me. Woe to me if I do not preach the gospel!" (1 Cor 9:16).

In this sense, the urgency of evangelization in the apostolic era was predicated not so much on the necessity for each individual to acquire knowledge of the Gospel in order to attain salvation, but rather on this grand conception of history: if the world was to arrive at its destiny, the Gospel had to be brought to all nations. At many stages in history, this sense of urgency has been markedly attenuated, but it has always revived, generating new dynamism for evangelization.

In this regard, the question of Israel's mission has always been present in the background. We realize today with horror how many misunderstandings with grave consequences have weighed down our history. Yet a new reflection can acknowledge that the beginnings of a correct understanding have always been there, waiting to be rediscovered, however deep the shadows.

Here I should like to recall the advice given by Bernard of Clairvaux to his pupil Pope Eugene III on this matter. He reminds the Pope that his duty of care extends not only to Christians, but: "You also have obligations toward unbelievers, whether Jew, Greek, or Gentile" (*De Consideratione* III/1, 2). Then he immediately corrects himself and observes more accurately: "Granted, with regard to the Jews, time excuses you; for them a determined point in time has been fixed, which cannot be anticipated. The full number of the Gentiles must come

44

in first. But what do you say about these Gentiles?...
Why did it seem good to the Fathers ... to suspend the
word of faith while unbelief was obdurate? Why do we
suppose the word that runs swiftly stopped short?" (*De
Consideratione* III/1, 3).

Hildegard Brem comments on this passage as follows:
"In the light of Romans 11:25, the Church must not concern herself with the conversion of the Jews, since she
must wait for the time fixed for this by God, 'until the
full number of the Gentiles come in' (Rom 11:25). On
the contrary, the Jews themselves are a living homily to
which the Church must draw attention, since they call
to mind the Lord's suffering (cf. *Ep* 363) ..." (quoted in
Sämtliche Werke, ed. Winkler, I, p. 834).

The prophecy of the time of the Gentiles and the corresponding mission is a core element of Jesus' eschatological
message. The special mission to evangelize the Gentiles, which Paul received from the risen Lord, is firmly
anchored in the message given by Jesus to his disciples
before his Passion. The time of the Gentiles—"the time
of the Church"—which, as we have seen, is proclaimed in
all the Gospels, constitutes an essential element of Jesus'
eschatological message.

3. *Prophecy and Apocalyptic in the Eschatological Discourse*

Before we address the strictly apocalyptic part of Jesus'
discourse, let us attempt a summary of what we have seen
so far.

First, we saw the prophecy of the destruction of the Temple and, in Luke, explicit reference also to the destruction of Jerusalem. Yet it became clear that the nucleus of Jesus' prophecy is concerned, not with the outward events of war and destruction, but with the demise of the Temple in salvation-historical terms, as it becomes a "deserted house". It ceases to be the locus of God's presence and the locus of atonement for Israel, indeed, for the world. The time of sacrifices, as regulated by the Law of Moses, is over.

We have seen that the early Church was aware of this profound watershed in history long before the outward demise of the Temple, and we have seen that amid all the difficult debates over which Jewish customs needed to be retained and imposed on Gentiles too, there was evidently no dissent over this point: with the Cross of Christ, the era of sacrifices was over.

Moreover, we have seen that the nucleus of Jesus' eschatological message includes the proclamation of an age of the nations, during which the Gospel must be brought to the whole world and to all people: only then can history attain its goal.

In the meantime, Israel retains its own mission. Israel is in the hands of God, who will save it "as a whole" at the proper time, when the number of the Gentiles is complete. The fact that the historical duration of this period cannot be calculated is self-evident and should not surprise us. But it was becoming increasingly clear that the evangelization of the Gentiles was now the disciples' particular task—thanks above all to the special commission given to Paul as a duty and a grace.

From this perspective, it can be understood that this "time of the Gentiles" is not yet the full Messianic age in terms of the great salvation promises, but it remains the time of present history and suffering; yet in a new way it is also a time of hope: "The night is far gone, the day is at hand" (Rom 13:12).

It seems obvious to me that several of Jesus' parables—such as the parable of the net with good and bad fish (Mt 13:47–50), the parable of the darnel in the field (Mt 13:24–30)—speak of this time of the Church; from the perspective of a purely imminent eschatology, they would make no sense.

As a subsidiary theme, we also came across the instruction to the Christians to flee from Jerusalem at the time of an as yet unspecified profanation of the Temple. The historicity of this flight to Pella in Transjordan cannot be seriously doubted. While for our purposes this may seem a peripheral detail, it has a theological significance that should not be underestimated: their refusal to take part in the military defense of the Temple, through which the sacred place itself became a fortress and an arena for cruel military actions, corresponds exactly to the approach taken by Jeremiah at the time of the Babylonian siege of Jerusalem (cf. Jer 7:1–15; 38:14–28, for example).

Joachim Gnilka emphasizes the link between this approach and the heart of Jesus' teaching: "It is most unlikely that the Christian believers in Jerusalem took any part in the war. It was Palestinian Christianity that transmitted Jesus' Sermon on the Mount. So they must have known Jesus' commandments regarding love of enemies and renunciation of violence. We also know that they did not take part in the revolt at the time of Emperor Hadrian" (*Nazarener*, p. 69).

A further key element of Jesus' eschatological discourse is the warning against false Messiahs and apocalyptic enthusiasm. Linked with this is the instruction to practice sobriety and vigilance, which Jesus developed further in a series of parables, especially in the story of the wise and foolish virgins (Mt 25:1–13) and in his sayings about the watchful doorkeeper (Mk 13:33–36). In this last passage we see clearly what is meant by "vigilance": not neglecting the present, speculating on the future, or forgetting the task in hand, but quite the reverse—it means doing what is right here and now, as is incumbent upon us in the sight of God.

Matthew and Luke recount the parable of the servant who noted his master's delay in returning and, thinking him absent, made himself master, beat the servants and maids, and gave himself over to fine living. On the other hand, the good servant remains a servant, knowing that he will be called to account. He gives to all their due and is praised by the master for so doing: acting with justice is true vigilance (cf. Mt 24:45–51; Lk 12:41–46). To be vigilant is to know that one is under God's watchful eye and to act accordingly.

In the Second Letter to the Thessalonians, Paul explained in stark and vivid terms what Christian vigilance involves: "For even when we were with you, we gave you this command: If any one will not work, let him not eat. For we hear that some of you are walking in idleness, mere busybodies, not doing any work. Now such persons we command and exhort in the Lord Jesus Christ to do their work in quietness and to earn their own living" (3:10–12).

A further important element of Jesus' eschatological discourse is the reference to the persecution that lies in store for his followers. Here, too, the time of the Gentiles is presupposed, for the Lord says that his disciples will be brought not only before courts and synagogues, but also before governors and kings (Mk 13:9): the proclamation of the Gospel will always be marked by the sign of the Cross—this is what each generation of Jesus' disciples must learn anew. The Cross is and remains the sign of "the Son of Man": ultimately, in the battle against lies and violence, truth and love have no other weapon than the witness of suffering.

Let us now turn to the strictly apocalyptic section of Jesus' eschatological discourse: to the prophecy of the end of the world, the second coming of the Son of Man, and the Last Judgment (Mk 13:24–27).

What is striking here is that this text is largely composed of Old Testament passages, especially from the Book of Daniel, but also from Ezekiel, Isaiah, and other scriptural texts. For their part, these passages are interconnected: old images are reinterpreted in situations of hardship and developed further; within the Book of Daniel itself one can observe such a process of rereading certain passages as history unfolds. Jesus places himself within this process of *relecture*, and hence it is understandable that, for their part, the community of believers—as we saw earlier—reread Jesus' words in the light of their new circumstances, naturally in such a way that the fundamental message remained intact. Yet the fact that Jesus spoke of the future, not in his own words, but by proclaiming the words of ancient prophecy in a new way is highly significant.

First, we must of course note the element that is genuinely new: the coming Son of Man, of whom Daniel had spoken (7:13–14), without being able to give him personal features, is now identical with the Son of Man addressing the disciples. The old apocalyptic text is given a personalist dimension: at its heart we now find the person of Jesus himself, who combines into one the lived present and the mysterious future. The real "event" is the person in whom, despite the passage of time, the present truly remains. In this person the future is already here. When all is said and done, the future will not place us in any other situation than the one to which our encounter with Jesus has already brought us.

In this way, the focusing of the cosmic images onto a person, who is now present and known to us, renders the cosmic context a secondary consideration. Even the question of time loses its importance: the person "is" in the midst of physically measurable things; he has his own "time"; he "remains".

This relativization of the cosmic, or, rather, its focusing onto the personal, is seen very clearly in the closing words of the apocalyptic section: "Heaven and earth will pass away, but my words will not pass away" (Mk 13:31). The word—which seems almost nothing in comparison to the mighty power of the immeasurable material cosmos, like a fleeting breath against the silent grandeur of the universe—the word is more real and more lasting than the entire material world. The word is the true, dependable reality: the solid ground on which we can stand, which holds firm even when the sun goes dark and the firmament disintegrates. The cosmic elements pass away; the word of Jesus is the true "firmament" beneath which we can stand and remain.

This personalistic focus, this transformation of the apocalyptic visions—which still corresponds to the inner meaning of the Old Testament images—is the original element in Jesus' teaching about the end of the world: this is what it is all about.

From this standpoint, we can understand the significance of Jesus choosing not to offer a description of the end of the world, but rather to proclaim it using words already found in the Old Testament. Speaking about things to come using words from the past strips these discourses of any temporal frame of reference. What we have here is not a newly formulated account of the future, such as one might expect from a clairvoyant, but a realignment of our perspective on the future within the previously given word of God, manifesting both the perennial validity and the open potentialities of that word. It becomes clear that the word of God from the past illumines the essential meaning of the future. Yet it does not offer us a description of that future: rather it shows us, just for today, the right path for now and for tomorrow.

Jesus' apocalyptic words have nothing to do with clairvoyance. Indeed, they are intended to deter us from mere superficial curiosity about observable phenomena (cf. Lk 17:20) and to lead us toward the essential: toward life built upon the word of God that Jesus gives us; toward an encounter with him, the living Word; toward responsibility before the Judge of the living and the dead.

CHAPTER THREE

The Washing of the Feet

After the teaching discourses that follow the account of Jesus' entrance into Jerusalem, the Synoptic Gospels resume the narrative thread with a precise chronological indication that leads into the Last Supper.

Mark says at the very beginning of chapter 14: "It was now two days before the Passover and the feast of Unleavened Bread" (14:1). Then he recounts the anointing at Bethany and Judas' conspiracy, and he continues: "On the first day of Unleavened Bread, when they sacrificed the Passover lamb, his disciples said to him, 'Where will you have us go and prepare for you to eat the Passover?'" (14:12).

John, on the other hand, simply says: "Before the feast of the Passover ... during supper" (13:1–2). The meal that John describes takes place "before the feast of the Passover", whereas the Synoptics present the Last Supper as a Passover meal, and thus they appear to be using a chronology that differs from John's by one day.

We will return to the much-debated questions about these differing chronologies and their theological significance when we consider Jesus' Last Supper and the institution of the Eucharist.

The hour of Jesus

For now, let us focus on the Fourth Gospel, where we find two uniquely Johannine elements in the account of Jesus' final evening with his disciples before the Passion. First, John tells us that Jesus administered the menial service of washing the disciples' feet. In this context, he also recounts the prophecies of Judas' betrayal and Peter's denial. The second element consists of Jesus' farewell discourse, culminating in the high-priestly prayer. These two key episodes will be considered in turn during the present chapter and the one following.

"Now before the feast of the Passover, when Jesus knew that his hour had come to depart out of this world to the Father, having loved his own who were in the world, he loved them to the end" (13:1). With the Last Supper, Jesus' "hour" has arrived, the goal to which his ministry has been directed from the beginning (2:4). The essence of this hour is described by John with two key words: it is the hour of his "departing" (*metabaínein* / *metábasis*); it is the hour of the love that reaches to the end (*agápē*).

The two concepts shed light on one another and are inseparable. Love is the very process of passing over, of transformation, of stepping outside the limitations of fallen humanity—in which we are all separated from one

another and ultimately impenetrable to one another—
into an infinite otherness. "Love to the end" is what
brings about the seemingly impossible *metábasis*: stepping
outside the limits of one's closed individuality, which is
what *agápē* is—breaking through into the divine.

The "hour" of Jesus is the hour of the great stepping-
beyond, the hour of transformation, and this metamor-
phosis of being is brought about through *agápē*. It is *agápē*
"to the end"—and here John anticipates the final word
of the dying Jesus: *tetélestai*—"it is finished" (19:30). This
end (*télos*), this totality of self-giving, of remolding the
whole of being—this is what it means to give oneself even
unto death.

When Jesus speaks here, as elsewhere in John's Gospel,
of having come from the Father and of returning to him,
one is perhaps reminded of the ancient model of *exitus*
and *reditus*, of exit and return, such as we find in the philosophy of Plotinus in particular. Nevertheless, the going
out and returning that John describes is something quite
different from what is meant in the philosophical model.
For Plotinus and his successors, the "going out", which is
their equivalent of the divine act of creation, is a descent
that ultimately leads to a fall: from the height of the "one"
down into ever lower regions of being. The return then
consists in purification from the material sphere, in a gradual ascent, and in purifications that strip away again what
is base and ultimately lead back to the unity of the divine.

Jesus' going out, on the other hand, presupposes that
creation is not a fall, but a positive act of God's will. It is

thus a movement of love, which in the process of descending demonstrates its true nature—motivated by love for the creature, love for the lost sheep—and so in descending it reveals what God is really like. On returning, Jesus does not strip away his humanity again as if it were a source of impurity. The goal of his descent was the adoption and assumption of all mankind, and his homecoming with all men is the homecoming of "all flesh".

Something new happens in this return: Jesus does not return alone. He does not strip away the flesh, but draws all to himself (cf. Jn 12:32). The *metábasis* applies to all. If in the Prologue of John's Gospel we read that "his own" (*ídioi*) did not accept him (cf. 1:11), we now hear that he loves "his own" to the end (cf. 13:1). In descending he has reassembled "his own"—the great family of God—from strangers he has made them "his own".

Let us listen to the evangelist as he continues: Jesus "rose from supper, laid aside his garments, and tied a towel around himself. Then he poured water into a basin, and began to wash the disciples' feet, and to wipe them with the towel that was tied around him" (Jn 13:4–5). Jesus performs for his disciples the service of a slave, he "emptied himself" (Phil 2:7).

What the Letter to the Philippians says in its great Christological hymn—namely, that unlike Adam, who had tried to grasp divinity for himself, Christ moves in the opposite direction, coming down from his divinity into humanity, taking the form of a servant and becoming obedient even to death on a cross (cf. 2:7–8)—all this is rendered visible in a single gesture. Jesus represents the whole of his saving ministry in one symbolic act. He divests himself of his divine splendor; he, as it were, kneels down before us; he washes and dries our soiled feet, in order to make us fit to sit at table for God's wedding feast.

When we read in the Book of Revelation the paradoxical statement that the redeemed have "washed their robes and made them white in the blood of the Lamb" (Rev 7:14), the meaning is that Jesus' love "to the end" is what cleanses us, washes us. The gesture of washing feet expresses precisely this: it is the servant-love of Jesus that draws us out of our pride and makes us fit for God, makes us "clean".

"You are clean"

In the passage about the washing of the feet, the word "clean" occurs three times. John is drawing upon a fundamental concept of the religious tradition of the Old Testament and of world religions in general. If man is to enter God's presence, to have fellowship with God, he must be "clean". Yet the more he moves into the light, the more he senses how defiled he is, how much he stands in need of cleansing. Religions have therefore created systems of "purification", intended to make it possible for man to approach God.

In the cultic ordering of all religions, purification regulations play a major part: they give man a sense of the holiness of God and of his own darkness, from which he must be liberated if he is to be able to approach God. The system of cultic purifications dominated the whole of life in observant Judaism at the time of Jesus. In chapter 7 of Mark's Gospel, we encounter Jesus' fundamental challenge to this concept of cultic purity obtained through ritual actions; and in Paul's letters, the question of "purity" before God is repeatedly debated.

In Mark's Gospel we see the radical transformation that Jesus brought to the concept of purity before God: it is not ritual actions that make us pure. Purity and impurity arise within man's heart and depend on the condition of his heart (Mk 7:14–23).

Yet the question immediately presents itself: How does the heart become pure? Who are the pure in heart, those who can see God (Mt 5:8)? Liberal exegesis has claimed that Jesus replaced the ritual concept of purity with a moral concept: in place of the cult and all that went with it, we have morality. In this view, Christianity is considered to be essentially about morality, a kind of moral "rearmament". But this does not do justice to the radically new dimension of the New Testament.

Its newness becomes clear in the Acts of the Apostles when Peter takes issue with the former Pharisees in the Christian community who insist that Gentile Christians must be circumcised and must "keep the law of Moses". Peter explains: God himself decided that "the Gentiles should hear the word of the gospel and believe.... He made no distinction between us and them, but cleansed their hearts by faith" (15:5–11). Faith cleanses the heart. It is the result of God's initiative toward man. It is not simply a choice that men make for themselves. Faith comes about because men are touched deep within by God's Spirit, who opens and purifies their hearts.

This broad theme of purification, which is merely mentioned in passing in Peter's address, is taken up and developed further by John both in the account of the washing of the feet and later, under the heading of "sanctification", in Jesus' high-priestly prayer. "You are already made clean by the word which I have spoken to you", Jesus assures his disciples in the parable of the vine (Jn 15:3). It is his word that penetrates them, transforms their intellect, their will, their "heart", and opens it up in such a way that it becomes a seeing heart.

In our reflection on the high-priestly prayer, we will encounter this idea again, albeit expressed in slightly different terms, when Jesus prays: "Sanctify them in the truth" (Jn 17:17). In priestly terminology, "to sanctify" means to render fit for divine worship. The word designates the ritual actions that the priest must carry out before he enters the presence of God. "Sanctify them in the truth"—Jesus here gives us to understand that the truth is now the "bath" that makes men fit for God. They must be immersed in it in order to be freed from the impurity that separates them from God. In this regard, we must remember that the truth John has in mind here is no abstract concept: he knows that Jesus himself is the truth.

In chapter 13 of the Gospel, it is the washing of feet by Jesus that serves as the way of purification. Here we encounter the same idea once again, but from a different perspective. The bath that cleanses us is Jesus' love to the point of death. Jesus' word is more than a word; it is his very self. His word is truth, and it is love.

Essentially Paul is expressing this same idea in a more roundabout way when he says, "We are now justified by his blood" (Rom 5:9; cf. Rom 3:25, Eph 1:7 et al.). And the same thing reappears in the exalted vision of Jesus' high priesthood that is set forth in the Letter to the Hebrews. In place of ritual purity, what we have now is not merely morality, but the gift of encounter with God in Jesus Christ.

Once again the comparison with Platonic philosophies of late antiquity suggests itself, philosophies that, as we saw in the case of Plotinus, revolve around the theme of purification. This purification is obtained, on the one hand, through ritual actions, but also and especially through man's gradual ascent to the heights of God. In this way man purifies himself from matter, becoming spirit and, hence, pure.

For the Christian faith, though, it is the incarnate God who makes us truly pure and draws creation into unity with God. Nineteenth-century piety brought back a one-sided notion of purity by reducing it to the sexual sphere, thereby burdening it once again with suspicion of material things, of the body. In terms of mankind's broader search for purity, Saint John's Gospel—and Jesus himself—shows us the way: he who is both God and man makes us fit for God. Being incorporated into his body, being pervaded by his presence is what matters.

Perhaps it is worth mentioning at this point that the shift in meaning of the notion of purity brought about by Jesus' message is a further illustration of what was said in chapter 2 about the end of the animal sacrifices, about worship and the new Temple. Just as the old sacrifices pointed toward the future that was awaited, receiving light and dignity from that eagerly anticipated future, so too the whole question of ritual purity associated with this worship was likewise—as the Fathers would say—"*sacramentum futuri*": a stage in the history of God with men, and of men with God, straining forward to the future, but obliged to step aside once the hour of the new had actually come.

Sacramentum *and* exemplum—*gift and task: The "new commandment"*

Let us return to chapter 13 of Saint John's Gospel. "You are clean", says Jesus to his disciples. The gift of purity is an act of God. Man cannot make himself fit for God, whatever systems of purification he may follow. "You are clean"—in Jesus' wonderfully simple statement, the grandeur of the mystery of Christ is somehow encapsulated. It is the God who comes down to us who makes us clean. Purity is a gift.

Yet an objection springs to mind. A few verses later, Jesus says: "If I, then, your Lord and Teacher, have washed your feet, you also ought to wash one another's feet. For I have given you an example, that you also should do as I have done to you" (Jn 13:14–15). Does this not after all suggest a purely moral conception of Christianity?

61

Rudolf Schnackenburg, as it happens, speaks of two opposing interpretations of the foot-washing in chapter 13: the first is "theologically more profound and in it the washing of the feet is seen as a symbolic action pointing to Jesus' death. The second is paradigmatic and is centered on the humble service of Jesus—itself based on the washing of the disciples' feet" (*The Gospel according to Saint John* III, p. 7). Schnackenburg holds that the second interpretation is an "editorial formation", and in his view "the second interpretation seems to have nothing to do with the first" (p. 12, cf. p. 24). But this is too narrow an approach, too closely tied to the thought patterns of our Western logic. For John, Jesus' gift and his subsequent ministry among the disciples form a unity.

The Fathers expressed the difference between these two aspects, as well as their mutual relationship, using the categories of *sacramentum* and *exemplum*: by *sacramentum* they mean, not any particular sacrament, but rather the entire mystery of Christ—his life and death—in which he draws close to us, enters us through his Spirit, and transforms us. But precisely because this *sacramentum* truly "cleanses" us, renewing us from within, it also unleashes a dynamic of new life. The command to do as Jesus did is no mere moral appendix to the mystery, let alone an antithesis to it. It follows from the inner dynamic of gift with which the Lord renews us and draws us into what is his.

This essential dynamic of gift, through which he now acts in us and our action becomes one with his, is seen with particular clarity in Jesus' saying: "He who believes in me will also do the works that I do; and greater works than these will he do, because I go to the Father" (Jn 14:12). This expresses exactly what is meant by "I have given you an example" from the account of the foot-washing: Jesus' action becomes ours, because he is acting in us.

On this basis we can understand the teaching about the "new commandment". After an interlude devoted to Judas' betrayal, Jesus returns to his instruction to the disciples to wash one another's feet, and he applies it more widely (13:34–35.). What is new about the new commandment? Since this question ultimately concerns the "newness" of the New Testament, that is to say, the "essence of Christianity", it is important to be very attentive.

It has been argued that the new element—moving beyond the earlier commandment to love one's neighbor—is revealed in the saying "love as I have loved you", in other words, loving to the point of readiness to lay down one's life for the other. If this were the specific and exclusive content of the "new commandment", then Christianity could after all be defined as a form of extreme moral effort. This is how many commentators explain the Sermon on the Mount: in contrast to the old way of the Ten Commandments—the way of the average man, one might say—Christianity, through the Sermon on the Mount, opens up the high way that is radical in its demands, revealing a new level of humanity to which men can aspire.

And yet who could possibly claim to have risen above the "average" way of the Ten Commandments, to have left them behind as self-evident, so to speak, and now to walk along the exalted paths of the "new law"? No, the newness of the new commandment cannot consist in the highest moral attainment. Here, too, the essential point is not the call to supreme achievement, but the new foundation of being that is given to us. The newness can come only from the gift of being-*with* and being-*in* Christ.

Saint Augustine actually began his exegesis of the Sermon on the Mount—his first cycle of homilies after priestly ordination—with the idea of a higher ethos, loftier and purer norms. But in the course of the homilies, the center of gravity shifts more and more. In a number of places he has to acknowledge that the older morality was already marked by a genuine completeness. With increasing clarity, preparation of the heart comes to replace the idea of the higher demand (cf. *De Serm. Dom. in Monte* I, 19, 59); the "pure heart" (cf. Mt 5:8) becomes more and more the focus of the exegesis. Over half of the entire cycle of homilies is shaped in terms of this basic idea of the purified heart. Hence the connection with the washing of the feet becomes visible in a surprising way: only by letting ourselves be repeatedly cleansed, "made pure", by the Lord himself can we learn to act as he did, in union with him.

It all depends on our "I" being absorbed into his ("it is no longer I who live, but Christ who lives in me"—Gal 2:20). This is why the second constantly recurring keyword in Augustine's exegesis of the Sermon on the Mount is *misericordia*—mercy. We must let ourselves be immersed in the Lord's mercy, then our "hearts", too, will discover the right path. The "new commandment" is not simply a new and higher demand: it is linked to the newness of Jesus Christ—to growing immersion in him.

Taking this line of argument farther, Thomas Aquinas observed: "The new law is the grace of the Holy Spirit" (*Summa Theologiae* I–II, q. 106, a. 1)—not a new norm, but the new interiority granted by the Spirit of God himself. This spiritual experience of the truly new element in Christianity was what Augustine succinctly expressed in the famous formula: "Da quod iubes et iube quod vis" (give what you command and command what you will; *Conf.* X, 29, 40).

The gift—the *sacramentum*—becomes an *exemplum*, an example, while always remaining a gift. To be a Christian is primarily a gift, which then unfolds in the dynamic of living and acting in and around the gift.

The mystery of the betrayer

The account of the washing of the feet presents us with two different human responses to this gift, exemplified by Judas and Peter. Immediately after the exhortation to follow his example, Jesus begins to speak of Judas. John tells us in this regard that Jesus was troubled in spirit and testified: "Truly, truly, I say to you, one of you will betray me" (13:21).

John speaks three times of Jesus' being "troubled": beside the grave of Lazarus (11:33, 38), on "Palm Sunday" after the saying about the dying grain of wheat in a scene reminiscent of Gethsemane (12:24–27), and finally here.

These are moments when Jesus encounters the majesty of death and rubs against the might of darkness, which it is his task to wrestle with and overcome. We shall return to this "troubling" of Jesus' spirit when we consider the night spent on the Mount of Olives.

Let us return to our text. Understandably, the prophecy of the betrayal produces agitation and curiosity among the disciples. "One of his disciples, whom Jesus loved, was lying close to the breast of Jesus: so Simon Peter beckoned to him and said, 'Tell us who it is of whom he speaks.' So lying thus, close to the breast of Jesus, he said to him: 'Lord, who is it?' Jesus answered: 'It is he to whom I shall give this morsel when I have dipped it'" (13:23–26).

In order to understand this text, it should be noted first of all that reclining at table was prescribed for the Passover meal. Charles K. Barrett explains the verse just quoted as follows: "Persons taking part in a meal reclined on the left side; the left arm was used to support the body, the right was free for use. The disciple to the right of Jesus would thus find his head immediately in front of Jesus and might accordingly be said to lie in his bosom. Evidently he would be in a position to speak intimately with Jesus, but his was not the place of greatest honor; this was to the left of the host. The place occupied by the beloved disciple was nevertheless the place of a trusted friend"; Barrett then makes reference to a passage from Pliny (*The Gospel according to Saint John*, p. 446).

Jesus' answer, as given here, is quite unambiguous. Yet the evangelist says that the disciples still did not understand

66

whom he meant. So we must assume that John retro-spectively attributed a clarity to the Lord's answer that it lacked at the time for those present. John 13:18 brings us onto the right track. Here Jesus says, "The Scripture must be fulfilled: 'He who ate my bread has lifted his heel against me'" (cf. Ps 41:9; Ps 55:13). This is Jesus' classic way of speaking: he alludes to his destiny using words from Scripture, thereby locating it directly within God's logic, within the logic of salvation history.

At a later stage, these words become fully transparent; it is seen that Scripture really does describe the path he is to tread—but for now the enigma remains. All that can be deduced at this point is that one of those at table will betray Jesus; it is clear that the Lord will have to endure to the end and to the last detail the suffering of the just, for which the Psalms in particular provide many different expressions. Jesus must experience the incomprehension and the infi-delity even of those within his innermost circle of friends and, in this way, "fulfill the Scripture". He is revealed as the true subject of the Psalms, the "David" from whom they come and through whom they acquire meaning.

John gives a new depth to the psalm verse with which Jesus spoke prophetically of what lay ahead, since instead of the expression given in the Greek Bible for "eating", he chooses the verb *trōgein*, the word used by Jesus in the great "bread of life" discourse for "eating" his flesh and blood, that is, receiving the sacrament of the Eucharist (Jn 6:54–58). So the psalm verse casts a prophetic shadow over the Church of the evangelist's own day, in which the Eucharist was celebrated, and indeed over the Church of all times: Judas' betrayal was not the last breach of fidelity that Jesus would suffer. "Even my bosom friend, in whom I trusted, who ate my bread, has lifted his heel against me" (Ps 41:9). The breach of friendship extends into the sacramental community of the Church, where people continue to take "his bread" and to betray him.

Jesus' agony, his struggle against death, continues until the end of the world, as Blaise Pascal said on the basis of similar considerations (cf. *Pensées* VII, 553). We could also put it the other way around: at this hour, Jesus took upon himself the betrayal of all ages, the pain caused by betrayal in every era, and he endured the anguish of history to the bitter end.

John does not offer any psychological interpretation of Judas' conduct. The only clue he gives is a hint that Judas had helped himself to the contents of the disciples' money box, of which he had charge (12:6). In the context of chapter 13, the evangelist merely says laconically: "Then after the morsel, Satan entered into him" (13:27).

For John, what happened to Judas is beyond psychological explanation. He has come under the dominion of another. Anyone who breaks off friendship with Jesus, casting off his "easy yoke", does not attain liberty, does not become free, but succumbs to other powers. To put it another way, he betrays this friendship because he is in the grip of another power to which he has opened himself.

True, the light shed by Jesus into Judas' soul was not completely extinguished. He does take a step toward conversion: "I have sinned", he says to those who commissioned him. He tries to save Jesus, and he gives the money back (Mt 27:3–5). Everything pure and great that he had received from Jesus remained inscribed on his soul—he could not forget it.

His second tragedy—after the betrayal—is that he can no longer believe in forgiveness. His remorse turns into despair. Now he sees only himself and his darkness; he no longer sees the light of Jesus, which can illumine and overcome the darkness. He shows us the wrong type of remorse: the type that is unable to hope, that sees only its own darkness, the type that is destructive and in no way authentic. Genuine remorse is marked by the certainty of hope born of faith in the superior power of the light that was made flesh in Jesus.

John concludes the passage about Judas with these dramatic words: "After receiving the morsel, he immediately went out; and it was night" (13:30). Judas goes out—in a deeper sense. He goes into the night; he moves out of light into darkness: the "power of darkness" has taken hold of him (cf. Jn 3:19; Lk 22:53).

Two conversations with Peter

In the case of Judas, we encountered the perennial danger that even those "who have once been enlightened, who have tasted the heavenly gift, and have become partakers of the Holy Spirit" (Heb 6:4) can perish spiritually through a series of seemingly small infidelities, ultimately passing from the light into the night, where they are no longer capable of conversion. In Peter we encounter another danger, that of a fall which is not definitive and which can therefore be healed through conversion.

John 13 recounts two exchanges between Jesus and Peter, in which two aspects of this danger become visible. Initially, Peter does not want to have his feet washed by Jesus. This goes against his understanding of the relationship between master and disciple and against his image of the Messiah, whom he recognizes in Jesus. His resistance to the foot-washing has ultimately the same meaning as his protest against Jesus' prophecy of the Passion after the great confession at Caesarea Philippi: "God forbid, Lord! This shall never happen to you" was how he put it on that occasion (Mt 16:22).

Now, from a similar standpoint, he says: "You shall never wash my feet" (Jn 13:8). It is the response to Jesus that we find throughout history: You are the victor, you are the strong one—you must not lower yourself or practice humility! Again and again Jesus has to help us recognize anew that God's power is different, that the Messiah must pass through suffering into glory and must lead others along the same path.

In the second exchange, which comes after Judas' departure and the teaching on the new commandment, the theme is martyrdom. It is expressed in terms of "going away", "going across" (hypágō). Jesus had spoken on two occasions in John's Gospel about "going away" to a place where the Jews could not come (7:34–36; 8:21–22). His hearers had tried to work out what he meant by this, and they had arrived at two different hypotheses. On the first occasion, they asked: "Does he intend to go to the Dispersion among the Greeks and teach the Greeks?" (7:35). And the second time: "Will he kill himself?" (8:22). In both cases, they have an inkling of what is meant, yet they completely miss the truth. Yes, his going away is a going unto death—yet not through suicide: rather, he transforms his violent death into the free offering of his life (cf. 10:18). And in the same way Jesus did not actually travel to Greece, yet through the Cross and Resurrection he did effectively come to the Greeks, and he revealed the Father, the living God, to the Gentile world.

During the washing of the feet, in the atmosphere of farewell that pervades the scene, Peter asks his master quite openly: "Lord, where are you going?" And again he receives a cryptic answer: "Where I am going you cannot follow me now; but you shall follow afterward" (13:36). Peter understands that Jesus is speaking of his imminent death, and he now wants to emphasize his radical fidelity even unto death: "Why can I not follow you now? I will lay down my life for you" (13:37). Indeed, shortly afterward on the Mount of Olives, he rushes in with his sword, ready to put his intention into effect. But he must learn that even martyrdom is no heroic achievement: rather, it is a grace to be able to suffer for Jesus. He must bid farewell to the heroism of personal deeds and learn the humility of the disciple. His desire to rush in—his heroism—leads to his denial. In order to secure his place by the fire in the forecourt of the high priest's palace, and in order to keep abreast of every development in Jesus' destiny as it happens, he claims not to know him. His heroism falls to pieces in a small-minded tactic. He must learn to await his hour. He must learn how to wait, how to persevere. He must learn the way of the disciple in order to be led, when his hour comes, to the place where he does not want to go (cf. Jn 21:18) and to receive the grace of martyrdom.

The two exchanges are essentially about the same thing: not telling God what to do, but learning to accept him as he reveals himself to us; not seeking to exalt ourselves to God's level, but in humble service letting ourselves be slowly refashioned into God's true image.

Washing of feet and confession of sin

As we conclude, we must consider one final detail from the account of the washing of the feet. After the Lord has explained to Peter the necessity of having his feet washed, Peter answers: if this be the case, then Jesus should wash not only his feet, but his hands and his head as well. Jesus' answer is once again enigmatic: "He who has bathed does not need to wash, except for his feet" (13:10). What does this mean?

Jesus evidently takes for granted that before coming to the meal, the disciples have already had a complete bath, so that at table it is only their feet that need to be washed. It is clear that John sees a deeper symbolic meaning in these words, which is not easy to recognize. Let us remind ourselves straightaway that the washing of feet—as argued above—is not an individual sacrament, but it signifies the whole of Jesus' saving ministry: the *sacramentum* of his love into which he immerses us in faith, his love, which is our true bath of purification.

Yet in this context, the washing of feet acquires another more concrete meaning, over and above its fundamental symbolism, one that points to the practicalities of life in the early Church. What is it? The complete bath that was taken for granted can only mean Baptism, by which man is immersed into Christ once and for all, acquiring his new identity as one who dwells in Christ. This fundamental event, by which we become Christians not through our own doing but through the action of the Lord in his Church, cannot be repeated. Yet in the life of Christians—for table fellowship with the Lord—it constantly requires completion: "washing of feet". What is this? There is no single undisputed answer. Yet it seems to me that the First Letter of John points us in the right direction and shows us what is meant. There we read: "If we say we have no sin, we deceive ourselves, and the truth is not in us. If we confess our sins, he is faithful and just, and will forgive our sins and cleanse us from all unrighteousness. If we say we have not sinned, we make him a liar, and his word is not in us" (1:8–10). Since even the baptized remain sinners, they need confession of sins, "which cleanses us from all unrighteousness".

This word "cleanse" signals the inner connection with the foot-washing passage. The same practice of confession of sin, which originally came from Judaism, is also mentioned in the Letter of James (5:16), as well as the *Didachē*. There we read: "In church, make confession of your faults" (4, 14) and again, "Assemble on the Lord's

73

day, and break bread and offer the Eucharist; but first make confession of your faults" (14, 1). In this regard, Franz Mussner, following Rudolf Knopf, says: "In both places a short, public, individual confession is envisaged" (*Jakobusbrief*, p. 226, n. 5). Admittedly, one cannot equate this confession of sin, found in the life of early Christian communities in areas influenced by Jewish Christianity, with the sacrament of Confession as it was to develop in the course of later Church history: it is merely a "step on the way" toward it (ibid., p. 226).

The point is this: guilt must not be allowed to fester in the silence of the soul, poisoning it from within. It needs to be confessed. Through confession, we bring it into the light, we place it within Christ's purifying love (cf. Jn 3:20–21). In confession, the Lord washes our soiled feet over and over again and prepares us for table fellowship with him.

Looking back over the whole chapter on the washing of the feet, we may say that in this humble gesture, expressing the entire ministry of Jesus' life and death, the Lord stands before us as the servant of God—he who for our sake became one who serves, who carries our burden and so grants us true purity, the capacity to draw close to God. In the second Suffering Servant Song from Isaiah, there is a phrase that in some sense anticipates the essence of John's theology of the Passion: The Lord "said to me, 'You are my servant, Israel, in whom I will be glorified'" (49:3; the Greek word in the Septuagint version is *doxasthēsomai*).

Indeed, Saint John's whole Passion narrative is built on this connection between humble service and glory (*dóxa*): it is in Jesus' downward path, in his abasement even to the Cross, that God's glory is seen, that the Father and, in him, Jesus are glorified. In a brief scene on "Palm Sunday"—in what might be termed the Johannine version of the Gethsemane story—all this is summed up: " 'Now is my soul troubled. And what shall I say? "Father, save me from this hour"? No, for this purpose I have come to this hour. Father, glorify your name.' Then a voice came from heaven, 'I have glorified it, and I will glorify it again' " (12:27–28). The hour of the Cross is the hour of the Father's true glory, the hour of Jesus' true glory.

CHAPTER FOUR

Jesus' High-Priestly Prayer

The washing of the feet is followed in Saint John's Gospel by Jesus' farewell discourses (chaps. 14–16), which culminate in chapter 17 with a great prayer for which the Lutheran theologian David Chytraeus (1530–1600) coined the name "high-priestly prayer". The priestly character of the prayer had already been highlighted in the time of the Fathers, especially by Cyril of Alexandria (d. 444). André Feuillet, in his monograph on John 17, quotes a text by Rupert of Deutz (d. 1129/30), in which the prayer's essential character is very beautifully summed up: "Haec pontifex summus propiator ipse et propitiatorium, sacerdos et sacrificium, pro nobis oravit" (the high priest who was himself the one making atonement as well as the expiatory offering, both priest and sacrifice, implored this for us; *Ioan.*, in *PL* 169, col. 764 B; cf. Feuillet, *The Priesthood of Christ and His Ministers*, p. 245).

1. *The Jewish Feast of Atonement as Biblical Background to the High-Priestly Prayer*

The key to a correct understanding of this great text seems to me to be given in the above-mentioned book by Feuillet. He shows that this prayer can be understood only against the background of the liturgy of the Jewish Feast of Atonement (*Yom ha-Kippurim*). The ritual of the feast, with its rich theological content, is realized in Jesus' prayer—"realized" in the literal sense: the rite is translated into the reality that it signifies. What had been represented in ritual acts now takes place in reality, and it takes place definitively.

In order to understand this, we must first consider the ritual of the Feast of Atonement that is described in Leviticus 16 and 23:26–32. On this day, the high priest is required, through the appropriate sacrifice (two male goats for a sin offering and one ram for a burnt offering, a young animal: cf. 16:5–6.), to make atonement, first for himself, then for "his house", in other words, for the priestly clan of Israel in general, and finally for the whole community of Israel (cf. 16:17). "Thus he shall make atonement for the holy place, because of the uncleannesses of the sons of Israel, and because of their transgressions, all their sins; and so he shall do for the tent of meeting, which abides with them in the midst of their uncleannesses" (16:16).

These rituals constitute the one occasion in the entire year when the high priest pronounces in God's presence the otherwise unutterable holy name that God had revealed at the burning bush—the name through which he had, as it were, placed himself within Israel's reach. Hence the object of the Day of Atonement is to restore to Israel, after the misdeeds of the previous year, its character as a "holy people", to lead it back once more to its designated position as God's people in the midst of the world (cf. Feuillet, *The Priesthood of Christ and His Ministers*, pp. 49, 70). In this sense it has to do with the innermost purpose of the whole of creation: to open up a space for response to God's love, to his holy will.

According to rabbinic theology, the idea of the covenant— the idea of establishing a holy people to be an interlocutor for God in union with him—is prior to the idea of the creation of the world and supplies its inner motive. The cosmos was created, not that there might be manifold things in heaven and earth, but that there might be a space for the "covenant", for the loving "yes" between God and his human respondent. Each year the Feast of Atonement restores this harmony, this inner meaning of the world that is constantly disrupted by sin, and it therefore marks the high point of the liturgical year.

The structure of the ritual described in Leviticus 16 is reproduced exactly in Jesus' prayer: just as the high priest makes atonement for himself, for the priestly clan, and for the whole community of Israel, so Jesus prays for himself, for the Apostles, and finally for all who will come to believe in him through their word—for the Church of all times (cf. Jn 17:20). He sanctifies "himself", and he obtains the sanctification of those who are his. The fact that, despite a certain demarcation from the "world" (cf. 17:9), this means the salvation of all, the "life of the world" as a whole (cf. 6:51), is something we will be considering later. Jesus' prayer manifests him as the high priest of the Day of Atonement. His Cross and his exaltation is the Day of Atonement for the world, in which the whole of world history—in the face of all human sin and its destructive consequences—finds its meaning and is aligned with its true purpose and destiny.

In this sense, the theology of John 17 corresponds exactly to the ideas that are worked out in detail in the Letter to the Hebrews. The interpretation put forward there of Old Testament worship in the light of Jesus Christ is what lies at the heart of the prayer of John 17. But Saint Paul's theology also converges on this center, which is clear in dramatically imploring form in the Second Letter to the Corinthians: "We beg you on behalf of Christ, be reconciled to God" (5:20).

And is it not the case that our need to be reconciled with God—the silent, mysterious, seemingly absent, and yet omnipresent God—is the real problem of the whole of world history?

Jesus' high-priestly prayer is the consummation of the Day of Atonement, the eternally accessible feast, as it were, of God's reconciliation with men. At this point, the question arises over the connection between Jesus' high-priestly prayer and the Eucharist. There have been attempts to portray this prayer as a kind of Eucharistic Prayer, to present it as John's version, so to speak, of the institution of the Sacrament. Such attempts are untenable. Yet on a deeper level, a connection does exist.

In the words addressed by Jesus to the Father, the ritual of the Day of Atonement is transformed into prayer. Here we find a concrete example of that cultic renewal toward which the cleansing of the Temple and Jesus' interpretation of it were pointing. Sacrificial animals are a thing of the past. In their place are what the Greek Fathers called *thysía logikē*—spiritual sacrifices [literally: sacrifices after the manner of the word]—and what Paul described in similar terms as *logikē latreía*, that is, worship shaped by the word, structured on reason (Rom 12:1).

Admittedly, this "word" that supplants the sacrificial offerings is no ordinary word. To begin with, it is no mere human speech, but rather the word of him who is "*the* Word", and so it draws all human words into God's inner dialogue, into his reason and his love. For this reason, though, let me reiterate that it is more than a word, because the eternal Word said: "Sacrifices and offerings you have not desired, but a body have you prepared for me" (Heb 10:5; cf. Ps 40:6). The Word is now flesh, and not only that: it is his body offered up, his blood poured out.

With the institution of the Eucharist, Jesus transforms his cruel death into "word", into the radical expression of his love, his self-giving to the point of death. So he himself becomes the "Temple". Insofar as the high-priestly prayer forms the consummation of Jesus' self-gift, it represents the new worship and has a deep inner connection with the Eucharist: when we consider the institution of the Eucharist, we shall return to this.

Before we consider the individual themes contained in Jesus' high-priestly prayer, one further Old Testament allusion should be mentioned, one that has again been studied by André Feuillet. He shows that the renewed and deepened spiritual understanding of the priesthood found in John 17 is already prefigured in Isaiah's Suffering Servant Songs, especially in Isaiah 53. The Suffering Servant, who has the guilt of all laid upon him (53:6), giving up his life as a sin-offering (53:10) and bearing the sins of many (53:12), thereby carries out the ministry of the high priest, fulfilling the figure of the priesthood from deep within. He is both priest and victim, and in this way he achieves reconciliation. Thus the Suffering Servant Songs continue along the whole path of exploring the deeper meaning of the priesthood and worship, in harmony with the prophetic tradition, especially Ezekiel.

Even if there is no direct reference in John 17 to the Suffering Servant Songs, nevertheless the vision of Isaiah 53 is fundamental for the new understanding of the priesthood and worship that is presented throughout John's Gospel and especially in the high-priestly prayer. We came across a clear manifestation of this connection in the chapter on the washing of the feet, and it is also evident in the Good Shepherd discourse, where Jesus says five times that the Good Shepherd lays down his life for the sheep (Jn 10:11, 15, 17, 18 [twice]), clearly echoing Isaiah 53:10.

The "newness" of the figure of Jesus Christ—made visible in the outward discontinuity with the Temple and its sacrifices—nevertheless maintains a deep inner unity with the salvation history of the Old Covenant. If we think of the figure of Moses, who intercedes for Israel's salvation by offering his life to God, then this unity becomes evident yet again, and it is an essential concern of John's Gospel to reveal it.

2. *Four Major Themes of the Prayer*

From the great wealth of material contained in John 17, I should now like to select four principal themes that draw out essential aspects of this great text and, hence, of John's message in general.

"This is eternal life . . ."

To begin with, there is verse 3: "This is eternal life, that they know you the only true God, and Jesus Christ whom you have sent."

The theme of "life" (*zōē*), which pervades the whole Gospel from verse 4 of the Prologue onward, is bound to feature also in the new liturgy of atonement that is realized in the high-priestly prayer. The thesis of Rudolf Schnackenburg and others that this verse is a later gloss, on the basis that the word "life" does not recur in John 17, seems to me to arise—just like the separation of sources in the chapter on the washing of the feet—from the kind of academic logic that takes the compositional form of modern scholarly texts as the criterion for something so utterly different in its expression and thought as John's Gospel.

"Eternal life" is not—as the modern reader might immediately assume—life after death, in contrast to this present life, which is transient and not eternal. "Eternal life" is life itself, real life, which can also be lived in the present age and is no longer challenged by physical death. This is the point: to seize "life" here and now, real life that can no longer be destroyed by anything or anyone.

This meaning of "eternal life" appears very clearly in the account of the raising of Lazarus: "He who believes in me, though he die, yet shall he live, and whoever lives and believes in me shall never die" (Jn 11:25–26). "Because I live, you will live also", says Jesus to his disciples at the Last Supper (Jn 14:19), and he thereby reveals once again that a distinguishing feature of the disciple of Jesus is the fact that he "lives": beyond the mere fact of existing, he has found and embraced the *real* life that everyone is seeking. On the basis of such texts, the early Christians called themselves simply "the living" (*hoi zōntes*). They had found what all are seeking—life itself, full and, hence, indestructible life.

Yet how does one obtain it? The high-priestly prayer gives an answer that may surprise us, even though in the context of biblical thought it was already present. "Eternal life" is gained through "recognition", presupposing here the Old Testament concept of recognition: recognizing creates communion; it is union of being with the one recognized. But of course the key to life is not *any kind of* recognition, but to "know *you* the only true God, and Jesus Christ whom you have sent" (17:3). This is a kind of summary creedal formula expressing the essential content of the decision to be a Christian—the recognition granted to us by faith. The Christian does not believe in a multiplicity of things. Ultimately he believes, quite simply, in God: he believes that there is only one true God.

This God becomes accessible to us through the one he sent, Jesus Christ: it is in the encounter with him that we experience the recognition of God that leads to communion and thus to "life". In the twofold expression "God and the one whom he sent", we hear echoes of a constantly recurring message, found especially in God's words in the Book of Exodus: they are to believe in "me", in God, and in Moses, the one he sent. God reveals his face in the one sent—definitively in his Son.

"Eternal life" is thus a relational event. Man did not acquire it from himself or for himself alone. Through relationship with the one who is himself life, man too comes alive.

Some preliminary steps toward this profoundly biblical idea can also be found in Plato, whose work draws upon very different traditions and reflections on the theme of immortality. His thought includes the idea that man can become immortal by uniting himself to the immortal. The more he takes truth into himself, binds himself to the truth and adheres to it, the more he is related to and filled with that which cannot be destroyed. Insofar as he himself, as it were, adheres to the truth, insofar as he is carried by that which endures, he may be sure of life after death—the fullness of life.

What these ideas explore only tentatively shines forth without a hint of ambiguity in the words of Jesus. Man has found life when he adheres to him who is himself Life. Then much that pertains to him can be destroyed. Death may remove him from the biosphere, but the life that reaches beyond it—real life—remains. This life, which John calls *zōē* as opposed to *bios*, is man's goal. The relationship to God in Jesus Christ is the source of a life that no death can take away.

Clearly, this "life in relation" refers to a thoroughly concrete manner of existence; faith and recognition are not like any other kind of human knowledge; rather, they are the very form of man's existence. Even if we are not yet speaking of love, it is clear that the "recognition" of him who is himself Love leads in turn to love, with all that it gives and all that it demands.

"Sanctify them in the truth ..."

As a second theme, I should like to explore the idea of sanctification and sanctifying, which points strongly toward the connection with the event of atonement and with the high priesthood.

In the prayer for the disciples, Jesus says: "Sanctify them in the truth; your word is truth.... For their sake I consecrate myself, that they also may be consecrated in truth" (Jn 17:17, 19). Let us also cite a passage from the controversy discourses that belongs in this context: here Jesus designates himself as the one sanctified and sent into the world by the Father (cf. 10:36). Hence we are dealing with a triple "sanctification": the Father has sanctified the Son and sent him into the world; the Son sanctifies himself; and he asks, on the basis of his own sanctification, that the disciples be sanctified in the truth.

What does it mean to "sanctify"? According to biblical understanding, sanctity or "holiness" in the fullest sense is attributable only to God. Holiness expresses his particular way of being, divine being as such. So the word "sanctify" (*qadoš* is the word for "holy" in the Hebrew Bible) means handing over a reality—a person or even a thing—to God, especially through appropriation for worship. This can take the form of consecration for sacrifice (cf. Ex 13:2; Deut 15:19); or, on the other hand, it can mean priestly consecration (cf. Ex 28:41), the designation of a man for God and for divine worship.

The process of consecration, "sanctification", includes two apparently opposed, but in reality deeply conjoined, aspects. On the one hand, "consecrating" as "sanctifying" means setting apart from the rest of reality that pertains to man's ordinary everyday life. Something that is consecrated is raised into a new sphere that is no longer under human control. But this setting apart also includes the essential dynamic of "existing for". Precisely because it is entirely given over to God, this reality is now there for the world, for men, it speaks for them and exists for their healing. We may also say: setting apart and mission form a single whole.

The connection between the two can be seen very clearly if we consider the special vocation of Israel: on the one hand, it is set apart from all other peoples, but for a particular reason—in order to carry out a commission for all peoples, for the whole world. That is what is meant when Israel is designated a "holy people".

Let us return to John's Gospel. What is the meaning of the three sanctifications (consecrations) that are spoken of there? First we are told that the Father sent his Son into the world and consecrated him (cf. 10:36). What does that mean? The exegetes suggest a certain parallel between this expression and the call of the Prophet Jeremiah: "Before I formed you in the womb I knew you, and before you were born I consecrated you; I appointed you a prophet to the nations" (Jer 1:5). Consecration means that God is exercising a total claim over this man, "setting him apart" for himself, yet at the same time sending him out for the nations.

In Jesus' words, too, consecration and mission are directly linked. Thus one may say that this consecration of Jesus by the Father is identical with the Incarnation: it expresses both total unity with the Father and total existence for the world. Jesus belongs entirely to God, and that is what makes him entirely "for all". "You are the Holy One of God", Peter said to him in the synagogue at Capernaum, and these words constitute a comprehensive Christological confession (Jn 6:69).

Once the Father has "consecrated" him, though, what is meant when he goes on to say "I consecrate (*hagiázō*) myself" (17:19)? Rudolf Bultmann gives a convincing answer to this question in his commentary on John's Gospel. "*Hagiázō*, put here in the farewell prayer at the beginning of the Passion, and used together with *hypèr autōn* (for them), means 'to make holy' in the sense of 'to consecrate for the sacrifice' "; Bultmann quotes in support a saying of Saint John Chrysostom: "I sanctify myself—I present myself as a sacrifice" (*The Gospel of John*, p. 510, n. 5; cf. also Feuillet, *The Priesthood of Christ and His Ministers*, pp. 35 and 44). If the first "sanctification" is related to the Incarnation, here the focus is on the Passion as sacrifice.

Bultmann has presented the inner connection between the two "sanctifications" very beautifully. The holiness that Jesus received from the Father is his "being for the world", or "being for his own". His holiness is "no static difference in substance from the world, but is something Jesus achieves only by completing the stand he has made for God and against the world. But this completion means sacrifice. In the sacrifice he is, in the manner of God, so *against* the world that he is at the same time *for* it" (*The Gospel of John*, p. 511). In this passage, one may object to the sharp distinction between substantial being and completion of the sacrifice: Jesus' "substantial" being is as such the entire dynamic of "being for"; the two are inseparable. But perhaps Bultmann meant this as well. He should, moreover, be given credit when he says of John 17:19 that "there is no disputing the allusion to the words of the Lord's supper" (ibid., p. 510 n. 5).

Thus, in these few words, we see before us the new atonement liturgy of Jesus Christ, the liturgy of the New Covenant, in its entire grandeur and purity. Jesus himself is the priest sent into the world by the Father; he himself is the sacrifice that is made present in the Eucharist of all times. Somehow Philo of Alexandria had correctly anticipated this when he spoke of the Logos as priest and high priest (*Leg. All.* III, 82; *De Somn.* I, 215; II, 183; reference found in Bultmann, ibid.). The meaning of the Day of Atonement is completely fulfilled in the "Word" that was made flesh "for the life of the world" (Jn 6:51).

Let us turn to the third sanctification that is spoken of in Jesus' prayer: "Sanctify them in the truth" (17:17). "I consecrate myself, that they also may be consecrated in truth" (17:19). The disciples are to be drawn into Jesus' sanctification; they too are included in this reappropriation into God's sphere and the ensuing mission for the world. "I consecrate myself, that they also may be consecrated in truth": their being given over to God, their "consecration", is tied to the consecration of Jesus Christ; it is a participation in his state of sanctification.

Between verses 17 and 19, which speak of the consecration of the disciples, there is a small but important difference. Verse 19 says that they are to be consecrated "in truth": not just ritually, but truly, in their whole being—this is doubtless how it should be translated. Verse 17, on the other hand, reads: "sanctify them in *the* truth". Here the truth is designated as the force of sanctification, as "their consecration".

According to the Book of Exodus, the priestly consecration of the sons of Aaron is accomplished when they are vested in sacred robes and anointed (29:1–9); the ritual of the Day of Atonement also speaks of a complete bath before the investiture with sacred robes (Lev 16:4). The disciples of Jesus are sanctified, consecrated "in the truth". The truth is the bath that purifies them; the truth is the robe and the anointing they need.

This purifying and sanctifying "truth" is ultimately Christ himself. They must be immersed in him; they must, so to speak, be "newly robed" in him, and thus they come to share in his consecration, in his priestly commission, in his sacrifice.

Judaism, likewise, after the demise of the Temple, had to discover a new meaning for the cultic prescriptions. It now saw "sanctification" in the fulfillment of the commandments—in being immersed in God's holy word and in God's will expressed therein (cf. Schnackenburg, *The Gospel according to Saint John* III, pp. 185f.).

In the Christian faith, Jesus is the Torah in person, and hence consecration takes place through union of will and union of being with him. If the disciples' sanctification in the truth is ultimately about sharing in Jesus' priestly mission, then we may recognize in these words of John's Gospel the institution of the priesthood of the Apostles, the institution of the New Testament priesthood, which at the deepest level is service to the truth.

"I have made your name known to them . . ."

A further fundamental theme of the high-priestly prayer is the revelation of God's name: "I have manifested your name to the men that you gave me out of the world" (Jn 17:6). "I made known to them your name, and I will make it known, that the love with which you have loved me may be in them, and I in them" (Jn 17:26).

With these words Jesus clearly presents himself as the new Moses, who brings to completion what began with

Moses at the burning bush. God revealed his "name" to Moses. That "name" was more than a word. It meant that God allowed himself to be invoked, that he had entered into communion with Israel. So in the course of Israel's faith history, it became ever clearer that the "name of God" meant his "immanence": his presence in the midst of men, in which he is entirely "there", while at the same time infinitely surpassing everything human, everything to do with this world.

"God's name" means: God present among men. It is said of the Temple in Jerusalem that God "[made] his name dwell" there (Deut 12:11, and elsewhere). Israel would never have dared to say simply: God lives there. Israel knew that God is infinitely great, that he surpasses and embraces the whole world. And yet he was truly present: he himself. That is what is meant by saying: "He [made] his name dwell there." He is truly present, yet always remains infinitely greater and beyond our reach. "God's name" is God himself insofar as he gives himself to us; however certain we are of his closeness and however much we rejoice over it, he always remains infinitely greater.

This is the understanding of God's name that lies behind Jesus' words. When he says he has manifested God's name and that he will manifest it further, he is not speaking of some new word that he has communicated to men as a particularly felicitous designation for God. The revelation of the name is a new mode of God's presence among men, a radically new way in which God makes his home with them. In Jesus, God gives himself entirely into

the world of mankind: whoever sees Jesus sees the Father
(cf. Jn 14:9).

If we may say that God's immanence in the Old Testament was effected in the form of the word and in the form
of liturgical celebration, that immanence has now become
ontological: in Jesus, God has truly become man. God has
entered our very being. In him God is truly "God-with-
us". The Incarnation, through which God's new being as
man was effected, becomes through his sacrifice an event
for the whole of mankind. As the Risen One, he comes
once more, in order to make all people into his body, the
new Temple. The "manifestation of the name" is meant
to ensure that "the love with which you have loved me
may be in them, and I in them" (17:26). It is aimed at the
transformation of the whole of creation, so that it may
become in a completely new way God's true dwelling
place in union with Christ.

Basil Studer has pointed out that at the beginning of
Christianity, "circles influenced by Judaism ... developed
a special name-Christology ... Name, Law, Covenant,
Beginning, and Day" now become Christological titles
(*Gott und unsere Erlösung*, pp. 56, 61). It is known that
Christ himself, in person, is God's "name", God's acces-
sibility to us.

"I made known to them your name, and I will make it
known." The self-gift of God in Christ is not a thing of
the past: "I will make it known". In Christ, God continually approaches men, so that they in turn can approach
him. To make Christ known is to make God known.

Through our encounter with Christ, God approaches us, draws us into himself (cf. Jn 12:32), in order, as it were, to lead us out beyond ourselves into the infinite breadth of his greatness and his love.

"That they may all be one ..."

Another major theme of the high-priestly prayer is the future unity of Jesus' disciples. Uniquely in the Gospels, Jesus' gaze now moves beyond the current community of disciples and is directed toward all those who "believe in me through their word" (Jn 17:20). The vast horizon of the community of believers in times to come opens up across the generations: the Church of the future is included in Jesus' prayer. He pleads for unity for his future disciples.

The Lord repeats this plea four times. Twice the purpose of this unity is indicated as being that the world may believe, that it may "recognize" that Jesus has been sent by the Father: "Holy Father, keep them in your name, which you have given me, that they may be one, even as we are one" (Jn 17:11). "That they may all be one; even as you, Father, are in me, and I in you, that they also may be in us, so that the world may believe that you have sent me" (Jn 17:21). "That they may be one even as we are one ... that they may become perfectly one, so that the world may know that you have sent me" (Jn 17:22–23).

No discourse on ecumenism ever lacks a reference to this "testament" of Jesus—to the fact that before he went to the Cross, he pleaded with the Father for the unity of his future disciples, for the Church of all times. And so it should be. Yet we have to ask with all the more urgency: For what unity was Jesus praying? What is his prayer for the community of believers throughout history?

It is instructive to hear Rudolf Bultmann once again on this question. He says first of all—as we read in the Gospel—that this unity is grounded in the unity of Father and Son, and then he continues: "That means it is not founded on natural or purely historical data, nor can it be manufactured by organization, institutions or dogma; these can at best only bear witness to the real unity, as on the other hand they can also give a false impression of unity. And even if the proclamation of the word in the world requires institutions and dogmas, these cannot guarantee the unity of true proclamation. On the other hand the actual disunion of the Church, which is, in passing, precisely the result of its institutions and dogmas, does not necessarily frustrate the unity of the proclamation. The word can resound authentically, wherever the tradition is maintained. Because the authenticity of the proclamation cannot be controlled by institutions or dogmas, and because the faith that answers the word is invisible, it is also true that the authentic unity of the community is invisible ... it is invisible because it is not a worldly phenomenon at all" (*The Gospel of John*, pp. 513–14).

These sentences are astonishing. Much of what they say might be called into question, the concept of "institutions" and "dogmas" to begin with, but even more so the concept of "proclamation", which is said to create unity by itself. Is it true that the Revealer in his unity with the Father is present in the proclamation? Is he not

94

often astonishingly absent? Now Bultmann gives us a certain criterion for establishing where the word resounds "authentically": "wherever the tradition is maintained". Which tradition? one might ask. Where does it come from; what is its content? Since not every proclamation is "authentic", how are we to recognize it? The "authentic proclamation" is said to create unity by itself. The "actual disunion" of the Church cannot hinder the unity that comes from the Lord, so Bultmann claims.

Does this mean that ecumenism is rendered superfluous, since unity is created in proclamation and is not hindered through the schisms of history? Perhaps it is also significant that Bultmann uses the word "Church" when he speaks of disunion, whereas he uses the word "community" when considering unity. The unity of proclamation is not verifiable, he tells us. Therefore the unity of the community is invisible, just as faith is invisible. Unity is invisible, because "it is not a worldly phenomenon at all."

Is this the correct exegesis of Jesus' prayer? It is certainly true that the unity of the disciples—of the future Church—for which Jesus prays "is not a worldly phenomenon". This the Lord says quite distinctly. Unity does not come from the world: on the basis of the world's own efforts, it is impossible. The world's own efforts lead to disunion, as we can all see. Inasmuch as the world is operative in the Church, in Christianity, it leads to schisms. Unity can only come from the Father through the Son. It has to do with the "glory" that the Son gives: with his presence, granted through the Holy Spirit, which is the fruit of the Cross, the fruit of Jesus' transformation through death and Resurrection.

Yet the power of God reaches into the midst of the world in which the disciples live. It must be of such a kind that the world can "recognize" it and thereby come to faith. While it does not come from the world, it can and must be thoroughly effective in and for the world, and it must be discernible by the world. The stated objective of Jesus' prayer for unity is precisely that through the unity of the disciples, the truth of his mission is made visible for men. Unity must be visible; it must be recognizable as something that does not exist elsewhere in the world; as something that is inexplicable on the basis of mankind's own efforts and that therefore makes visible the workings of a higher power. Through the humanly inexplicable unity of Jesus' disciples down the centuries, Jesus himself is vindicated. It can be seen that he is truly the "Son". Hence God can be recognized as the creator of a unity that overcomes the world's inherent tendency toward fragmentation.

For this the Lord prayed: for a unity that can come into existence only from God and through Christ and yet is so concrete in its appearance that in it we are able to see God's power at work. That is why the struggle for the visible unity of the disciples of Jesus Christ remains an urgent task for Christians of all times and places. The invisible unity of the "community" is not sufficient.

Is there more that we can discern about the nature and content of the unity for which Jesus prayed? One essential element of this unity has already emerged from our considerations thus far: it depends on faith in God and in the one whom he sent: Jesus Christ. The unity of the future Church therefore rests on the faith that Peter proclaimed in the name of the Twelve in the synagogue at Capernaum, after other disciples had turned away: "We have believed, and have come to know, that you are the Holy One of God" (Jn 6:69).

This confession is very close in content to the high-priestly prayer. Here Jesus encounters us as the one whom the Father has sanctified, who sanctifies himself for the disciples, who sanctifies the disciples in the truth. Faith is something more than a word, an idea: it involves entering into communion with Jesus Christ and through him with the Father. Faith is the real foundation of the disciples' communion, the basis for the Church's unity.

In its nucleus, this faith is "invisible". But because the disciples unite themselves to the one Christ, faith becomes "flesh" and knits the individual believers together into a real "body". The Incarnation of the *Logos* is perpetuated until the measure of Christ's "full stature" is attained (cf. Eph 4:13).

Faith in Jesus Christ as the one sent by the Father includes mission as its second structural element. We have seen that holiness, that is to say, belonging to the living God, signifies mission.

Throughout John's Gospel, then, and especially in chapter 17, Jesus, the Holy One of God, is the one sent by God. His whole identity is "being sent". What this means becomes clear from a passage in chapter 7, where the Lord says: "My teaching is not mine" (7:16). He lives totally "from the Father", and there is nothing else, nothing purely of his own, that he brings to the Father. In the farewell discourses, this characteristic identity of the Son is extended to include the Holy Spirit: "He will not speak on his own authority, but whatever he hears he will speak" (16:13). The Father sends the Spirit in Jesus' name (14:26); Jesus sends him from the Father (15:26).

After the Resurrection, Jesus draws the disciples into this dynamic of mission: "As the Father has sent me, even so I send you" (20:21). A defining characteristic of the community of disciples in every age must be their "being sent" by Jesus. This will always mean that for them, too, "my teaching is not mine"; the disciples do not proclaim themselves, but they say what they have heard. They represent Christ, just as Christ represents the Father. They follow the guidance of the Holy Spirit, knowing that in this total fidelity a process of maturing is simultaneously at work: "The Spirit of truth … will guide you into all the truth" (16:13).

In this quality of "being sent", characteristic of Christ's disciples, and inasmuch as they were bound to his word and to the power of his Spirit, the early Church was able to recognize the form of "apostolic succession". The continuation of the mission is "sacramental", that is to say, it is not self-generating, nor is it something man-made, but it is a matter of being incorporated into the "Word that existed from the beginning" (cf. 1 Jn 1:1), into the communion of witnesses called forth by the Spirit. The Greek word for succession—*diadochē*—refers to both structure and content. It points to the continuation of the mission in the witnesses; but it also points to the content of their testimony, to the word that is handed down, to which the witness is bound by the "sacrament".

Together with "apostolic succession", the early Church discovered (she did *not* invent) two further elements fundamental for her unity: the canon of Scripture and the so-called *regula fidei*, or "rule of faith". This was a short summary—not definitively tied down in every detail to specific linguistic formulations—of the essential content of the faith, which in the early Church's different baptismal confessions took on a liturgical form. This rule of faith, or creed, constitutes the real "hermeneutic" of Scripture, the key derived from Scripture itself by which the sacred text can be interpreted according to its spirit.

The unity of these three constitutive elements of the Church—the sacrament of succession, Scripture, the rule of faith (creed)—is the true guarantee that "the word can resound authentically", that "the tradition is maintained" (cf. Bultmann). Of course John's Gospel does not speak in so many words of these three pillars of the community of disciples, of the Church, but with its references to Trinitarian faith and to "being sent", it lays the foundations for them.

Let us return to Jesus' prayer that, through the unity of the disciples, the world may recognize him as the one sent by the Father. This recognizing and believing is not something merely intellectual; it is about being touched

99

by God's love and therefore changed; it is about the gift of true life.

The universality of Jesus' mission is made visible; it concerns not just a limited circle of chosen ones—its scope is the whole of creation, the world in its entirety. Through the disciples and their mission, the world as a whole is to be torn free from its alienation, it is to rediscover unity with God.

This universal horizon of Jesus' mission can also be seen in two other important texts from the Fourth Gospel: first, in Jesus' nocturnal conversation with Nicodemus: "God so loved the world that he gave his only-begotten Son" (3:16), and then—with the emphasis here on the sacrifice of his life—in the bread of life discourse at Capernaum: "The bread which I shall give for the life of the world is my flesh" (6:51).

But how do we reconcile this universalism with the harsh words found in verse 9 of the high-priestly prayer: "I am praying for them; I am not praying for the world"? In order to grasp the inner unity of the apparently contradictory prayers, we must remember that John uses the word "cosmos"—world—in two different senses. On the one hand, it refers to the whole of God's good creation, especially to men: his creatures, whom he loves to the point of the gift of himself in the Son. On the other hand, the word refers to the human world as it has evolved in history. Corruption, lies, and violence have, as it were, become "natural" to it. Blaise Pascal speaks of a second nature that in the course of history has supplanted the first. Modern philosophers have described this historical state of mankind in various ways, as for example when Martin Heidegger speaks of being reduced to the impersonal, of existing in "inauthenticity". These same issues are presented in a very different way when Karl Marx expounds man's alienation.

Philosophy in these instances is ultimately describing what is known to faith as "original sin". The present "world" has to disappear; it must be changed into God's world. That is precisely what Jesus' mission is, into which the disciples are taken up: leading "the world" away from the condition of man's alienation from God and from himself, so that it can become God's world once more and so that man can become fully himself again by becoming one with God. Yet this transformation comes at the price of the Cross; it comes at the price of readiness for martyrdom on the part of Christ's witnesses.

If we take one last look back over the whole of the prayer for unity, we can say that the founding of the Church takes place during this passage, even though the word Church does not appear. For what else is the Church, if not the community of disciples who receive their unity through faith in Jesus Christ as the one sent by the Father and are drawn into Jesus' mission to lead the world toward the recognition of God—and in this way to redeem it?

The Church is born from Jesus' prayer. But this prayer is more than words; it is the act by which he "sanctifies" himself, that is to say, he "sacrifices" himself for the life of the world. We can also put it the other way around: in this prayer, the cruel event of the Cross becomes "word", it becomes the Feast of Atonement between God and the world. From here the Church emerges as the community of those who believe in Christ on the strength of the Apostles' word (cf. 17:20).

CHAPTER FIVE

The Last Supper

Even more than Jesus' eschatological discourse, which we considered in chapter 2 of this book, the accounts of the Last Supper and the institution of the Eucharist are caught up in a dense undergrowth of mutually contradictory hypotheses, which seem to make access to the real event virtually impossible. Since the text in question concerns the very heart of Christianity and does indeed raise difficult historical questions, this is not surprising.

I shall attempt to follow the same path as in the case of the eschatological discourse. This book does not seek to address the many perfectly justifiable specific questions about every detail of text and history: our task instead is to become acquainted with the figure of Jesus, and we leave the details to the experts. All the same, we cannot prescind from the question of the actual historicity of the key events.

The New Testament message is not simply an idea; essential to it is the fact that these events actually occurred in the history of this world: biblical faith does not recount stories as symbols of meta-historical truths; rather, it bases itself upon history that unfolded upon this earth (cf. Part One, p. xv). If Jesus did *not* give his disciples bread and wine as his body and blood, then the Church's eucharistic celebration is empty—a pious fiction and not a reality at the foundation of communion with God and among men.

This naturally raises once more the question of possible and appropriate forms of historical verification. We must be clear about the fact that historical research can at most establish high probability but never final and absolute certainty over every detail. If the certainty of faith were dependent upon scientific-historical verification alone, it would always remain open to revision.

Let me take an example from the recent history of exegetical research. Amid the growing confusion of academic hypotheses, the great German exegete Joachim Jeremias set out with the utmost historical and philological erudition and with the greatest methodological precision to identify the *ipsissima verba Iesu*, Jesus' own words, from the abundance of material handed down, hoping to find in them the bedrock of faith: surely we can build on what Jesus himself actually said. Even though Jeremias' results are still relevant and of considerable importance in academic circles, there are well-founded critical questions that show at least that there are limits to the certainty he attained.

So what may we expect? And what may we not expect? From a theological standpoint, it must be said that if the historicity of the key words and events could be scientifically disproved, then the faith would have lost its foundation. Conversely, we may not expect, as mentioned earlier, to find absolutely certain proof of every detail, given the nature of historical knowledge. The important thing for us, then, is to ascertain whether the basic convictions of the faith are historically plausible and credible when today's exegetical knowledge is taken in all seriousness.

Many details may remain open. Yet the "*factum est*" of John's Prologue (1:14) is a basic Christian category, and it applies not only to the Incarnation: it must also be invoked for the Last Supper, the Cross, and the Resurrection. Jesus' Incarnation is ordered toward his offering of himself for men, and this in turn is ordered toward the Resurrection: were it otherwise, Christianity would not be true. The reality of this "*factum est*" cannot—as we have seen—be viewed through the lens of absolute historical certainty, but its gravity can be recognized through correct reading of the Scripture as such.

It is faith that gives us the ultimate certainty upon which we base our whole lives—a humble commonality of belief in company with the Church of every age under the guidance of the Holy Spirit. On this basis, moreover, we can serenely examine exegetical hypotheses that all too often make exaggerated claims to certainty, claims that are already undermined by the existence of diametrically opposed positions put forward with an equal claim to scientific certainty.

On the basis of these methodological presuppositions, I shall attempt to select the questions that are essential for the faith from across the whole range of the debate. They will be grouped into four sections. In the first place, we will consider the dating of Jesus' Last Supper, which is essentially the question of whether or not it was a Passover meal. Secondly, we will consider the texts that recount Jesus' Last Supper, together with the question of their historical credibility. In third place, I should like to attempt an exegesis of the essential theological content of the Last Supper tradition. Finally, in the fourth section, we must briefly look beyond the New Testament tradition to the emergence of the Church's Eucharist—the development that Augustine described as the passage from the Last Supper to the "morning offering" (cf. *En. in Ps.* 140, 5).

1. *The Dating of the Last Supper*

The problem of dating Jesus' Last Supper arises from the contradiction on this point between the Synoptic Gospels, on the one hand, and Saint John's Gospel, on the other. Mark, whom Matthew and Luke follow in essentials, gives us a precise dating: "On the first day of Unleavened Bread, when they sacrificed the Passover lamb, his disciples said to him, 'Where will you have us go and prepare for you to eat the Passover?' ... And when it was evening he came with the Twelve" (14:12, 17). The evening of the first day of Unleavened Bread, on which the Paschal lambs are slaughtered in the Temple, is the vigil of the Passover feast. According to the chronology of the Synoptics, this was a Thursday.

After sunset, the Passover began, and then the Passover meal was taken—by Jesus and his disciples, as indeed by all the pilgrims who had come to Jerusalem. On the night leading into Friday, then—still according to the Synoptic chronology—Jesus was arrested and brought before the court; on Friday morning he was condemned to death by Pilate, and subsequently, "around the third hour" (ca. 9:00 A.M.), he was led to the Cross. Jesus died at the ninth hour (ca. 3:00 P.M.). "And when evening had come, since it was the day of Preparation, that is, the day before the sabbath, Joseph of Arimathea ... took courage and went to Pilate, and asked for the body of Jesus" (Mk 15:42–43). The burial had to take place before sunset, because then the Sabbath would begin. The Sabbath is the day when Jesus rested in the tomb. The Resurrection took place on the morning of the "first day of the week", on Sunday.

This chronology suffers from the problem that Jesus' trial and crucifixion would have taken place on the day of the Passover feast, which that year fell on a Friday. True, many scholars have tried to show that the trial and crucifixion were compatible with the prescriptions of the Passover. But despite all academic arguments, it seems questionable whether the trial before Pilate and the crucifixion would have been permissible and possible on such an important Jewish feast day. Moreover, there is a comment reported by Mark that militates against this hypothesis. He tells us that two days before the Feast of Unleavened Bread, the chief priests and scribes were looking for an opportunity to bring Jesus under their control by stealth and kill him, but in this regard, they declared: "not during the feast, lest there be a tumult of the people" (14:1–2). According to the Synoptic chronology, the execution of Jesus would indeed have taken place on the very day of the feast.

Let us now turn to John's chronology. John goes to great lengths to indicate that the Last Supper was not a Passover meal. On the contrary: the Jewish authorities who led Jesus before Pilate's court avoided entering the praetorium, "so that they might not be defiled, but might eat the Passover" (18:28). The Passover, therefore, began only in the evening, and at the time of the trial the Passover meal had not yet taken place; the trial and crucifixion took place on the day before the Passover, on the "day of preparation", not on the feast day itself. The Passover feast in the year in question accordingly ran from Friday evening until Saturday evening, not from Thursday evening until Friday evening.

Otherwise the sequence of events remains the same: Thursday evening—Jesus' Last Supper with the disciples, but not a Passover meal; Friday, the vigil of the feast, not the feast itself—trial and execution; Saturday—rest in the tomb; Sunday—Resurrection. According to this chronology, Jesus dies at the moment when the Passover lambs are being slaughtered in the Temple. Jesus dies as the real lamb, merely prefigured by those slain in the Temple.

This theologically significant connection, that Jesus' death coincides with the slaughter of the Passover lambs, has led many scholars to dismiss John's presentation as a theological chronology. John, they claim, altered the chronology in order to create this theological connection, which admittedly is not made explicit in the Gospel. Today, though, it is becoming increasingly clear that John's chronology is more probable historically than the Synoptic chronology. For as mentioned earlier: trial and execution on the feast seem scarcely conceivable. On the other hand, Jesus' Last Supper seems so closely tied to the Passover tradition that to deny its Passover character is problematic.

Frequent attempts have been made, therefore, to reconcile the two chronologies with one another. A most important and indeed fascinating attempt to harmonize the two traditions was made by the French scholar Annie Jaubert, who developed her theory in a series of publications starting in 1953. We need not go into the details of this proposal here; let us confine ourselves to the essentials.

Jaubert bases herself primarily on two early texts, which seem to suggest a solution to the problem. First she refers to an ancient priestly calendar handed down in the *Book of Jubilees*, which was a Hebrew text produced in the second half of the second century before Christ. This calendar leaves the cycles of the moon out of consideration and bases itself upon a year of 364 days, divided into four seasons, each consisting of three months, two of them thirty days long and one thirty-one days long. Each quarter year, then, has ninety-one days, which is exactly thirteen weeks, and each year has exactly fifty-two weeks. Accordingly, the liturgical feasts fall on the same weekday every year. For the Passover, this means that the fifteenth day of Nisan is always a Wednesday and the Passover meal is held after sunset on Tuesday evening. According to Jaubert, Jesus celebrated the Passover following this calendar, that is, on Tuesday evening, and was arrested during the night leading into Wednesday.

Jaubert sees here the solution to two problems: first, Jesus celebrated a real Passover meal, as the Synoptic tradition maintains; yet John is also right, in that the Jewish authorities, following their own calendar, did not celebrate the Passover until after Jesus' trial, and Jesus was therefore executed on the vigil of the real Passover, not on the feast itself. Both the Synoptic and the Johannine traditions thus appear to be correct on the basis of the discrepancy between two different calendars.

The second advantage emphasized by Annie Jaubert shows at the same time the weakness of this attempted solution. She points out that the traditional chronologies (Synoptic *and* Johannine) have to compress a whole series of events into a few hours: the hearing before the Sanhedrin, Jesus being sent over to Pilate, Pilate's wife's dream, Jesus being handed over to Herod, his return to Pilate, the scourging, the condemnation to death, the way of the Cross, and the crucifixion. To accomplish all this in the space of a few hours seems scarcely possible, according to Jaubert. Her solution, though, provides a time frame from the night leading into Wednesday to the morning of Good Friday.

She also argues that Mark gives a precise sequence of events for "Palm Sunday", Monday, and Tuesday, but then leaps directly to the Passover meal. According to the traditional dating, then, two days remain of which nothing is recounted. Finally, Jaubert reminds us that, if her theory is correct, the Jewish authorities could have succeeded in their plan to kill Jesus in good time before the feast. Pilate then delayed the crucifixion until Friday, so the theory goes, through his hesitations.

One argument against this redating of the Last Supper to Tuesday, of course, is the long tradition assigning it to Thursday, which we find clearly established as early as the second century. Jaubert responds by pointing to the second text on which her theory is based: the so-called *Didascalia Apostolorum*, a text from the early third century that places the Last Supper on Tuesday. She tries to show that this book preserved an old tradition, traces of which are also found in other texts.

In reply it must be said that the traces of tradition to which she refers are too weak to be convincing. The other difficulty is that Jesus is unlikely to have used a calendar associated principally with Qumran. Jesus went to the Temple for the great feasts. Even if he prophesied its demise and confirmed this with a dramatic symbolic action, he still followed the Jewish festal calendar, as is evident from John's Gospel in particular. True, one can agree with Jaubert that the Jubilees calendar was not strictly limited to Qumran and the Essenes. Yet this is not sufficient to justify applying it to Jesus' Passover. Thus it is understandable that Annie Jaubert's theory—so fascinating on first sight—is rejected by the majority of exegetes.

I have presented it in some detail because it offers an insight into the complexity of the Jewish world at the time of Jesus, a world that we can reconstruct only to a limited degree, despite all the knowledge of sources now available to us. So while I would not reject this theory outright, it cannot simply be accepted at face value, in view of the various problems that remain unresolved.

So what are we to say? The most meticulous evaluation I have come across of all the solutions proposed so far is found in the book *A Marginal Jew: Rethinking the Historical Jesus*, by John P. Meier, who at the end of his first volume presents a comprehensive study of the chronology of Jesus' life. He concludes that one has to choose between the Synoptic and Johannine chronologies, and he argues, on the basis of the whole range of source material, that the weight of evidence favors John.

John is right when he says that at the time of Jesus' trial before Pilate, the Jewish authorities had not yet eaten the Passover and, thus, had to keep themselves ritually pure. He is right that the crucifixion took place, not on the feast, but on the day before the feast. This means that Jesus died at the hour when the Passover lambs were being slaughtered in the Temple. That Christians later saw this as no coincidence, that they recognized Jesus as the true Lamb, that in this way they came to see the true meaning of the ritual of the lambs—all this seems to follow naturally.

The question remains: Why did the Synoptics speak of a Passover meal? What is the basis for this strand of tradition? Not even Meier can give a truly convincing answer to this question. He makes an attempt—like many other exegetes—through redaction criticism and literary criticism. He argues that Mark 14:1a and 14:12–16—the only passages in which Mark mentions the Passover—were later additions. In the actual account of the Last Supper itself, he claims, there is no reference to the Passover.

This argument, however many major figures have come out in support of it, is artificial. Yet Meier is right to point out that in the description of the meal itself, the Synoptics recount as little of the Passover ritual as John. Thus with certain reservations, one can agree with his conclusion: "The entire Johannine tradition, from early to late, agrees perfectly with the primitive Synoptic tradition on the non-Passover character of the meal" (*A Marginal Jew* I, p. 398).

We have to ask, though, what Jesus' Last Supper actually was. And how did it acquire its undoubtedly early attribution of Passover character? The answer given by Meier is astonishingly simple and in many respects convincing: Jesus knew that he was about to die. He knew that he would not be able to eat the Passover again. Fully aware of this, he invited his disciples to a Last Supper of a very special kind, one that followed no specific Jewish ritual but, rather, constituted his farewell; during the meal he gave them something new: he gave them himself as the true Lamb and thereby instituted *his* Passover.

In all the Synoptic Gospels, the prophecy of Jesus' death and Resurrection form part of this meal. Luke presents it in an especially solemn and mysterious form: "I have earnestly desired to eat this Passover with you before I suffer; for I tell you I shall not eat it until it is fulfilled in the kingdom of God" (22:15–16). The saying is ambiguous. It can mean that Jesus is eating the usual Passover meal with his disciples for the last time. But it can also mean that he is eating it no longer but, rather, is on his way to the new Passover.

One thing emerges clearly from the entire tradition: essentially, this farewell meal was not the old Passover, but the new one, which Jesus accomplished in this context. Even though the meal that Jesus shared with the Twelve was not a Passover meal according to the ritual prescriptions of Judaism, nevertheless, in retrospect, the inner connection of the whole event with Jesus' death and Resurrection stood out clearly. It was Jesus' Passover. And in this sense he both did and did not celebrate the Passover: the old rituals could not be carried out—when their time came, Jesus had already died. But he had given himself, and thus he had truly celebrated the Passover with them. The old was not abolished; it was simply brought to its full meaning.

The earliest evidence for this unified view of the new and the old, providing a new explanation of the Passover character of Jesus' meal in terms of his death and Resurrection, is found in Saint Paul's First Letter to the Corinthians: "Cleanse out the old leaven that you may be new dough, as you really are unleavened. For Christ, our Paschal Lamb, has been sacrificed" (5:7; cf. Meier, *A Marginal Jew* I, pp. 429–30). As in Mark 14:1, so here the first day of Unleavened Bread and the Passover follow in rapid succession, but the older ritual understanding is transformed into a Christological and existential interpretation. Unleavened bread must now refer to Christians themselves, who are freed from sin by the addition of yeast. But the sacrificial lamb is Christ. Here Paul is in complete harmony with John's presentation of events. For him the death and Resurrection of Christ have become the Passover that endures.

On this basis one can understand how it was that very early on, Jesus' Last Supper—which includes not only a prophecy, but a real anticipation of the Cross and Resurrection in the eucharistic gifts—was regarded as a Passover: as *his* Passover. And so it was.

2. *The Institution of the Eucharist*

The so-called institution narrative, namely, the words and actions by which Jesus gave himself to the disciples in the form of bread and wine, lies at the heart of the Last Supper tradition. In addition to the three Synoptic Gospels (Matthew, Mark, and Luke), Saint Paul's First Letter to the Corinthians provides a further institution narrative (11:23–26). The four accounts are very similar in essentials, yet there are differences in detail that have understandably received a great deal of attention in exegetical literature.

Two basic models can be distinguished: first there is Mark's account, which is broadly similar to Matthew's; then there is Paul's text, which is related to Luke's. The Pauline account is the oldest in literary terms: the First Letter to the Corinthians was written around the year 56. Mark's Gospel in its written form came later, but it is widely agreed that his text is based upon very early tradition. The argument among exegetes is concerned

with the attempt to establish which of the two models—
Mark's or Paul's—is the older.

Rudolf Pesch has argued impressively for the greater
antiquity of Mark's tradition, which he dates back to the
30s. But Paul's account has its roots in the same decade.
Paul states that he is handing on the tradition that he himself received concerning the Lord. The institution narrative and the Resurrection tradition (1 Cor 15:3–8) occupy
a special place in Paul's letters: they are preexistent texts
that the Apostle has already "received" and that he takes
pains to hand on literally. In both places he states that he
is handing on what he has received. In 1 Corinthians 15,
he insists explicitly on the exact wording, as it is necessary
for salvation that this be preserved. It follows that Paul
received the words of the Last Supper from within the
early community in a manner that left him quite certain
of their authenticity—quite certain that these were the
Lord's own words.

Pesch bases his argument for the historical priority of
Mark's account on the fact that his is still a simple narrative, whereas Pesch regards 1 Corinthians 11 as "etiology of worship", that is to say, it is shaped by and for
the liturgy (cf. *Markusevangelium* II, pp. 364–77, esp. 369).
He certainly has a point. Nevertheless, it seems to me
that, as far as their historical and theological character is
concerned, there is ultimately no significant difference
between the two texts.

It is true that Paul is using normative language to speak
about the celebration of the Christian liturgy; if *that* is

what is meant by "etiology of worship", then I can agree. But what makes the text normative for worship in Paul's eyes is the very fact that it reproduces the Lord's testament literally. Hence there is no contradiction between holding that the text is intended for the liturgy, having been crafted earlier with the liturgy in mind, and holding that it represents a strict tradition of the Lord's own words and intentions. Quite the contrary: it is normative precisely because it is true and authentic. At the same time, accuracy of transmission does not exclude a degree of concentration and selection. Yet whatever selection and shaping of material took place could never, in Paul's mind, be allowed to misrepresent what the Lord entrusted to his disciples that night.

Similar selection and shaping of material for liturgical purposes took place in Mark's Gospel as well. For neither can this "narrative" prescind from its normative function vis-à-vis the Church's liturgy: it, too, presupposes an already established liturgical tradition. Both strands of tradition set out to transmit the Lord's testament to us accurately. Between them, they allow us to recognize the depth of the theological implications of the events of that night, and at the same time they highlight what was radically new in Jesus' action.

Given the uniquely powerful event described in the Last Supper accounts, in terms of its theological significance and its place in the history of religions, it could hardly fail to be called into question in modern theology: something so utterly extraordinary was scarcely compatible with the picture of the friendly rabbi that many exegetes draw of Jesus. It is "not to be believed of him". Neither, of course, does it match the picture of Jesus as a political revolutionary. Much present-day exegesis, then, disputes the claim that the words of institution go back to Jesus himself. As this concerns the very heart of Christianity and the essence of the figure of Jesus, we must take a somewhat closer look.

The principal argument against the historical authenticity of the words and actions of the Last Supper may be summarized as follows: There is an insoluble contradiction between Jesus' message about the kingdom of God and the notion of his vicarious expiatory death. Yet the key element in the words of institution is the "for you—for many", the vicarious self-offering of Jesus including the idea of expiation. Whereas John the Baptist had called people to conversion in the face of the threat of judgment, Jesus, as the messenger of joy, proclaimed that God's lordship and unconditional readiness to forgive were close at hand, that the dominion of God's goodness and mercy had arrived. "The final word spoken by God through his final messenger (the messenger of joy following the last messenger of judgment, John) is a word of salvation. Jesus' proclamation is characterized by an unambiguously prior orientation toward God's promise of salvation, by the eclipse of the approaching God of judgment by the present God of goodness." In these words, Pesch summarizes the essential content of the case for incompatibility between the Last Supper tradition and all that was new and specific in Jesus' proclamation (*Abendmahl*, p. 104).

Peter Fiedler takes this argument to extremes by point-ing out, first: "Jesus taught that the Father is *unconditionally* ready to pardon", and going on to ask: "Yet perhaps he was not so magnanimous with his grace or so sovereign after all, since he demanded expiation" (*Sünde und Verge-bung*, p. 569; cf. Pesch, *Abendmahl*, pp. 16, 106). Fiedler then claims that the idea of expiation is incompatible with Jesus' image of God, and here many exegetes and system-atic theologians would agree with him.

This is the real reason why a good number of modern theologians (not only exegetes) reject the idea that the words of the Last Supper go back to Jesus himself. It is not on the basis of historical evidence: as we have seen, the eucharis-tic texts belong to the earliest strand of tradition. From the point of view of historical evidence, nothing could be more authentic than this Last Supper tradition. But the idea of expiation is incomprehensible to the modern mind. Jesus, with his proclamation of the kingdom of God, must surely be diametrically opposed to such a notion. At issue here is our image of God and our image of man. To this extent, the whole discussion only *appears* to be concerned with history.

The real question is: What is expiation? Is it compat-ible with a pure image of God? Is it not a phase in man's religious development that we need to move beyond? If Jesus is to be the new messenger of God, should he not be opposing this notion? So the actual point at issue is whether the New Testament texts—if read rightly—articulate an understanding of expiation that we too can accept, whether we are prepared to listen to the whole of the message that it offers us.

We will have to provide an answer to this question in the chapter on Jesus' death on the Cross. Naturally this will require of us a readiness not only to form a "critical" assessment of the New Testament, but also to learn from it and to let ourselves be led by it: not to dismantle the texts according to our preconceived ideas, but to let our own ideas be purified and deepened by his word.

Meanwhile, by listening in this way, let us try to take some tentative steps toward an understanding. Here the first question to consider is this: Is there really a contradiction between the Galilean proclamation of the kingdom of God and Jesus' final teaching upon arrival in Jerusalem?

Some notable exegetes—Rudolf Pesch, Gerhard Lohfink, Ulrich Wilckens—do indeed see an important difference, but not an insoluble antithesis between the two. They argue that Jesus began by offering the good news of God's kingdom and his unconditional forgiveness, but that he had to acknowledge the rejection of this offer and so came to identify his mission with that of the Suffering Servant. They argue that after his offer was refused, he realized that the only remaining path was that of vicarious expiation: that he had to take upon himself the disaster looming over Israel, thereby obtaining salvation for many.

What is our response to this? From the perspective of the whole structure of the biblical image of God and salvation history, a progression of this kind, a move toward a new path of love after the initial offer was rejected, is entirely plausible. This "flexibility" on God's part is utterly characteristic of the paths that he treads with his people, as recounted for us in the Old Testament—he waits for man's free choice, and whenever the answer is "no", he opens up a new path of love. He responds to Adam's "no" with a new overture toward man. He responds to Babel's "no" with a fresh initiative in history—the choice of Abraham. When the Israelites ask for a king, it is initially out of spite toward God, who prefers to reign directly over his people. Yet in the promise to David he transforms this spite into a path leading directly to Christ, David's Son. So a similar two-stage process in Jesus' approach to the people is entirely plausible.

Chapter 6 of John's Gospel seems to suggest just such a change in Jesus' dealings with men. The people and many of his disciples turn away from him after the eucharistic discourse. Only the Twelve stay with him. There is a similar turning point in Mark's Gospel after the second miracle of the multiplication of loaves and Peter's confession (8:27–30), when Jesus begins the prophecies of the Passion and sets out on the road to Jerusalem, toward his final Passover.

In 1929, Erik Peterson wrote an article on the Church—one that is still well worth reading—in which he argued that the Church came into existence only because "the Jews as God's chosen people did not become believers in the Lord." Had they accepted Jesus, then "the Son of Man would have come again and the Messianic kingdom would have been inaugurated, with the Jews occupying the most important place" (*Theologische Traktakte*, p. 247). Romano

Guardini in his writings about Jesus took up this idea and reworked it. For him, Jesus' message clearly begins with the offer of the kingdom; Israel's "no" leads to the new phase in salvation history to which the Lord's death and Resurrection and the Church of the Gentiles belong.

What are we to make of all this? First of all, a certain development in Jesus' message with a change of strategy is entirely plausible. Admittedly, Peterson himself does not locate the shift in the message of Jesus himself, but in the post-Easter period, when to begin with the disciples were still struggling to obtain a "yes" from Israel. Only to the extent that this attempt proved a failure did they turn to the Gentiles. This second stage is clearly described for us in the New Testament texts.

On the other hand, developments in Jesus' path can only ever be posited with a greater or lesser degree of probability, not with total clarity. The sharp contrast that some modern exegetes draw between the proclamation of God's kingdom and the Jerusalem teaching simply does not exist. We have already noted the evidence that points toward a certain development in Jesus' path. Yet now we must acknowledge (as John P. Meier has clearly maintained) that the format of the Synoptic Gospels does not permit us to establish the chronology of Jesus' proclamation. It is true that there is a growing emphasis on the necessity of Jesus' death and Resurrection as the narrative unfolds. But the material overall is not chronologically ordered in a way that would permit a clear distinction between earlier and later elements.

A few examples must suffice. In Mark's Gospel, as early as chapter 2 during the dispute over the disciples' fasting, Jesus prophesies: "The days will come, when the bridegroom is taken away from them, and then they will fast in that day" (2:20). Still more important is the definition of his mission concealed beneath his speaking in parables—parables that convey to the people his message about the kingdom of God. Jesus identifies his mission with the one that Isaiah received after his encounter with the living God in the Temple: the Prophet was told that initially his mission would merely lead to further hardening of hearts, and only through this could salvation then follow. Even during the early phase of his preaching, Jesus tells the disciples that his own path will follow exactly the same pattern (Mk 4:10–12; cf. Is 6:9–10).

In this way all the parables, the whole proclamation of God's kingdom, are placed under the sign of the Cross. Viewed through the lens of the Last Supper and the Resurrection, we could describe the Cross as the most radical expression of God's unconditional love, as he offers himself despite all rejection on the part of men, taking men's "no" upon himself and drawing it into his "yes" (cf. 2 Cor 1:19). This interpretation of the parables and their proclamation of God's kingdom in terms of the theology of the Cross is also found in the parallel passages of the other two Synoptic Gospels (Mt 13:10–17; Lk 8:9–10).

The fact that Jesus' message was shaped by the Cross from the outset can be seen in other ways in the Synoptic Gospels. I shall limit myself to two examples.

Matthew begins his account of Jesus' ministry with the Sermon on the Mount, which opens solemnly with the beatitudes. These are colored throughout by the language of the Cross, expressed most vividly in the final beatitude: "Blessed are those who are persecuted for righteousness' sake, for theirs is the kingdom of heaven. Blessed are you when men revile you and persecute you and utter all kinds of evil against you falsely on my account. Rejoice and be glad, for your reward is great in heaven, for so men persecuted the prophets who were before you" (Mt 5:10–12).

Finally, at the beginning of Saint Luke's account of Jesus' ministry, we read of his rejection in Nazareth (cf. Lk 4:16–19). Jesus proclaims that Isaiah's promise of a year of the Lord's favor is being fulfilled: "He has anointed me to preach good news to the poor. He has sent me to proclaim release to the captives and recovering of sight to the blind, to set at liberty those who are oppressed" (4:18). In response to this claim, his compatriots immediately become angry and drive him out of the town: they "led him to the brow of the hill on which their city was built, that they might throw him down headlong" (4:29). At the very moment when Jesus announces the message of grace, the perspective of the Cross opens up. Luke, who took great care over the composition of his Gospel, used this episode quite deliberately to set the scene for Jesus' entire ministry.

There is no contradiction between Jesus' proclamation of joy and his acceptance of death on the Cross for many. On the contrary: only through this acceptance and transformation of death does the message of grace acquire its full depth. Moreover, the idea that the Eucharist origi-nated within the "community" is quite absurd, even from a historical point of view. Who could possibly have dreamed up such an idea, such a reality? How could the first generation of Christians—as early as the 30s—have accepted such an invention without anyone calling it into question?

Rightly, Pesch comments that "so far, it has not been possible to come up with any convincing alternative explanation of the Last Supper tradition" (*Abendmahl*, p. 21). No such explanation exists. Only from the mind of Jesus himself could such an idea have emerged. Only he could so authoritatively weave together the strands of the Law and the Prophets—remaining entirely faithful to Scripture while expressing the radically new quality of his sonship. Only because he himself spoke and acted thus could the Church in her various manifestations "break bread" from the very beginning, as Jesus did on the night he was betrayed.

3. *The Theology of the Words of Institution*

After all these reflections on the historical background and authenticity of Jesus' words of institution, it is now time to consider their content. First we should remind ourselves that the four accounts of the Eucharist can be grouped according to two strands of tradition with dif-fering characteristics. Without examining the differences in detail, we should briefly draw attention to the most important ones.

Whereas Mark (14:22) and Matthew (26:26) give the words spoken over the bread simply as "This is my body", Paul extends this to "This is my body which is for you" (1 Cor 11:24), and Luke fills out the sense further: "This is my body which is given for you" (22:19). For Luke and Paul, this is immediately followed by the instruction to repeat the action: "Do this in remembrance of me", but no such instruction is found in the accounts of Matthew and Mark. The words over the chalice, in Mark's account, are: "This is my blood of the covenant, which is poured out for many" (14:24); Matthew adds: "for many, for the forgiveness of sins" (26:28). In Paul's account, though, Jesus says: "This chalice is the new covenant in my blood. Do this, as often as you drink it, in remembrance of me" (1 Cor 11:25). Luke uses a similar formulation, but with slight differences: "This chalice which is poured out for you is the new covenant in my blood" (22:20). There is no second instruction to repeat.

It is important to note two clear differences between Paul/Luke, on the one hand, and Mark/Matthew, on the other: Mark and Matthew make "the blood" the subject: "This is my blood", whereas Paul and Luke say: This is "the new covenant in my blood". Many see here an acknowledgment of Jewish abhorrence at the idea of consuming blood: here the direct content of what is to be drunk is not "blood" but "the new covenant". This leads us now to the second difference: whereas Mark and Matthew speak simply of "blood of the covenant" and thus point to Exodus 24:8, the sealing of the Covenant on Sinai, Paul and Luke speak of a new covenant and thus refer to Jeremiah 31:31—yet another strand of Old Testament background. Moreover, Mark and Matthew speak of the shedding of the blood "for many" and thus point to Isaiah 53:12, whereas Paul and Luke say "for you", bringing the community of disciples directly to mind.

Not surprisingly, there is a great deal of debate among exegetes over what Jesus' actual words were. Rudolf Pesch has shown that there are forty-six *prima facie* possibilities, and this figure can be doubled by exchanging the introductory formulae (cf. *Das Evangelium in Jerusalem*, pp. 134ff.). These efforts are not without importance, but they cannot detain us here.

We take it as a given that the tradition of Jesus' words would not exist without reception by the early Church, which was conscious of a strict obligation to faithfulness in essentials, but also recognized that the enormous resonance of these words, with their subtle references to Scripture, permitted a degree of nuanced redaction. The New Testament writers heard echoes of both Exodus 24 and Jeremiah 31 in Jesus' words and could choose to place the accent more on the one or on the other, without thereby being unfaithful to the Lord's words, which in barely audible yet unmistakable ways gathered within themselves the Law and the Prophets. With these considerations we have already crossed over into the realm of interpretation.

In all four versions, the institution narratives begin by recounting two actions of Jesus that have taken on an essential meaning for the Church's reception of this whole tradition. We are told that Jesus took the bread, saying over it the prayer of blessing and thanksgiving, and that then he broke and distributed the bread. For the first action we find the word *eucharistía* (Paul/Luke) or *eulogia* (Mark/Matthew): each of these words indicates the *berakah*, the Jewish tradition's great prayer of thanksgiving and blessing, which belongs both to the Passover ritual and to other meals. No one ever eats without first thanking God for his gifts: for the bread that he brings forth from the earth and for the fruit of the vine.

The two different Greek words used by Mark/Matthew, on the one hand, and Paul/Luke, on the other, point to the two strands contained within this prayer: it is thanks and praise for God's gift. Yet this praise returns as blessing over the gift, as we read in 1 Timothy 4:4–5: "Everything created by God is good, and nothing is to be rejected if it is received with thanksgiving (*eucharistía*); for then it is consecrated by the word of God and prayer." At the Last Supper (and earlier at the multiplication of loaves, Jn 6:11), Jesus takes up this tradition. The words of institution belong within this context of prayer; the thanksgiving leads to blessing and to transformation.

From her earliest days, the Church has understood the words of consecration not simply as a kind of quasi-magical command, but as part of her praying in and with Jesus; as a central part of the praise and thanksgiving through which God's earthly gift is given to us anew in the form of Jesus' body and blood, as God's gift of himself in his Son's self-emptying love. Louis Bouyer has attempted to trace the development of the Christian *eucharistía*—the Eucharistic Prayer—from the Jewish *berakah*. Thus we can understand how the name "Eucharist" came to be applied to the whole of the new act of worship given to us by Jesus. We will return to this theme later, in the fourth section of this chapter.

The second action to note is that Jesus "broke the bread". The breaking of bread for all is in the first instance a function of the head of the family, who by this action in some sense represents God the Father, who gives us everything, through the earth's bounty, that we need for life. It is also a gesture of hospitality, through which the stranger is given a share in what is one's own; he is welcomed into table fellowship. Breaking and distributing: it is the act of distributing that creates community. This archetypally human gesture of giving, sharing, and uniting acquires an entirely new depth in Jesus' Last Supper through his gift of himself. God's bountiful distribution of gifts takes on a radical quality when the Son communicates and distributes himself in the form of bread.

This gesture of Jesus has thus come to symbolize the whole mystery of the Eucharist: in the Acts of the Apostles and in early Christianity generally, the "breaking of bread" designates the Eucharist. In this sacrament we enjoy the hospitality of God, who gives himself to us in Jesus Christ, crucified and risen. Thus breaking bread and distributing it—the act of attending lovingly to those in need—is an intrinsic dimension of the Eucharist.

"*Caritas*", care for the other, is not an additional sector of Christianity alongside worship; rather, it is rooted in it and forms part of it. The horizontal and the vertical are inseparably linked in the Eucharist, in the "breaking of bread". In this dual action of praise/thanksgiving and breaking/distributing that is recounted at the beginning of the institution narrative, the essence of the new worship established by Christ through the Last Supper, Cross, and Resurrection is made manifest: here the old Temple worship is abolished and at the same time brought to its fulfillment.

Let us now turn to the words spoken over the bread. The accounts of Mark and Matthew simply say: "This is my body", whereas Paul and Luke add: "which is given for you". This addition makes explicit what is contained in the act of distributing. When Jesus speaks of his body, he is obviously not referring to the body as opposed to the soul or the spirit, but to the whole, flesh-and-blood person. In this sense, as Rudolf Pesch rightly observes: "Jesus' interpretation of the bread presupposes the particular meaning of his person. The disciples could understand that he was saying: this is I myself, the Messiah" (*Markusevangelium* II, p. 357).

But how can this be? Jesus, after all, is standing there in the midst of his disciples—what is he doing? He is bringing to fulfillment what he had said in the Good Shepherd discourse: "No one takes [my life] from me, but I lay it down of my own accord" (Jn 10:18). His life will be taken from him on the Cross, but here he is already laying it down. He transforms his violent death into a free act of self-giving for others and to others.

And he also says: "I have power to lay [my life] down, and I have power to take it again" (ibid.). He gives his life, knowing that in so doing he is taking it up again. The act of giving his life includes the Resurrection. Therefore, by way of anticipation, he can already distribute himself, because he is already offering his life—himself—and in the process receiving it again. So it is that he can already institute the sacrament in which he becomes the grain of wheat that dies, the sacrament in which he distributes himself to men through the ages in the real multiplication of loaves.

The words spoken over the chalice, which we must now consider, are of extraordinary theological depth. As indicated earlier, three Old Testament texts are woven together in these few words, so that the whole of earlier salvation history is summarized in them and once more made present.

First there is Exodus 24:8—the sealing of the Covenant on Sinai; then there is Jeremiah 31:31—the promise of the New Covenant amid the crisis of the Covenant's history, a crisis whose clearest manifestations were the destruction of the Temple and the Babylonian exile; finally there is Isaiah 53:12—the mysterious promise of the Suffering Servant, who bears the sins of many and so brings about their salvation.

Let us now try to understand these three texts in their individual meanings and in terms of their new interrelationship. According to the account of Exodus 24, the Sinai Covenant rested on two elements: first, on the "blood of the covenant", the blood of sacrificed animals with which the altar—as the symbol of God—and the people were sprinkled, and second, on God's word and Israel's promise of obedience: "Behold the blood of the covenant which the LORD has made with you in accordance with all these words", as Moses said solemnly after the ritual sprinkling. Immediately before this, the people had responded to the reading of the book of the covenant: "All that the LORD has spoken we will do, and we will be obedient" (Ex 24:7–8).

This promise of obedience, which is an indispensable element of the Covenant, was broken immediately afterward while Moses was on the mountain, through the worship of the golden calf. The entire history that follows is a tale of repeated violations of the promise of obedience, as can be seen both in the historical books of the Old Testament and in the books of the Prophets. The rupture seems beyond repair when God hands his people over to exile and the Temple to destruction.

At this moment, the hope of a "new covenant" arises, one that is no longer built upon the perennially fragile fidelity of the human will but that is written indestructibly on men's hearts (cf. Jer 31:33). In other words, the New Covenant must be founded on an obedience that is irrevocable and inviolable. This obedience, now located at the very root of human nature, is the obedience of the Son, who made himself a servant and took all human disobedience upon himself in his obedience even unto death, suffered it right to the end, and conquered it.

God cannot simply ignore man's disobedience and all the evil of history; he cannot treat it as if it were inconsequential or meaningless. Such "mercy", such "unconditional forgiveness" would be that "cheap grace" to which Dietrich Bonhoeffer rightly objected in the face of the appalling evil encountered in his day. That which is wrong, the reality of evil, cannot simply be ignored; it cannot just be left to stand. It must be dealt with; it must be overcome. Only this counts as true mercy. And the fact that God now confronts evil himself, because men are incapable of doing so—therein lies the "unconditional" goodness of God, which can never be opposed to truth or the justice that goes with it. "If we are faithless, he remains faithful—for he cannot deny himself", writes Paul to Timothy (2 Tim 2:13).

This faithfulness of his means that he acts not only as God toward men, but also as man toward God, in this way establishing the Covenant irrevocably. So the figure of the Suffering Servant who bears the sins of many (Is 53:12) goes hand in hand with the promise of the new and indestructible covenant. This planting of the covenant in men's hearts, in mankind itself, in such a way that it can no longer be destroyed, takes place through the vicarious suffering of the Son who has become a servant. Ever since, standing against the whole flood of filth and evil is the obedience of the Son, in whom God himself suffered, and hence this obedience always infinitely surpasses the growing mass of evil (cf. Rom 5:16–20).

The blood of animals could neither "atone" for sin nor bring God and men together. It could only be a sign of hope, anticipating a greater obedience that would be truly redemptive. In Jesus' words over the chalice, all this is summed up and fulfilled: he gives us the "new covenant in his blood". "His blood"—that is, the total gift of himself, in which he suffers to the end all human sinfulness and repairs every breach of fidelity by his unconditional fidelity. This is the new worship, which he establishes at the Last Supper, drawing mankind into his vicarious obedience. Our participation in Christ's body and blood indicates that his action is "for many", for us, and that we are drawn into the "many" through the sacrament.

Now there is one further expression in Jesus' words of institution that needs to be explained, one that has been extensively debated in recent times. According to Mark and Matthew, Jesus said that his blood would be shed "for many", echoing Isaiah 53, whereas in Paul and Luke we read of the blood being given or poured out "for you".

Recent theology has rightly underlined the use of the word "for" in all four accounts, a word that may be considered the key not only to the Last Supper accounts, but to the figure of Jesus overall. His entire being is expressed by the word "pro-existence"—he is there, not for himself, but for others. This is not merely a dimension of his existence, but its innermost essence and its entirety. His very being is a "being-for". If we are able to grasp this, then we have truly come close to the mystery of Jesus, and we have understood what discipleship is.

But what does "poured out for many" mean? In his seminal work *The Eucharistic Words of Jesus* (1935), Joachim Jeremias set out to demonstrate that the word "many" in the institution narratives is a Semitism and must therefore be read, not in terms of Greek usage, but in terms of the corresponding Old Testament texts. He tried to prove that the word "many" in the Old Testament means "the totality" and is therefore most accurately translated as "all". This thesis quickly gained ground at the time and became part of received theological thinking. On this basis, during the words of consecration, the word "many" has been translated in a number of languages as "all". "Shed for you and for all" is how the faithful in many countries today hear the words of Jesus during the Mass.

Meanwhile, though, this consensus among exegetes has broken down once more. The prevailing opinion today is that "many" in Isaiah 53 and similar passages does indeed indicate a totality, but it cannot simply be equated with "all". On the basis of Qumranic usage, it is now generally held that "many" in Isaiah and on the lips of Jesus means the "totality" of Israel (cf. Pesch, *Abendmahl*, pp. 99–100; Wilckens, *Theologie des Neuen Testaments* I/2, p. 84). It was only when the Gospel was brought to the Gentiles that the universal horizon of Jesus' death and atonement came to the fore, embracing Jews and Gentiles equally.

Recently the Viennese Jesuit Norbert Baumert together with Maria-Irma Seewann has put forward an interpretation of "for many" that in its principal outline had already been developed by Joseph Pascher in his book *Eucharistia* (1947). The essence of the thesis is this: according to the linguistic structure of the text, "being poured out" refers, not to the blood, but to the cup; on this interpretation, "the passage refers to an active outpouring of the blood from the chalice, by which divine life itself is liberally bestowed, without any reference to the action of executioners" (Baumert and Seewann, "Eucharistie", *Gregorianum* 89/3:507). The words spoken over the chalice would relate, not to the event of Jesus' death on the Cross and its consequences, but to the sacramental action, and this would also shed light on the word "many": whereas Jesus' death applies "for all", the range of the sacrament is more limited. It comes to many, but not to all (cf. ibid., especially p. 511).

From a strictly philological point of view, this solution can be successfully applied to Mark's text in 14:24. If Matthew's version is deemed simply to reproduce Mark's, then it would appear that the words spoken at the Last Supper have been convincingly explained. The allusion to the difference between the range of the Eucharist and the universal range of Jesus' death on the Cross is helpful in any case and can take us a step farther. But the problem of the word "many" is still only partly explained.

For we have yet to consider Jesus' fundamental interpretation of his mission in Mark 10:45, which likewise features the word "many": "For the Son of man also came not to be served but to serve, and to give his life as a ransom for many." Here he is clearly speaking of the sacrifice of his life, and so it is obvious that Jesus is taking up the Suffering Servant prophecy from Isaiah 53 and linking it to the mission of the Son of Man, giving it a new interpretation.

What are we to make of this? It strikes me as both presumptuous and naive to seek to shed light on Jesus' consciousness and to try to explain it in terms of what he could or could not have thought, given our knowledge of the period and its theological outlook. The most we can say is that he knew that the mission of the Suffering Servant and the mission of the Son of Man were being fulfilled in himself. This linking together of the two elements also represented an expansion of the mission of the Suffering Servant in terms of universalization, giving it greater breadth and depth.

We can see, then, that the infant Church was slowly arriving at a deeper understanding of Jesus' mission and that the disciples' "remembering", under the guidance of God's Spirit (cf. Jn 14:26), was gradually beginning to grasp the whole of the mystery behind Jesus' words. First Timothy 2:6 speaks of Jesus Christ as the one mediator between God and men "who gave himself as a ransom *for all*". The universal salvific meaning of Jesus' death is here made crystal clear.

In the writings of Paul and John we can find answers to the question about the scope of Jesus' saving work, answers that are historically differentiated yet fully in harmony with one another and that indirectly answer the many/all problem. Paul tells the Romans that the Gentiles "in full number" (*plērōma*) must attain salvation and that all Israel will be saved (cf. 11:25–26). John says that Jesus will die "for the people" (the Jews), but not only for the people: also in order to gather together into unity the scattered children of God (cf. 11:50–52). Jesus died for Jews and Gentiles, for the whole of mankind.

If Isaiah used the word "many" to refer essentially to the totality of Israel, then as the Church responds in faith to Jesus' new use of the word, it becomes increasingly clear that he did indeed die for all.

In 1921, the Protestant theologian Ferdinand Kattenbusch tried to show that Jesus' words of institution at the Last Supper constituted the act of founding the Church. With these words, he argued, Jesus gave his disciples something new that bound them together and made them into a community. Kattenbusch was right: with the Eucharist, the Church herself was established. Through Christ's body, the Church became one, she became herself, and at the same time, through his death, she was opened up to the breadth of the world and its history.

The Eucharist is also a visible process of gathering. In each locality, as well as beyond all localities, it involves entering into communion with the living God, who inwardly draws people together. The Church comes into being from the Eucharist. She receives her unity and her mission from the Eucharist. She is derived from the Last Supper, that is to say, from Christ's death and Resurrection, which he anticipated in the gift of his body and blood.

4. *From the Last Supper to the Sunday Morning Eucharist*

In Paul and Luke, the words "This is my body which is given for you" are followed by the instruction to repeat the action: "Do this in remembrance of me!" Paul repeats the instruction in a more detailed form after the words over the chalice. Mark and Matthew make no reference to this instruction, but since the concrete form of their accounts is shaped by liturgical usage, it is clear that they too understood these words to be instituting something: they understood that what happened here for the first time was to be continued in the community of disciples.

Yet we may ask: What exactly did the Lord instruct them to repeat? Certainly not the Passover meal (if that is what Jesus' Last Supper was). The Passover was an annual feast, whose recurring celebration in Israel was clearly regulated through hallowed tradition and tied to a specific date. Even if what happened that evening was not an actual Passover meal according to Jewish law, but Jesus' last meal on earth before his death, still, that is not what they were told to repeat.

The instruction to repeat refers simply to what was new in Jesus' actions that evening: the breaking of bread, the prayer of blessing and thanksgiving accompanied by the words of consecration of bread and wine. We might say: through these words our "now" is taken up into the hour of Jesus. What Jesus had proclaimed in John 12:32 is here fulfilled: from the Cross he draws all men to himself, into himself.

Through Jesus' words and actions, then, the essentials of the new "worship" was given, but no definitive liturgical form had yet been established—this was still to evolve in the life of the Church. It seems likely that at first people celebrated a communal meal after the pattern of the Last Supper and then added the Eucharist. Rudolf Pesch has shown that, according to the social structure of the early

Church and the customs of the time, the meal probably consisted only of bread, without any other food.

In the First Letter to the Corinthians (11:20–22, 34), we see how in another society things happened differently: the wealthy brought their own food and helped themselves enthusiastically, whereas the poor once again had nothing but bread. Experiences like this led very early to the separation of the Lord's Supper from the regular meal and, at the same time, hastened the development of a distinctive liturgical shape. We should not suppose for a moment that the "Lord's Supper" ever consisted simply of reciting the words of consecration. From the time of Jesus himself, these words have always been a part of his *berakah*, his prayer of praise and thanksgiving.

For what was Jesus giving thanks? That his prayer was "heard" (cf. Heb 5:7). He gave thanks in advance that the Father did not abandon him in death (cf. Ps 16:10). He gave thanks for the gift of the Resurrection, and on that basis he could already give his body and blood in the form of bread and wine as a pledge of resurrection and eternal life (cf. Jn 6:53–58).

We may think of the structure of the "vow-psalms", in which the one suffering tribulation announces that after he has been rescued he will thank God and will proclaim God's saving deed before the great assembly. The great "Passion Psalm" (Ps 22), which begins with the words: "My God, my God, why have you forsaken me", ends with a promise that anticipates the granting of the prayer: "From you comes my praise in the great congregation; my vows I will pay before those who fear him. The afflicted shall eat and be satisfied; those who seek him shall praise the LORD" (vv. 25–26). In truth, these words are fulfilled now: "the afflicted shall eat". What they receive is more than earthly food; they receive the true manna: communion with God in the risen Christ.

Naturally these connections dawned on the disciples only gradually. Yet from Jesus' words of thanksgiving, which gave a new focus to the Jewish *berakah*, we see the new thanksgiving prayer, the *eucharistía*, gradually emerging as the definitive form, the liturgical shape that gives the words of institution their meaning. Here the new worship is established that brings the Temple sacrifices to an end: God is glorified in word, but in a Word that took flesh in Jesus, a Word that, by means of this body which has now passed through death, is able to draw in the whole man, the whole of mankind—thus heralding the beginning of the new creation.

Josef Andreas Jungmann, the great scholar of the history of eucharistic celebration and one of the architects of the liturgical reform, summarizes this argument as follows: "The fundamental element is the thanksgiving prayer over the bread and wine. The liturgy of the Mass was derived from the thanksgiving prayer after the meal on that last evening, not from the meal itself, which was held to be so inessential and so easily detachable that it quickly died out in the early Church. On the other hand, the liturgy in all its manifestations has developed further the thanksgiving prayer spoken over the bread and wine. . . .

What the Church celebrates in the Mass is not the Last Supper; no, it is what the Lord instituted in the course of the Last Supper and entrusted to the Church: the memorial of his sacrificial death" (*Messe im Gottesvolk*, p. 24).

A similar conclusion may be drawn from Jungmann's historical statement to the effect "that in the entire Christian tradition, from the time when the Eucharist was separated from an actual meal (indicated by such terms as 'breaking of bread' or 'Lord's Supper') until the sixteenth-century Reformation, no name meaning 'meal' was ever used to designate the eucharistic celebration" (p. 23, n. 73).

In the evolution of Christian worship, though, there is a further decisive moment. In his certainty that his prayer would be heard, the Lord gave his body and blood to the disciples during the Last Supper in anticipation of the Resurrection: both Cross and Resurrection are intrinsic to the Eucharist—without them there would be no Eucharist. Yet because Jesus' gift is essentially rooted in the Resurrection, the celebration of the sacrament had necessarily to be connected with the memorial of the Resurrection. The first encounter with the risen Lord took place on the morning of the first day of the week—the third day after Jesus' death—that is to say, Sunday morning. The morning of the first day thus naturally became the time for Christian worship—Sunday became the "Lord's day".

This fixed time for the Christian liturgy, which is of defining importance for its character and its format, was established very early on. Thus in the eyewitness account related in Acts 20:6–11 of the journey of Saint Paul and his companions to Troas, we read this: "On the first day of the week, when we were gathered together to break bread" (20:7). In other words, the "breaking of bread" was already fixed for the morning of the day of Resurrection in the apostolic age—the Eucharist was already celebrated as an encounter with the risen Lord.

In this context, it is also significant that Paul arranges for the Jerusalem collection to be taken on the "first day of every week" (1 Cor 16:2). While there is no talk of the eucharistic celebration here, it is clear that Sunday is the day when the Corinthian community came together, and so there can be little doubt that it was also the day of their worship. Finally, in Revelation 1:10 we find the first use of the expression "the Lord's day" for Sunday. The new Christian ordering of the week has clearly taken shape. The day of Resurrection is the Lord's day, and thus it is also the day of his disciples, the day of the Church. At the end of the first century, the tradition is already clearly established. For example, the *Teaching of the Twelve Apostles* (*Didachē*, ca. 100) states quite unambiguously: "Assemble on the Lord's day and break bread and offer the Eucharist, but first make confession of your faults" (14, 1). For Ignatius of Antioch (d. ca. 110), life "ordered by the Lord's day" is already a distinguishing feature of Christians in contrast to those who celebrate the Sabbath (*Ad Magn.* 9:1).

It was logical that the liturgy of the Word—reading of Scripture, commentary on the reading, and prayer—which at first still took place in the synagogue, came to be joined to the celebration of the Eucharist. Thus by the beginning of the second century, the evolution of the essential elements of Christian worship was already complete. This gestation process forms an intrinsic part of the institution of the Eucharist. As we have seen, the institution of the Eucharist presupposes the Resurrection and hence also the living community that, under the guidance of God's Spirit, gives form to the Lord's gift in the life of the faithful.

A "purist" attempt to cut out the Resurrection and its dynamic and simply to imitate the Last Supper would not in any way correspond to the nature of the Lord's gift to his disciples. The Day of Resurrection is the exterior and interior locus of Christian worship, and the thanksgiving prayer as Jesus' creative anticipation of the Resurrection is the Lord's way of uniting us with his thanksgiving, blessing us in the gift and drawing us into the process of transformation that starts with the gifts, moves on to include us, and then spreads out to the world "until he comes" (1 Cor 11:26).

Gethsemane

1. On the Way to the Mount of Olives

"When they had sung a hymn, they went out to the Mount of Olives." With these words, Matthew and Mark conclude their accounts of the Last Supper (Mt 26:30; Mk 14:26). Jesus' final meal—whether or not it was a Passover meal—was first and foremost an act of worship. At its heart was the prayer of praise and thanksgiving, and at the end it led back into prayer. Still praying, Jesus goes out into the night with his disciples, reminding us of the night when the first-born of Egypt were struck down and Israel was saved through the blood of the lamb (cf. Ex 12). Jesus goes out into the night during which he will have to take upon himself the destiny of the lamb.

We may suppose that, in keeping with the Passover that he had celebrated in his own way, Jesus may have sung some of the Hallel Psalms (113–18 and 136). These are hymns of thanksgiving to God for liberating Israel from Egypt, but they also speak of the stone rejected by the builders that wondrously turned out to be the cornerstone. In these Psalms, past history constantly comes into the present. Thanksgiving for liberation is at the same time a plea for help in the face of ever new tribulations and threats; and in the reference to the stone that was rejected, the darkness and the promise of this night are simultaneously brought into the present.

Jesus prays the Psalms of Israel with his disciples: this element is fundamental for understanding the figure of Jesus, but also for understanding the Psalms themselves, which in him could be said to acquire a new subject, a new mode of presence, and an extension beyond Israel into universality.

We also see a new vision of the figure of David emerging here: in the canonical Psalter, David is regarded as the principal author of the Psalms. He thus appears as the one who leads and inspires the prayer of Israel, who sums up all Israel's sufferings and hopes, carries them within himself, and expresses them in prayer. So Israel can continue praying with David, expressing itself in the Psalms, which constantly offer new hope, however deep the surrounding darkness. In the early Church, Jesus was immediately hailed as the new David, the real David, and so the Psalms could be recited in a new way—yet without discontinuity—as prayer in communion with Jesus Christ. Augustine offered a perfect explanation of this Christian way of praying the Psalms—a way that evolved very early on—when he said: it is always Christ who is speaking in the

Psalms—now as the head, now as the body (for example, cf. *En. in Ps.* 60:1–2: 61:4; 85:1, 5). Yet through him— through Jesus Christ—all of us now form a single subject, and so, in union with him, we can truly speak to God.

This process of appropriation and reinterpretation, which begins with Jesus' praying of the Psalms, is a typical illustration of the unity of the two Testaments, as taught to us by Jesus. When he prays, he is completely in union with Israel, and yet he is Israel in a new way: the old Passover now appears as a great foreshadowing. The new Passover, though, is Jesus himself, and the true "liberation" is taking place now, through his love that embraces all mankind.

This combination of fidelity to tradition and novelty, which we observe in the figure of Jesus in every chapter of this book, appears now in a further detail of the Mount of Olives narrative. On each of the previous nights, Jesus has withdrawn to Bethany. On this night, which he celebrates as his Passover night, he follows the instruction to remain within the city of Jerusalem, whose boundary was extended outward for the night, so as to offer all pilgrims the opportunity to keep this law. Jesus observes the norm, and in full knowledge of what he is doing, he approaches the betrayer and the hour of the Passion.

If at this point we look back once more over Jesus' entire path, we encounter the same combination of fidelity and utter novelty: Jesus is "observant". He celebrates the Jewish feasts with others. He prays in the Temple. He follows Moses and the Prophets. Yet at the same time his whole outlook is new: from his explanation of the Sabbath (Mk 2:27; cf. also pp. 106–12 in Part One) and his position on the purity regulations (Mk 7) to the reinterpretation of the Decalogue given in the Sermon on the Mount (Mt 5:17–48) and the cleansing of the Temple (Mt 21:12–13 and parallel passages), which anticipates the demise of the stone Temple and proclaims the new Temple, the new worship "in spirit and truth" (Jn 4:24).

This action, as we have seen, is in profound continuity with God's primordial will, and at the same time it marks the decisive turning point in the history of religions, a turning point that becomes a reality on the Cross. It was this action—the cleansing of the Temple—that contributed significantly to Jesus' condemnation to death on the Cross, thereby fulfilling his prophecy and heralding the new worship.

"They went to a place which was called Gethsemane; and he said to his disciples, 'Sit here, while I pray'" (Mk 14:32). Gerhard Kroll comments as follows: "At the time of Jesus, in this terrain on the slopes of the Mount of Olives, there was a farmstead with an oil press for crushing the olives.... The farmstead was named Gethsemane on account of the oil press.... Nearby was a large natural cave, which could have offered Jesus and his disciples a safe, if not particularly comfortable place to spend the night" (*Auf den Spuren Jesu*, p. 404). We know from the pilgrim Egeria that by the end of the fourth century there was a "magnificent church" here, which was reduced to ruins by the turmoil of the times but was rediscovered by the Franciscans in the twentieth century. "Completed in 1924, the present-day Church of Jesus' Agony not only encompasses the site of the 'ecclesia elegans' [Egeria's church]: it once more surrounds the rock on which tradition tells us that Jesus prayed" (Kroll, *Auf den Spuren Jesu*, p. 410).

This is one of the most venerable sites of Christianity. True, the trees do not date from the time of Jesus; Titus cut down all the trees within a wide radius during the siege of Jerusalem. Yet it is still the same Mount of Olives. Anyone who spends time here is confronted with one of the most dramatic moments in the mystery of our Savior: it was here that Jesus experienced that final loneliness, the whole anguish of the human condition. Here the abyss of sin and evil penetrated deep within his soul. Here he was to quake with foreboding of his imminent death. Here he was kissed by the betrayer. Here he was abandoned by all the disciples. Here he wrestled with his destiny for my sake.

Saint John takes up all these experiences and gives a theological interpretation to the place when he says: "across the Kidron valley, where there was a garden" (18:1). This same highly evocative word comes back at the end of the Passion narrative: "In the place where he was crucified there was a garden, and in the garden a new tomb where no one had ever been laid" (19:41). John's use of the word "garden" is an unmistakable reference to the story of Paradise and the Fall. That story, he tells us, is being resumed here. It is in the "garden" that Jesus is betrayed, but the garden is also the place of the Resurrection. It was in the garden that Jesus fully accepted the Father's will, made it his own, and thus changed the course of history.

After praying the psalms with his disciples, while still on the way to the place where they were intending to rest for the night, Jesus makes three prophecies.

He applies to himself the prophecy of Zechariah, who had said that "the shepherd" would be struck down— killed, in other words—and then the sheep would be scattered (Zech 13:7; Mt 26:31). Zechariah, in a mysterious vision, had spoken of a Messiah who suffers death, after which Israel is once again dispersed. Only after going through these extreme tribulations does he await redemption from God. Jesus gives concrete form to this dark vision of an unknown future. Yes, the shepherd is struck down. Jesus himself is the shepherd of Israel, the shepherd of humanity. And he takes injustice upon himself; he shoulders the destructive burden of guilt. He allows himself to be struck down. He takes up the cause of all who are struck down in the course of history. Now, at this hour, there is the further consequence that the community of disciples is scattered, the newly formed family of God falls apart before it has been properly established. "The good shepherd lays down his life for the sheep" (Jn 10:11). Zechariah sheds new light upon this saying of Jesus: its hour has come.

The prophecy of doom is followed by the promise of salvation: "After I am raised up, I will go before you to Galilee" (Mk 14:28). "Go before" is a typical expression to apply to a shepherd. Jesus, having passed through death, will live again. As the risen Lord, he is now in the fullest sense the shepherd who leads, through death, to the path of life. The Good Shepherd does both: he offers up his life, and he goes before. Indeed, the offering up of his life *is* the going before. It is through these actions that he leads us. It is through these actions that he opens the door onto the vast panorama of reality. Having experienced dispersal, the sheep can now be definitively reassembled. So right at the beginning of the night spent on the Mount of Olives, we find the dark saying about striking down and scattering, but also the promise that through these events, Jesus will reveal himself as the true shepherd who gathers together the scattered ones and leads them to God, to life.

The third prophecy is a further development of the exchanges with Peter that occurred during the Last Supper. Peter does not hear the prophecy of the Resurrection. He only registers the reference to death and dispersal, and this prompts him to declare his unshakable courage and his radical fidelity to Jesus. Because he wants to bypass the Cross, he cannot accept the saying about the Resurrection, and as we saw in the earlier episode at Caesarea Philippi, he would like the victory without the Cross. He is relying on his own resources.

Who could deny that his approach illustrates the constant temptation for Christians, indeed, for the Church: to seek victory without the Cross? Thus it is that his weakness, his threefold denial, has to be held up to him. No one is strong enough to travel the entire path of salvation unaided. All have sinned, all need the Lord's mercy, the love of the Crucified One (cf. Rom 3:23–24).

2. The Prayer of Jesus

The prayer on the Mount of Olives, which follows next, has come down to us in five versions: first, there are the accounts in the three Synoptic Gospels (Mt 26:36–46; Mk 14:32–42; Lk 22:39–46); then there is a short text in the Fourth Gospel that John places among the collection of Jesus' sayings in the Temple on "Palm Sunday" (12:27–28); and finally there is one based on a separate tradition in the Letter to the Hebrews (5:7–10). Let us now attempt, by examining these texts together, to approach as close as we can to the mystery of this hour of Jesus.

After the common recitation of the psalms, Jesus prays alone—as on so many previous nights. Yet close by is the group of three disciples—Peter, James, and John: a trio known to us from other contexts, especially from the account of the Transfiguration. These three disciples, even though they are repeatedly overcome by sleep, are the witnesses of Jesus' night of anguish. Mark tells us that Jesus "began to be greatly distressed and troubled". The Lord says to his disciples: "My soul is very sorrowful, even to death; remain here, and watch" (14:33–34).

The summons to vigilance has already been a major theme of Jesus' Jerusalem teaching, and now it emerges directly with great urgency. And yet, while it refers specifically to Gethsemane, it also points ahead to the later history of Christianity. Across the centuries, it is the drowsiness of the disciples that opens up possibilities for the power of the Evil One. Such drowsiness deadens the soul, so that it remains undisturbed by the power of the Evil One at work in the world and by all the injustice and suffering ravaging the earth. In its state of numbness, the soul prefers not to see all this; it is easily persuaded that things cannot be so bad, so as to continue in the self-satisfaction of its own comfortable existence. Yet this deadening of souls, this lack of vigilance regarding both God's closeness and the looming forces of darkness, is what gives the Evil One power in the world. On beholding the drowsy disciples, so disinclined to rouse themselves, the Lord says: "My soul is very sorrowful, even to death." This is a quotation from Psalm 43:5, and it calls to mind other verses from the Psalms.

In the Passion, too—on the Mount of Olives and on the Cross—Jesus uses passages from the Psalms to speak of himself and to address the Father. Yet these quotations have become fully personal; they have become the intimate words of Jesus himself in his agony. It is he who truly prays these psalms; he is their real subject. Jesus' utterly personal prayer and his praying in the words of faithful, suffering Israel are here seamlessly united.

After this admonition to vigilance, Jesus goes a short distance away. This is where the prayer on the Mount of Olives actually begins. Matthew and Mark tell us that Jesus falls on his face—the prayer posture of extreme submission to the will of God, of radical self-offering to him.

In the Western liturgy, this posture is still adopted on Good Friday, at monastic professions, and at ordinations.

Luke, however, has Jesus kneeling to pray. In terms of praying posture, then, he draws Jesus' night of anguish into the context of the history of Christian prayer: Stephen sinks to his knees in prayer as he is being stoned (Acts 7:60); Peter kneels before he wakes Tabitha from death (Acts 9:40); Paul kneels to bid farewell to the Ephesian elders (Acts 20:36) and again when the disciples tell him not to go up to Jerusalem (Acts 21:5). Alois Stöger says on this subject: "When they were confronted with the power of death, they all prayed kneeling down. Martyrdom can be overcome only by prayer. Jesus is the model of martyrs" (*The Gospel according to Saint Luke* II, p. 199).

There now follows the prayer itself, in which the whole drama of our redemption is made present. In Mark's account, Jesus begins by asking that, if it were possible, the hour might pass from him (14:35). This is then filled out by a statement of the essential content of the prayer: "Abba, Father, all things are possible to you; remove this chalice from me; yet not what I will, but what you will" (14:36).

We may distinguish three elements in this prayer of Jesus. First there is the primordial experience of fear, quaking in the face of the power of death, terror before the abyss of nothingness that makes him tremble to the point that, in Luke's account, his sweat falls to the ground like drops of blood (cf. 22:44). In the equivalent passage in Saint John's Gospel (12:27), this horror is expressed, as in the

Synoptics, in terms reminiscent of Psalm 43:5, but using a word that emphasizes the dark depths of Jesus' fear: *tetáraktai*—it is the same verb, *tarássein*, that John uses to describe Jesus' deep emotion at the tomb of Lazarus (cf. 11:33) as well as his inner turmoil at the prophecy of Judas' betrayal in the Upper Room (cf. 13:21).

In this way John is clearly indicating the primordial fear of created nature in the face of imminent death, and yet there is more: the particular horror felt by him who is Life itself before the abyss of the full power of destruction, evil, and enmity with God that is now unleashed upon him, that he now takes directly upon himself, or rather into himself, to the point that he is "made to be sin" (cf. 2 Cor 5:21).

Because he is the Son, he sees with total clarity the whole foul flood of evil, all the power of lies and pride, all the wiles and cruelty of the evil that masks itself as life yet constantly serves to destroy, debase, and crush life. Because he is the Son, he experiences deeply all the horror, filth, and baseness that he must drink from the "chalice" prepared for him: the vast power of sin and death. All this he must take into himself, so that it can be disarmed and defeated in him.

As Bultmann rightly observes: Jesus here is "not simply the prototype, in whom the behavior demanded of man becomes visible in an exemplary manner ... he is also and above all the Revealer, whose decision alone makes possible in such an hour the human decision for God" (*The Gospel of John,* p. 428). Jesus' fear is far more radical than the fear that everyone experiences in the face of death:

it is the collision between light and darkness, between life and death itself—the critical moment of decision in human history. With this understanding, following Pascal, we may see ourselves drawn quite personally into the episode on the Mount of Olives: my own sin was present in that terrifying chalice. "Those drops of blood I shed for you", Pascal hears the Lord say to him during the agony on the Mount of Olives (cf. *Pensées* VII, 553).

The two parts of Jesus' prayer are presented as the confrontation between two wills: there is the "natural will" of the man Jesus, which resists the appalling destructiveness of what is happening and wants to plead that the chalice pass from him; and there is the "filial will" that abandons itself totally to the Father's will. In order to understand this mystery of the "two wills" as much as possible, it is helpful to take a look at John's version of the prayer. Here, too, we find the same two prayers on Jesus' lips: "Father, save me from this hour ... Father, glorify your name" (Jn 12:27–28).

The relationship between these two prayers in John's account is essentially no different from what we find in the Synoptics. The anguish of Jesus' human soul ("I am troubled"; Bultmann translates it as: "I am afraid", p. 427) impels him to pray for deliverance from this hour. Yet his awareness of his mission, his knowledge that it was for this hour that he came, enables him to utter the second prayer—the prayer that God glorify his name: it is Jesus' acceptance of the horror of the Cross, his ignominious experience of being stripped of all dignity and suffering a shameful death, that becomes the glorification of God's name. For in this way, God is manifested as he really is: the God who, in the unfathomable depth of his self-giving love, sets the true power of good against all the powers of evil. Jesus uttered both prayers, but the first one, asking for deliverance, merges into the second one, asking for God to be glorified by the fulfillment of his will—and so the conflicting elements blend into unity deep within the heart of Jesus' human existence.

3. Jesus' Will and the Will of the Father

What does this mean? What is "my" will as opposed to "your" will? Who is speaking to whom? Is it the Son addressing the Father? Or the man Jesus addressing the triune God? Nowhere else in sacred Scripture do we gain so deep an insight into the inner mystery of Jesus as in the prayer on the Mount of Olives. So it is no coincidence that the early Church's efforts to arrive at an understanding of the figure of Jesus Christ took their final shape as a result of faith-filled reflection on his prayer on the Mount of Olives.

At this point we should undertake a rapid overview of the early Church's Christology, in order to grasp its understanding of the interrelation between the divine will and the human will in the figure of Jesus Christ. The Council of Nicea (325) had clarified the Christian concept of God. The three persons—Father, Son, and Holy Spirit—are one, in the one "substance" of God. More than a century later, the Council of Chalcedon

(451) sought to articulate the relation between divinity and humanity in Jesus Christ by adopting the formula that the one person of the Son of God embraces and bears the two natures—human and divine—"without confusion and without separation".

Thus the infinite difference between God and man, between Creator and creature is preserved: humanity remains humanity, divinity remains divinity. Jesus' humanity is neither absorbed nor reduced by his divinity. It exists in its fullness, while subsisting in the divine person of the Logos. At the same time, in the continuing distinction of natures, the expression "*one* person" conveys the radical unity that God in Christ has entered into with man. The formula of Pope Leo the Great—two natures, one person—expresses an insight that transcended by far the historical moment, and for that reason it was enthusiastically accepted by the Council Fathers.

Yet it was ahead of its time: its concrete meaning had not yet been fully set forth. What is meant by "nature"? But more importantly, what is meant by "person"? Since this was by no means clear, many bishops after Chalcedon said that they would rather think like fishermen than like Aristotle. The formula remained obscure. Therefore the reception of Chalcedon was an extremely complex process, and fierce battles were fought over it. In the end it led to division: only the Churches of Rome and Byzantium definitively accepted the Council and its formula. Alexandria in Egypt preferred to remain with the formula of "one divinized nature"

(monophysitism); while farther east, Syria remained scep-
tical about the notion of one person, as it appeared to
compromise Jesus' true humanity (Nestorianism). It was
not simply ideas that were at issue here: more significantly,
contrasting forms of devotion burdened the debate with
the weight of religious sensibilities, rendering it insoluble.

The Ecumenical Council of Chalcedon continues to
indicate, to the Church of all ages, the necessary pathway into the mystery of Jesus Christ. That said, it has
to be appropriated anew in the context of contemporary
thought, since the concepts of "nature" and "person"
have acquired quite different meanings from those they
had at the time. This task of reappropriation must go hand
in hand with ecumenical dialogue with the pre-Chalce-
donian Churches, so that our lost unity may be regained
in the core of our faith—in our confession of the God
who became man in Jesus Christ.

The great battle that was fought after Chalcedon, especially in the Byzantine East, was essentially concerned
with the question: If there is only one divine person in
Jesus, embracing both natures, then what is the status of
his human nature? If it subsists within the one divine person, can it be said to have any real, specific existence in
itself? Must it not inevitably be absorbed by the divine, at
least at its highest point, the will? This leads us to the last
of the great Christological heresies, known as "monotheletism". There can be only *one* will within the unity of a
person, its adherents maintained; a person with two wills
would be schizophrenic: ultimately it is in the will that

a person manifests himself, and where there is only one person, then ultimately there can be only *one* will. Yet an objection comes to mind: What kind of man has no human will? Is a man without a will really a man? Did God in Jesus truly become man, if this man had no will?

The great Byzantine theologian Maximus the Confessor (d. 662) formulated an answer to this question by struggling to understand Jesus' prayer on the Mount of Olives. Maximus is first and foremost a determined opponent of monotheletism: Jesus' human nature is not amputated through union with the Logos; it remains complete. And the will is part of human nature. This irreducible duality of human and divine willing in Jesus must not, however, be understood to imply the schizophrenia of a dual personality. Nature and person must be seen in the mode of existence proper to each. In other words: in Jesus the "natural will" of the human nature is present, but there is only *one* "personal will", which draws the "natural will" into itself. And this is possible without annihilating the specifically human element, because the human will, as created by God, is ordered to the divine will. In becoming attuned to the divine will, it experiences its fulfillment, not its annihilation. Maximus says in this regard that the human will, by virtue of creation, tends toward synergy (working together) with the divine will, but that through sin, opposition takes the place of synergy: man, whose will attains fulfillment through becoming attuned to God's will, now has the sense that his freedom is compromised by God's will. He regards consenting to God's will, not as his opportunity to become fully himself, but as a threat to his freedom against which he rebels.

The drama of the Mount of Olives lies in the fact that Jesus draws man's natural will away from opposition and back toward synergy, and in so doing he restores man's true greatness. In Jesus' natural human will, the sum total of human nature's resistance to God is, as it were, present within Jesus himself. The obstinacy of us all, the whole of our opposition to God is present, and in his struggle, Jesus elevates our recalcitrant nature to become its real self.

Christoph Schönborn says in this regard that "the transition between the two wills from opposition to union is accomplished through the sacrifice of obedience. In the agony of Gethsemane, this transition occurs" (*God's Human Face*, pp. 126–27). Thus the prayer "not my will, but yours" (Lk 22:42) is truly the Son's prayer to the Father, through which the natural human will is completely subsumed into the "I" of the Son. Indeed, the Son's whole being is expressed in the "not I, but you"—in the total self-abandonment of the "I" to the "you" of God the Father. This same "I" has subsumed and transformed humanity's resistance, so that we are all now present within the Son's obedience; we are all drawn into sonship.

This brings us to one final point regarding Jesus' prayer, to its actual interpretative key, namely, the form of address: "Abba, Father" (Mk 14:36). In 1966 Joachim Jeremias wrote an important article about the use of this term in Jesus' prayer, from which I should like to quote two essential insights: "Whereas there is not a single instance of God being addressed as *Abba* in the literature of Jewish prayer, Jesus always addressed him in this way (with the exception of the cry from the Cross, Mark 15:34 and parallel passages). So we have here a quite unmistakable characteristic of the *ipsissima vox Jesu*" (*Abba*, p. 57). Moreover, Jeremias shows that this word *Abba* belongs to the language of children—that it is the way a child addresses his father within the family. "To the Jewish mind it would have been disrespectful and therefore inconceivable to address God with this familiar word. For Jesus to venture to take this step was something new and unheard of. He spoke to God like a child to his father ... Jesus' use of *Abba* in addressing God reveals the heart of his relationship with God" (p. 62). It is therefore quite mistaken on the part of some theologians to suggest that the man Jesus was addressing the Trinitarian God in the prayer on the Mount of Olives. No, it is the Son speaking here, having subsumed the fullness of man's will into himself and transformed it into the will of the Son.

4. *Jesus' Prayer on the Mount of Olives in the Letter to the Hebrews*

Finally we must turn our attention to the passage from the Letter to the Hebrews that points toward the Mount of Olives. There we read: "In the days of his flesh, Jesus offered up prayers and supplications, with loud cries and tears, to him who was able to save him from death, and he was heard for his godly fear" (5:7). Here we may identify an independent tradition concerning the Gethsemane event, for there is no mention of loud cries or tears in the Gospels.

We have to admit that the author of the Letter is c learly not referring exclusively to the night in Gethsemane, but has in mind the whole of Jesus' *via dolorosa* right up to the crucifixion, that is to say, to the moment when, according to Matthew and Mark, Jesus "cried out with a loud voice" the opening words of Psalm 22; these two evangelists also tell us that Jesus expired with a loud cry; Matthew expressly uses the word "cried" at this point, meaning "cry out" (cf. 27:50). John speaks of Jesus' tears at the death of Lazarus, and this in the context of his being "troubled" in spirit—for which, as we have seen, John uses the word that was to reappear in the "Palm Sunday" passage corresponding to the Mount of Olives tradition.

Each time, it is a question of Jesus' encounter with the powers of death, whose ultimate depths he as the Holy One of God can sense in their full horror. The Letter to the Hebrews views the whole of Jesus' Passion—from the Mount of Olives to the last cry from the Cross—as thoroughly permeated by prayer, one long impassioned plea to God for life in the face of the power of death.

If the Letter to the Hebrews treats the entire Passion as a prayer in which Jesus wrestles with God the Father and at the same time with human nature, it also sheds new light on the theological depth of the Mount of Olives prayer. For these cries and pleas are seen as Jesus' way of exercising his high priesthood. It is through his cries, his tears, and his prayers that Jesus does what the high priest is meant to do: he holds up to God the anguish of human existence. He brings man before God.

There are two particular words with which the author of the Letter to the Hebrews underlines this dimension of Jesus' prayer. The verb "bring" (*prosphérein*: bring before God, bear aloft—cf. Heb 5:1) comes from the language of the sacrificial cult. What Jesus does here lies right at the heart of what sacrifice is. "He offered himself to do the will of the Father", as Albert Vanhoye comments (*Let Us Confidently Welcome Christ Our High Priest*, p. 60). The second word that is important for our purposes tells us that through his sufferings Jesus learned obedience and was thus "made perfect" (Heb 5:8–9). Vanhoye points out that in the Pentateuch, the five books of Moses, the expression "make perfect" (*teleioũn*) is used exclusively to mean "consecrate as priest" (p. 62). The Letter to the Hebrews takes over this terminology (cf. 7:11, 19, 28). So the passage in question tells us that Christ's obedience, his final "yes" to the Father accomplished on the Mount of Olives, as it were, "consecrated him as a priest"; it tells us that precisely in this act of self-giving, in this bearing-aloft of human existence to God, Christ truly became a priest "according to the order of Melchizedek" (Heb 5:9–10; cf. Vanhoye, pp. 61–62).

At this point, though, we must move on toward the heart of what the Letter to the Hebrews has to say concerning the prayer of the suffering Lord. The text states that Jesus pleaded with him who had the power to save him from death and that, on account of his godly fear (cf. 5:7), his prayer was granted. But was it granted? He still died on the Cross! For this reason Harnack maintained that the word "not" must have been omitted here, and Bultmann agrees. But an exegesis that turns a text into its opposite is no exegesis. Rather, we must attempt to understand this mysterious form of "granting" so as to come closer to grasping the mystery of our own salvation.

We may distinguish different aspects of this "granting". One possible translation of the text would be: "He was heard and delivered from his fear." This would correspond to Luke's account, which says that an angel came and comforted him (cf. 22:43). It would then refer to the inner strength given to Jesus through prayer, so that he was able to endure the arrest and the Passion resolutely. Yet the text obviously says more: the Father raised him from the night of death and, through the Resurrection, saved him definitively and permanently from death: Jesus dies no more (cf. Vanhoye, *Let Us Confidently Welcome Christ Our High Priest*, p. 60). Yet surely the text means *even more*: the Resurrection is not just Jesus' personal rescue from death. He did not die for himself alone. His was a dying "for others"; it was the conquest of death itself.

Hence this "granting" may also be understood in terms of the parallel text in John 12:27–28, where in answer to Jesus' prayer: "Father, glorify your name!" a voice from heaven replies: "I have glorified it, and I will glorify it again." The Cross itself has become God's glorification, the glory of God made manifest in the love of the Son. This glory extends beyond the moment into the whole sweep of history. This glory is life. It is on the Cross that we see it, hidden yet powerful: the glory of God, the transformation of death into life.

From the Cross, new life comes to us. On the Cross, Jesus becomes the source of life for himself and for all. On the Cross, death is conquered. The granting of Jesus' prayer concerns all mankind: his obedience becomes life for all. This conclusion is spelled out for us in the closing words of the passage we have been studying: "He became the source of eternal salvation to all who obey him, being designated by God a high priest according to the order of Melchizedek" (Heb 5:9–10; cf. Ps 110:4).

CHAPTER SEVEN

The Trial of Jesus

All four Gospels tell us that Jesus' night of prayer was brought to an end when an armed group of soldiers, sent by the Temple authorities and led by Judas, came and arrested him, leaving the disciples unharmed.

This arrest—evidently ordered by the Temple authorities and ultimately by the high priest Caiaphas—how did it come about? How did it come to pass that Jesus was handed over to the tribunal of the Roman Governor Pilate and condemned to death on the Cross?

The Gospels allow us to distinguish three stages in the juridical process leading to the sentence of death: a meeting of the Council in the house of Caiaphas, Jesus' hearing before the Sanhedrin, and finally the trial before Pilate.

1. *Preliminary Discussion in the Sanhedrin*

In the early stages of his ministry, the Temple authorities had evidently shown little interest in the figure of

Jesus or in the movement that formed around him; it all seemed a rather provincial affair—one of those movements that arose in Galilee from time to time and did not warrant much attention. The situation changed on "Palm Sunday". The Messianic homage paid to Jesus on his entrance into Jerusalem; the cleansing of the Temple with the interpretation he gave to it, which seemed to indicate the end of the Temple altogether and a radical change in the cult, contrary to the ordinances established by Moses; Jesus' teaching in the Temple, from which there emerged a claim to authority that seemed to channel Messianic hopes in a new direction, threatening Israel's monotheism; the miracles that Jesus worked publicly and the growing multitude that gathered around him—all this added up to a situation that could no longer be ignored.

In the days surrounding the Passover feast, when the city was overflowing with pilgrims and Messianic hopes could easily turn into political dynamite, the Temple authorities had to acknowledge their responsibility and establish clearly in the first instance how to interpret all this and then how to respond to it. Only John explicitly recounts a session of the Sanhedrin, which served to form opinion and to shape an eventual decision on the case of Jesus (11:47–53). John dates it, incidentally, before "Palm Sunday" and sees as its immediate occasion the popular movement generated by the raising of Lazarus. Without such a deliberate process, the arrest of Jesus during the night of Gethsemane would have been inconceivable. Evidently John is preserving a historical memory here, to which the Synoptics also refer briefly (cf. Mk 14:1, Mt 26:3–4; Lk 22:1–2).

John tells us that the chief priests and the Pharisees were gathered together. These were the two leading groups within Judaism at the time of Jesus, and on many points they were opposed to one another. But their common fear was this: "The Romans will come and destroy both our holy place [that is, the Temple, the holy place for divine worship] and our nation" (11:48). One is tempted to say that the motive for acting against Jesus was a political concern shared by the priestly aristocracy and the Pharisees, though they arrived at it from different starting points; yet this political interpretation of the figure of Jesus and his ministry caused them to miss completely what was most characteristic and new about him. Through the message that he proclaimed, Jesus had actually achieved a separation of the religious from the political, thereby changing the world: this is what truly marks the essence of his new path.

Nevertheless, we must not be too hasty in condemning the "purely political" outlook of his opponents. For in the world they inhabited, the two spheres—political and religious—were inseparable. The "purely" political existed no more than the "purely" religious. The Temple, the Holy City, and the Holy Land with its people: these were neither purely political nor purely religious realities. Anything to do with Temple, nation, and land involved both the religious foundation of politics and its religious consequences. The defense of the "place" and the "nation" was ultimately a religious affair, because it was concerned with God's house and God's people.

It is important to distinguish between this underlying religious and political motivation on the part of Israel's leaders and the specific power-interests of the dynasty of Annas and Caiaphas, which effectively precipitated the catastrophe of the year 70 and so caused precisely the outcome it had been their task to avoid. To this extent the death sentence passed against Jesus is characterized by a curious overlapping of two layers: the legal concern to protect the Temple and the nation, on the one hand, and the ambitious power seeking of the ruling group, on the other.

It is an overlap that corresponds to what we discovered in the cleansing of the Temple. Jesus fights there, on the one hand, as we saw, against self-serving abuse of the sacred space, but his prophetic gesture and the interpretation he gave to it go much deeper: the old cult of the stone Temple has come to an end. The hour of the new worship in "spirit and truth" has come. The Temple of stone must be destroyed, so that the new one, the New Covenant with its new style of worship, can come. Yet at the same time, this means that Jesus himself must endure crucifixion, so that, after his Resurrection, he may become the new Temple.

This brings us back to the question of the interweaving and the separation of religion and politics. In his teaching and in his whole ministry, Jesus had inaugurated a non-political Messianic kingdom and had begun to detach these two hitherto inseparable realities from one another, as we said earlier. But this separation—essential to Jesus' message—of politics from faith, of God's people from politics, was ultimately possible only through the Cross. Only through the total loss of all external power, through the radical stripping away that led to the Cross, could this new world come into being. Only through faith in the Crucified One, in him who was robbed of all worldly power and thereby exalted, does the new community arise, the new manner of God's dominion in the world.

This means, though, that the Cross corresponded to a divine "necessity" and that Caiaphas, in making the decision he did, was ultimately carrying out God's will, even if his motivation was impure and reflected, not God's will, but his own purposes.

John expressed with great clarity this striking combination in Caiaphas of carrying out God's will and blind self-seeking. While the Council members were perplexed as to what should be done in view of the danger posed by the movement surrounding Jesus, he made the decisive intervention: "You do not understand that it is expedient for you that one man should die for the people, and that the whole nation should not perish" (11:50). John designates this statement expressly as a "prophetic utterance" that Caiaphas formulated through the charism of his office as high priest, and not of his own accord.

The immediate consequence of Caiaphas' statement was this: until that moment, the assembled Council had held back in fear from a death sentence, looking for other ways out of the crisis, admittedly without finding a solution. Only a theologically motivated declaration from the high priest, spoken with the authority of his office, could dispel their doubts and prepare them in principle for such a momentous decision.

This passage in Saint John's Gospel—which recognizes as the decisive moment in salvation history the exercise of the charism pertaining to his office by this unworthy officeholder—corresponds to a saying of Jesus recounted by Matthew: "The scribes and the Pharisees sit on Moses' seat; so practice and observe whatever they tell you, but not what they do" (23:2-3). Both Matthew and John wanted to recall this distinction to the Church of their own day, for at that time, too, there was a contradiction between authority of office and manner of life, between "what they say" and "what they do".

On the surface, the content of Caiaphas' "prophecy" is thoroughly pragmatic, and, considered in those terms, it seems reasonable from his point of view: if the people can be saved through the death of one man (and in no other way), then this individual's death might seem the lesser evil and the politically correct path. But what on the surface sounds and is intended to be merely pragmatic acquires an entirely new depth on the basis of its "prophetic" quality. The one man, Jesus, dies for the nation: the mystery of vicarious atonement shines forth, and it is this that constitutes the most profound content of Jesus' mission.

The idea of vicarious atonement pervades the entire history of religions. In many different ways people have tried to deflect the threat of disaster from the king, from the people, from their own lives, by transferring it to a substitute. Evil must be atoned for, and in this way jus-tice must be restored. The punishment, the unavoid-able misfortune, is offloaded onto others in an effort to liberate oneself. Yet this substitution through animal or even human sacrifice ultimately lacks credibility. What is offered by way of substitution is still a mere proxy for one's own offering and can in no way take the place of the one needing to be redeemed. A proxy is not a substitute, yet the whole of history is searching for the one who can truly stand in for us, the one who is truly able to take us up with him and so lead us to salvation.

In the Old Testament, the idea of vicarious atonement occupies a central place when Moses says to the angry God, after the people's idolatry on Sinai: "But now, if you will forgive their sin—and if not, blot me, I beg you, out of your book which you have written" (Ex 32:32). While it is true that God replies: "Whoever has sinned against me, him will I blot out of my book" (32:33), neverthe-less Moses somehow remains the substitute, the one who bears the fate of the people and through pleading on their behalf is able to change it again and again. Finally, the Book of Deuteronomy presents Moses vicariously suffer-ing for Israel and likewise dying outside the Holy Land for Israel (cf. von Rad, *Old Testament Theology* I, p. 295). This idea of vicarious atonement is fully developed in the figure of the Suffering Servant in Isaiah 53, who takes the guilt of many upon himself and thereby makes them just (53:11). In Isaiah, this figure remains mysterious; the Song of the Suffering Servant is like a gaze into the future in search of the one who is to come. The one dies for the many—this prophetic utterance of the high priest Caiaphas brings together all the longing of the world's religious history and Israel's great faith traditions and applies them to Jesus. The whole of his living and dying is concealed within the word "for"; as Heinz Schürmann in particular has repeatedly emphasized, it is "pro-existence".

After this pronouncement of Caiaphas, which was tantamount to a death sentence, John added a further comment from the perspective of the disciples' faith. First he makes it clear—as we have seen—that the reference to dying for the people was a prophetic utterance, and then he goes on to say that Jesus would die, "not for the nation only, but to gather into one the children of God who are scattered abroad" (11:52). On first sight this seems a thoroughly Jewish manner of speaking. It expresses the hope that, in the Messianic age, the Israelites scattered around the world would be gathered together in their own land (cf. Barrett, *The Gospel according to Saint John*, p. 407).

On the lips of the evangelist, though, this saying takes on a new meaning. The gathering is oriented no longer toward a specific geographical territory, but toward the growth into unity of the children of God: we immediately hear echoes of the central element of Jesus' high-priestly prayer. The gathering is directed toward the unity of all believers, and thus it points ahead to the community of the Church and even beyond, toward definitive eschatological unity.

The scattered children of God are no longer exclusively Jews, but children of Abraham in the wider sense that

Paul expounded: people who, like Abraham, focus their gaze upon God; people who are ready to listen to him and to respond to his call—Advent people, we might say. The new community of Jews and Gentiles is taking shape here (cf. Jn 10:16). So a further window is opened onto our Lord's reference at the Last Supper to the "many", for whom he would lay down his life: he was referring to the gathering of the "children of God", that is to say, all those who are willing to hear his call.

2. *Jesus before the Sanhedrin*

The fundamental decision to take action against Jesus, reached during that meeting of the Sanhedrin, was put into effect on the night leading from Thursday to Friday with his arrest on the Mount of Olives. Jesus was led, still by night, to the high priest's palace, where the Sanhedrin with its three constituent groups—chief priests, elders, scribes—was evidently already assembled.

Jesus' two "trials", before the Sanhedrin and before the Roman Governor Pilate, have been analyzed by legal historians and exegetes down to the last detail. There is no need here to enter into all these subtle historical questions, the more so since, as Martin Hengel has emphasized, we do not know the details of the Sadducees' criminal law, and retrospective conclusions based on the later Mishna-treatise *Sanhedrin* cannot legitimately be applied to the time of Jesus (cf. Hengel and Schwemer, *Jesus und das Judentum*, p. 592). It now seems reasonable to assume that what took place when Jesus was brought before the Sanhedrin was not a proper trial, but more of a cross-examination that led to the decision to hand him over to the Roman Governor for sentencing.

Let us now take a closer look at the Gospel accounts, still with the intention of gaining a better knowledge and understanding of the figure of Jesus. We have already seen that after the cleansing of the Temple, two charges against Jesus were in circulation. The first had to do with his interpretation of the prophetic gesture of driving cattle and traders out of the Temple, which seemed like an attack on the Holy Place itself and, hence, on the Torah, on which Israel's life was built.

I consider it important that it was not the cleansing of the Temple as such for which Jesus was called to account, but only the interpretation he gave to his action. We may conclude that the symbolic gesture itself remained within acceptable limits and did not give rise to public unrest, such as would have supplied a motive for legal intervention. The danger lay in the interpretation, in the seeming attack on the Temple, and in the authority that Jesus was claiming to possess.

From the Acts of the Apostles we know that a similar charge was brought against Stephen, who had quoted Jesus' Temple prophecy; this led to him being stoned, which indicates that it was considered blasphemous. In Jesus' trial, witnesses came forward who wanted to report what Jesus had said. But there was no consistent version: his actual words could not be unequivocally established. The fact that this particular charge was then dropped reveals a concern to observe juridically correct procedure.

On the basis of Jesus' teaching in the Temple, a second charge was in circulation: that Jesus had made a Messianic claim, through which he somehow put himself on a par with God and thus seemed to contradict the very basis of Israel's faith—the firm belief that there is only one God. We should note that both charges are of a purely theological nature. Yet given the inseparability of the religious and political realms, of which we spoke earlier, the charges do also have a political dimension. As the place of Israel's sacrifices, to which the whole people comes on pilgrimage for great feasts, the Temple is the basis of Israel's inner unity. The Messianic claim is a claim to kingship over Israel. Hence the placing of the charge "King of the Jews" above the Cross, to indicate the reason for Jesus' execution.

As the events of the Jewish War show, there were certain circles within the Sanhedrin that would have favored the liberation of Israel through political and military means. But the way in which Jesus presented his claim seemed to them clearly unsuited to the effective advancement of their cause. So the status quo was preferable, since Rome at least respected the religious foundations of Israel, with the result that the survival of Temple and nation could be considered more or less secure.

After the vain attempt to establish a clear and well-founded charge against Jesus on the basis of his statement about the destruction and renewal of the Temple, we come to the dramatic encounter between the serving high priest of Israel, the highest authority of the chosen people, and Jesus himself, in whom Christians recognize the "high priest of the good things to come" (Heb 9:11), the definitive high priest "according to the order of Melchizedek" (Ps 110:4; Heb 5:6, and so on).

In all four Gospels, this decisive moment in world history is presented as a drama in which three different levels intersect—they must be considered together if the event is to be grasped in all its complexity (cf. Mt 26:57–75, Mk 14:53–72; Lk 22:54–71; Jn 18:12–27). During Caiaphas' interrogation of Jesus, which culminates in the question about his Messianic identity, Peter is sitting in the palace forecourt and denying Jesus. John's narrative brings out the chronological interplay of the two scenes with particular vividness; Matthew's account of the Messianic question highlights the inner connection between Jesus' confession and Peter's denial. Directly interwoven with the interrogation of Jesus, however, there is also the element of mockery by the Temple servants (or could it have been the Sanhedrin members themselves?); in the course of the trial before Pilate, this is followed by further mockery on the part of the Roman soldiers.

Let us come to the decisive point: to Caiaphas' question and Jesus' answer. With regard to the precise formulations, Matthew, Mark, and Luke differ in detail; their respective versions of the text are shaped by the overall context of each Gospel and by consideration of the particular perspectives of the audience being addressed. As we saw regarding the words used at the Last Supper, so here an exact reconstruction of Caiaphas' question and Jesus' answer is not possible. The essential content of the exchange nevertheless emerges quite unequivocally from the three different accounts. There are good reasons for assuming that Saint Mark's version offers us the most authentic form of this dramatic dialogue. But in the variations that Matthew and Luke provide, further important elements emerge that help us to arrive at a deeper understanding of the whole episode.

According to Mark, the high priest's question is: "Are you the Christ, the Son of the Blessed?" And Jesus answers: "I am; and you will see the Son of man sitting at the right hand of Power, and coming with the clouds of heaven" (14:62). The fact that God's name and the word "God" are avoided and replaced by "the Blessed" and "Power" is a sign of the text's authenticity. The high priest questions Jesus about his Messiahship and refers to it in terms of Psalm 2:7 (cf. Ps 110:3), using the expression "Son of the Blessed"—Son of God. In the context of the question, this expression refers to the Messianic tradition, while leaving open the form of sonship involved. One may assume that Caiaphas not only based the question on theological tradition, but also formulated it specifically in terms of Jesus' preaching, which had come to his attention.

Matthew gives a particular coloring to the formulation of the question. In his account, Caiaphas asks: "Tell us if you are the Christ, the Son of God" (26:63). He thus directly echoes the language of Peter's confession at Caesarea Philippi: "You are the Christ, the Son of the living

God" (16:16). At the very moment when the high priest addresses a question to Jesus using the terms of Peter's confession, Peter himself, separated only by a door from Jesus, declares that he does not know him. While Jesus is making "the good confession" (cf. 1 Tim 6:13), the one who had originally articulated this same confession is denying what he had then received from the "Father in heaven"; now it is only "flesh and blood" that is speaking in him (cf. Mt 16:17).

In Mark's account, Jesus answered the question that would determine his fate quite simply and clearly: "I am" (could there be an echo here of Exodus 3:14, "I AM WHO I AM"?). Jesus then explains more closely, basing himself on Psalm 110:1 and Daniel 7:13, how Messiahship and sonship are to be understood. Matthew has Jesus answer more indirectly: "You have said so. But I tell you ..." (26:64). Jesus does not contradict Caiaphas, but in response to the high priest's formulation he explains how he himself wants his mission to be understood—using words from Scripture. Luke, finally, presents two distinct questions (22:67, 70). In response to the Sanhedrin's challenge: "If you are the Christ, tell us", the Lord speaks enigmatically, neither openly agreeing nor explicitly denying it. This is followed by his own confession, combining Psalm 110 and Daniel 7, and then—after the Sanhedrin's insistent question: "Are you the Son of God, then?" he answers: "You say that I am."

From all this we may conclude that Jesus accepted the title Messiah, with all the meanings accruing to it from the tradition, but at the same time he qualified it in a way that could only lead to a guilty verdict, which he could have avoided either by rejecting it or by proposing a milder form of Messianism. He left no room for political or military interpretations of the Messiah's activity. No, the Messiah—he himself—will come as the Son of Man on the clouds of heaven. Objectively this is quite close to what we find in John's account when Jesus says: "My kingship is not of this world" (18:36). He claims to sit at the right hand of the Power, that is to say, to come from God in the manner of Daniel's Son of Man, in order to establish God's definitive kingdom.

This must have struck the members of the Sanhedrin as politically absurd and theologically unacceptable, for it meant that Jesus was claiming to be close to the "Power", to participate in God's own nature, and this would have been understood as blasphemy. However, Jesus had merely pieced a few scriptural quotations together and had expressed his mission "according to the Scriptures", in language drawn from the Scriptures themselves. But to the members of the Sanhedrin, the application of the noble words of Scripture to Jesus evidently appeared as an intolerable attack on God's otherness, on his uniqueness.

In any event, as far as the high priest and the members of the assembly were concerned, the evidence for blasphemy was supplied by Jesus' answer, at which Caiaphas "tore his robes, and said: 'He has uttered blasphemy'" (Mt 26:65). "The tearing of the high priest's garment does not occur through anger; rather, it is the action prescribed for the officiating judge as a sign of outrage upon hearing a blasphemy" (Gnilka, *Matthäusevangelium* II, p. 429). There now erupts over Jesus, who had prophesied his coming in glory, the brutal mockery of those who know they are in a position of strength: they make him feel their power, their utter contempt. He whom they had feared only days before was now in their hands. The cowardly conformism of weak souls feels strong in attacking him who now seems utterly powerless.

It does not occur to them that by mocking and striking Jesus, they are causing the destiny of the Suffering Servant to be literally fulfilled in him (cf. Gnilka, *Matthäusevangelium* II, p. 430). Abasement and exaltation are mysteriously intertwined. As the one enduring blows, he is the Son of Man, coming in the cloud of concealment from God and establishing the kingdom of the Son of Man, the kingdom of the humanity that proceeds from God. "Hereafter you will see ...", Jesus had said in Matthew's account (26:64), in a striking paradox. Hereafter— something new is beginning. All through history, people look upon the disfigured face of Jesus, and there they recognize the glory of God.

While this is happening, Peter insists for the third time that he has nothing to do with Jesus. "Immediately the cock crowed a second time. And Peter remembered ..." (Mk 14:72). The crowing of the cock was regarded as a sign of the end of the night. It opened the day. For Peter, too, cockcrow marked the end of the night of the soul, into which he had sunk. What Jesus had said about his denial before the cock crowed suddenly came back to him—in all its terrifying truth. Luke adds the detail that at this moment the chained and condemned Jesus is led off, to be brought before Pilate's court. Jesus and Peter encounter one another. Jesus' gaze meets the eyes and the soul of the unfaithful disciple. And Peter "went out and wept bitterly" (Lk 22:62).

3. Jesus before Pilate

Jesus' interrogation before the Sanhedrin had concluded in the way Caiaphas had expected: Jesus was found guilty of blasphemy, for which the penalty was death. But since only the Romans could carry out the death sentence, the case now had to be brought before Pilate and the political dimension of the guilty verdict had to be emphasized. Jesus had declared himself to be the Messiah; hence he had laid claim to the dignity of kingship, albeit in a way peculiarly his own. The claim to Messianic kingship was a political offense, one that had to be punished by Roman justice. With cockcrow, daybreak had arrived. The Roman Governor used to hold court early in the morning.

So Jesus is now led by his accusers to the praetorium and is presented to Pilate as a criminal who deserves to die. It is the "day of preparation" for the Passover feast. The lambs are slaughtered in the afternoon for the evening meal. Hence cultic purity must be preserved; so the priestly accusers may not enter the Gentile praetorium, and they negotiate with the Roman Governor outside the building. John, who provides this detail (18:28–29), thereby highlights the contradiction between the scrupulous attitude to regulations for cultic purity and the question of real inner purity: it simply does not occur to Jesus' accusers that impurity does not come from entering a Gentile house, but rather from the inner disposition of the heart. At the same time the evangelist emphasizes that the Passover meal had not yet taken place and that the slaughter of the lambs was still to come.

In all essentials, the four Gospels harmonize with one another in their accounts of the progress of the trial. Only John reports the conversation between Jesus and Pilate, in which the question about Jesus' kingship, the reason for his death, is explored in depth (18:33–38). The historicity of this tradition is of course contested by exegetes. While Charles H. Dodd and Raymond E. Brown judge it positively, Charles K. Barrett is extremely critical: "John's additions and alterations do not inspire confidence in his historical reliability" (*The Gospel according to Saint John*, p. 530). Certainly no one would claim that John set out to provide anything resembling a transcript of the trial. Yet we may assume that he was able to explain with great precision the core question at issue and that he presents us with a true account of the trial. Barrett also says "that John has with keen insight picked out the key of the Passion narrative in the kingship of Jesus, and has made its meaning clearer, perhaps, than any other New Testament writer" (ibid., p. 531).

Now we must ask: Who exactly were Jesus' accusers? Who insisted that he be condemned to death? We must take note of the different answers that the Gospels give to this question. According to John it was simply "the Jews". But John's use of this expression does not in any way indicate—as the modern reader might suppose—the people of Israel in general, even less is it "racist" in character. After all, John himself was ethnically a Jew, as were Jesus and all his followers. The entire early Christian community was made up of Jews. In John's Gospel this word has a precise and clearly defined meaning: he is referring to the Temple aristocracy. So the circle of accusers who instigate Jesus' death is precisely indicated in the Fourth Gospel and clearly limited: it is the Temple aristocracy—and not without certain exceptions, as the reference to Nicodemus (7:50–52) shows.

In Mark's Gospel, the circle of accusers is broadened in the context of the Passover amnesty (Barabbas or Jesus): the *"ochlos"* enters the scene and opts for the release of Barabbas. *"Ochlos"* in the first instance simply means a crowd of people, the "masses". The word frequently has a pejorative connotation, meaning "mob". In any event, it does not refer to the Jewish people as such. In the case of the Passover amnesty (which admittedly is not attested in other sources, but even so need not be doubted), the people, as so often with such amnesties, have a right to put forward a proposal, expressed by way of "acclamation". Popular acclamation in this case has juridical character (cf. Pesch, *Markusevangelium* II, p. 466). Effectively this "crowd" is made up of the followers of Barabbas who have been mobilized to secure the amnesty for him: as a rebel against Roman power he could naturally count on a good number of supporters. So the Barabbas party, the "crowd", was conspicuous, while the followers of Jesus remained hidden out of fear; this meant that the *vox populi*, on which Roman law was built, was represented one-sidedly. In Mark's account, then, in addition to "the Jews", that is to say the dominant priestly circle, the *ochlos* comes into play, the circle of Barabbas' supporters, but not the Jewish people as such.

An extension of Mark's *ochlos*, with fateful consequences, is found in Matthew's account (27:25), which speaks of "all the people" and attributes to them the demand for Jesus' crucifixion. Matthew is certainly not recounting historical fact here: How could the whole people have been present at this moment to clamor for Jesus' death? It seems obvious that the historical reality is correctly described in John's account and in Mark's. The real group of accusers are the current Temple authorities, joined in the context of the Passover amnesty by the "crowd" of Barabbas' supporters.

Here we may agree with Joachim Gnilka, who argues that Matthew, going beyond historical considerations, is attempting a theological etiology with which to account for the terrible fate of the people of Israel in the Jewish War, when land, city, and Temple were taken from them (cf. *Matthäusevangelium* II, p. 459). Matthew is thinking here of Jesus' prophecy concerning the end of the Temple: "O Jerusalem, Jerusalem, killing the prophets and stoning those who are sent to you! How often would I have gathered your children together as a hen gathers her brood under her wings, and you would not! Behold, your house is forsaken ..." (Mt 23:37–38: cf. Gnilka, *Matthäusevange-lium*, the whole of the section entitled "*Gerichtsworte*", II, pp. 295–308).

These words—as argued earlier, in the chapter on Jesus' eschatological discourse—remind us of the inner similarity between the Prophet Jeremiah's message and that of Jesus. Jeremiah—against the blindness of the then dominant circles—prophesied the destruction of the Temple and Israel's exile. But he also spoke of a "new covenant": punishment is not the last word; it leads to healing. In the same way Jesus prophesies the "deserted house" and proceeds to offer the New Covenant "in his blood": ultimately it is a question of healing, not of destruction and rejection.

When in Matthew's account the "whole people" say: "His blood be on us and on our children" (27:25), the Christian will remember that Jesus' blood speaks a differ-ent language from the blood of Abel (Heb 12:24): it does not cry out for vengeance and punishment; it brings rec-onciliation. It is not poured out *against* anyone; it is poured out *for* many, for all. "All have sinned and fall short of the glory of God ... *God* put [Jesus] forward as an expiation by his blood" (Rom 3:23, 25). Just as Caiaphas' words about the need for Jesus' death have to be read in an entirely new light from the perspective of faith, the same applies to Matthew's reference to blood: read in the light of faith, it means that we all stand in need of the purifying power of love which is his blood. These words are not a curse, but rather redemption, salvation. Only when understood in terms of the theology of the Last Supper and the Cross, drawn from the whole of the New Testament, does this verse from Matthew's Gospel take on its correct meaning.

Let us move now from the accusers to the judge: the Roman Governor Pontius Pilate. While Flavius Josephus and especially Philo of Alexandria paint a rather negative picture of him, other sources portray him as decisive, pragmatic, and realistic. It is often said that the Gospels presented him in an increasingly positive light out of a politically motivated pro-Roman tendency and that they shifted the blame for Jesus' death more and more onto the Jews. Yet there were no grounds for any such tendency in the historical circumstances of the evangelists: by the time the Gospels were written, Nero's persecution had already revealed the cruel side of the Roman State and the great arbitrariness of imperial power. If we may date the Book of Revelation to approximately the same period as John's Gospel, then it is clear that the Fourth Gospel did not come to be written in a context that could have given rise to a pro-Roman stance.

The image of Pilate in the Gospels presents the Roman Prefect quite realistically as a man who could be brutal when he judged this to be in the interests of public order. Yet he also knew that Rome owed its world dominance not least to its tolerance of foreign divinities and to the capacity of Roman law to build peace. This is how he comes across to us during Jesus' trial.

The charge that Jesus claimed to be king of the Jews was a serious one. Rome had no difficulty in recognizing regional kings like Herod, but they had to be legitimated by Rome and they had to receive from Rome the definition and limitation of their sovereignty. A king without such legitimation was a rebel who threatened the *Pax Romana* and therefore had to be put to death.

Pilate knew, however, that no rebel uprising had been instigated by Jesus. Everything he had heard must have made Jesus seem to him like a religious fanatic, who may have offended against some Jewish legal and religious rulings, but that was of no concern to him. The Jews themselves would have to judge that. From the point of view of the Roman juridical and political order, which fell under his competence, there was nothing serious to hold against Jesus.

At this point we must pass from considerations about the person of Pilate to the trial itself. In John 18:34–35 it is clearly stated that, on the basis of the information in his possession, Pilate had nothing that would incriminate Jesus. Nothing had come to the knowledge of the Roman authority that could in any way have posed a risk to law and order. The charge came from Jesus' own people, from the Temple authority. It must have astonished Pilate that Jesus' own people presented themselves to him as defenders of Rome, when the information at his disposal did not suggest the need for any action on his part.

Yet during the interrogation we suddenly arrive at a dramatic moment: Jesus' confession. To Pilate's question: "So you are a king?" he answers: "You say that I am a king. For this I was born, and for this I have come into the world, to bear witness to the truth. Every one who is of the truth hears my voice" (Jn 18:37). Previously Jesus had said: "My kingship is not of this world; if my kingship were of this world, my servants would fight, that I might not be handed over to the Jews; but my kingship is not from the world" (18:36).

This "confession" of Jesus places Pilate in an extraordinary situation: the accused claims kingship and a kingdom (*basileía*). Yet he underlines the complete otherness of his kingship, and he even makes the particular point that must have been decisive for the Roman judge: No one is fighting for this kingship. If power, indeed military power, is characteristic of kingship and kingdoms, there is no sign of it in Jesus' case. And neither is there any threat to Roman order. This kingdom is powerless. It has "no legions".

With these words Jesus created a thoroughly new concept of kingship and kingdom, and he held it up to Pilate, the representative of classical worldly power. What is Pilate to make of it, and what are we to make of it, this concept of kingdom and kingship? Is it unreal, is it sheer fantasy that can be safely ignored? Or does it somehow affect us?

In addition to the clear delimitation of his concept of kingdom (no fighting, earthly powerlessness), Jesus had introduced a positive idea, in order to explain the nature and particular character of the power of this kingship: namely, truth. Pilate brought another idea into play as the dialogue proceeded, one that came from his own world and was normally connected with "kingdom": namely, power—authority (*exousía*). Dominion demands power; it even defines it. Jesus, however, defines as the essence of his kingship witness to the truth. Is truth a political category? Or has Jesus' "kingdom" nothing to do with politics? To which order does it belong? If Jesus bases his concept of kingship and kingdom on truth as the fundamental category, then it is entirely understandable that the pragmatic Pilate asks him: "What is truth?" (18:38).

It is the question that is also asked by modern political theory: Can politics accept truth as a structural category? Or must truth, as something unattainable, be relegated to the subjective sphere, its place taken by an attempt to build peace and justice using whatever instruments are available to power? By relying on truth, does not politics, in view of the impossibility of attaining consensus on truth, make itself a tool of particular traditions that in reality are merely forms of holding on to power?

And yet, on the other hand, what happens when truth counts for nothing? What kind of justice is then possible? Must there not be common criteria that guarantee real justice for all—criteria that are independent of the arbitrariness of changing opinions and powerful lobbies? Is it not true that the great dictatorships were fed by the power of the ideological lie and that only truth was capable of bringing freedom?

What is truth? The pragmatist's question, tossed off with a degree of scepticism, is a very serious question, bound up with the fate of mankind. What, then, is truth? Are we able to recognize it? Can it serve as a criterion for our intellect and will, both in individual choices and in the life of the community?

The classic definition from scholastic philosophy designates truth as "adaequatio intellectus et rei" (conformity between the intellect and reality; Thomas Aquinas, *Summa Theologiae* I, q. 21, a. 2c). If a man's intellect reflects a thing as it is in itself, then he has found truth: but only a small fragment of reality—not truth in its grandeur and integrity.

We come closer to what Jesus meant with another of Saint Thomas' teachings: "Truth is in God's intellect properly and firstly (proprie et primo); in human intellect it is present properly and derivatively (proprie quidem et secundario)" (*De Verit.*, q. 1, a. 4c). And in conclusion we arrive at the succinct formula: God is "ipsa summa et prima veritas" (truth itself, the sovereign and first truth; *Summa Theologiae* I, q. 16, a. 5c).

This formula brings us close to what Jesus means when he speaks of the truth, when he says that his purpose in coming into the world was to "bear witness to the truth". Again and again in the world, truth and error, truth and untruth, are almost inseparably mixed together. *The truth* in all its grandeur and purity does not appear. The world is "true" to the extent that it reflects God: the creative logic, the eternal reason that brought it to birth. And it becomes more and more true the closer it draws to God. Man becomes true, he becomes himself, when he grows in God's likeness. Then he attains to his proper nature. God is the reality that gives being and intelligibility.

"Bearing witness to the truth" means giving priority to God and to his will over against the interests of the world and its powers. God is the criterion of being. In this sense, truth is the real "king" that confers light and greatness upon all things. We may also say that bearing witness to the truth means making creation intelligible and its truth accessible from God's perspective—the perspective of creative reason—in such a way that it can serve as a criterion and a signpost in this world of ours, in such a way that the great and the mighty are exposed to the power of truth, the common law, the law of truth.

Let us say plainly: the unredeemed state of the world consists precisely in the failure to understand the meaning of creation, in the failure to recognize truth; as a result, the rule of pragmatism is imposed, by which the strong arm of the powerful becomes the god of this world.

At this point, modern man is tempted to say: Creation has become intelligible to us through science. Indeed, Francis S. Collins, for example, who led the Human Genome Project, says with joyful astonishment: "The language of God was revealed" (*The Language of God*, p. 122). Indeed, in the magnificent mathematics of creation, which today we can read in the human genetic code, we recognize the language of God. But unfortunately not the whole language. The functional truth about man has been discovered. But the truth about man himself—who he is, where he comes from, what he should do, what is right, what is wrong—this unfortunately cannot be read in the same way. Hand in hand with growing knowledge of functional truth there seems to be an increasing blindness toward "truth" itself—toward the question of our real identity and purpose.

What is truth? Pilate was not alone in dismissing this question as unanswerable and irrelevant for his purposes. Today too, in political argument and in discussion of the foundations of law, it is generally experienced as disturbing. Yet if man lives without truth, life passes him by; ultimately he surrenders the field to whoever is the stronger. "Redemption" in the fullest sense can only consist in the truth becoming recognizable. And it becomes recognizable when God becomes recognizable. He becomes recognizable in Jesus Christ. In Christ, God entered the world and set up the criterion of truth in the midst of history. Truth is outwardly powerless in the world, just as Christ is powerless by the world's standards: he has no legions; he is crucified. Yet in his very powerlessness, he is powerful: only thus, again and again, does truth become power.

In the dialogue between Jesus and Pilate, the subject matter is Jesus' kingship and, hence, the kingship, the "kingdom", of God. In the course of this same conversation it becomes abundantly clear that there is no discontinuity between Jesus' Galilean teaching—the proclamation of the kingdom of God—and his Jerusalem teaching. The center of the message, all the way to the Cross—all the way to the inscription above the Cross—is the kingdom of God, the new kingship represented by Jesus. And this kingship is centered on truth. The kingship proclaimed by Jesus, at first in parables and then at the end quite openly before the earthly judge, is none other than the kingship of truth. The inauguration of this kingship is man's true liberation.

At the same time it becomes clear that between the pre-Resurrection focus on the kingdom of God and the post-Resurrection focus on faith in Jesus Christ as Son of God there is no contradiction. In Christ, God—the Truth—entered the world. Christology is the concrete form acquired by the proclamation of God's kingdom.

After the interrogation, Pilate knew for certain what in principle he had already known beforehand: this Jesus was no political rebel; his message and his activity posed no threat for the Roman rulers. Whether Jesus had offended against the Torah was of no concern to him as a Roman.

Yet Pilate seems also to have experienced a certain superstitious wariness concerning this remarkable figure. True, Pilate was a sceptic. As a man of his time, though, he did not exclude the possibility that gods or, at any rate, god-like beings could take on human form. John tells us that "the Jews" accused Jesus of making himself the Son of God, and then he adds: "When Pilate heard these words, he was even more afraid" (19:8).

I think we must take seriously the idea of Pilate's fear: Perhaps there really was something divine in this man? Perhaps Pilate would be opposing divine power if he were to condemn him? Perhaps he would have to reckon with the anger of the deity? I think his attitude during the trial can be explained not only on the basis of a certain commitment to see justice done, but also on the basis of such considerations as these.

Jesus' accusers obviously realize this, and so they now play off one fear against another. Against the superstitious fear of a possible divine presence, they appeal to the entirely practical fear of forfeiting the emperor's favor, being removed from office, and thus plunging into a downward spiral. The declaration: "If you release this man, you are not Caesar's friend" (Jn 19:12) is a threat. In the end, concern for career proves stronger than fear of divine powers.

Before the final verdict, though, there is a further dramatic and painful interlude in three acts, which we must consider at least briefly.

The first act sees Pilate presenting Jesus as a candidate for the Passover amnesty and seeking in this way to release him. In doing so, he puts himself in a fatal situation. Anyone put forward as a candidate for the amnesty is in principle already condemned. Otherwise, the amnesty would make no sense. If the crowd has the right of acclamation, then according to their response, the one they do *not* choose is to be regarded as condemned. In this sense, the proposed release on the basis of the amnesty already tacitly implies condemnation.

Regarding the juxtaposition of Jesus and Barabbas and the theological significance of the choice placed before the crowd, I have already written in some detail in Part One of this book (pp. 40–41). Here I shall merely recall the essentials. According to our translations, John refers to Barabbas simply as a robber (18:40). In the political context of the time, though, the Greek word that John uses had also acquired the meaning of terrorist or freedom fighter. It is clear from Mark's account that this is the intended meaning: "And among the rebels in prison, who had committed murder in the insurrection, there was a man called Barabbas" (15:7).

Barabbas ("Son of the Father") is a kind of Messianic figure. Two interpretations of Messianic hope are juxtaposed here in the offer of the Passover amnesty. In terms of Roman law, it is a case of two criminals convicted of the same offense—two rebels against the *Pax Romana*. It is clear that Pilate prefers the nonviolent "fanatic" that he sees in Jesus. Yet the crowd and the Temple authorities have different categories. If the Temple aristocracy felt constrained to declare: "We have no king but Caesar" (Jn 19:15), this only *appears* to be a renunciation of Israel's Messianic hope: "We do not want *this* king" is what they mean. They would like to see a different solution to the problem. Again and again, mankind will be faced with this same choice: to say yes to the God who works only through the power of truth and love, or to build on something tangible and concrete—on violence.

Jesus' followers are absent from the place of judgment, absent through fear. But they are also absent in the sense that they fail to step forward *en masse*. Their voice will make itself heard on the day of Pentecost in Peter's preaching, which cuts "to the heart" the very people who had earlier supported Barabbas. In answer to the question "Brethren, what shall we do?" they receive the answer: "Repent"—renew and transform your thinking, your being (cf. Acts 2:37–38). This is the summons which, in view of the Barabbas scene and its many recurrences throughout history, should tear open our hearts and change our lives.

The second act is succinctly summarized by John as follows: "Then Pilate took Jesus and scourged him" (19:1). In Roman criminal law, scourging was the punishment that accompanied the death sentence (Hengel and Schwemer, *Jesus und das Judentum*, p. 609). In John's Gospel, however, it is presented as an act during the interrogation, a measure that the Prefect was empowered to take on the basis of his responsibility for law enforcement. It was an extremely barbaric punishment; the victim was "struck by several torturers for as long as it took for them to grow tired, and for the flesh of the criminal to hang down in bleeding shreds" (Blinzler, *Der Prozess Jesu*, p. 321). Rudolf Pesch notes in this regard: "The fact that Simon of Cyrene has to carry the cross-beam for Jesus and that Jesus dies so quickly may well be attributable to the torture of scourging, during which other criminals sometimes would already have died" (*Markusevangelium* II, p. 467).

The third act is the crowning with thorns. The soldiers are playing cruel games with Jesus. They know that he claims to be a king. But now he is in their hands; now it pleases them to humiliate him, to display their power over him, and perhaps to offload vicariously onto him their anger against their rulers. Him whose whole body is torn and wounded, they vest, as a caricature, with the tokens of imperial majesty: the purple robe, the crown plaited from thorns, and the reed scepter. They pay homage to him: "Hail, King of the Jews"; their homage consists of blows to his head, through which they once more express their utter contempt for him (Mt 27:28–30; Mk 15:17–19; Jn 19:2–3).

The history of religions knows the figure of the mock king—related to the figure of the "scapegoat". Whatever may be afflicting the people is offloaded onto him: in this way it is to be driven out of the world. Without realizing it, the soldiers were actually accomplishing what those rites and ceremonies were unable to achieve: "Upon him was the chastisement that made us whole, and with his stripes we are healed" (Is 53:5). Thus caricatured, Jesus is led to Pilate, and Pilate presents him to the crowd—to all mankind: "Ecce homo", "Here is the man!" (Jn 19:5). The Roman judge is no doubt distressed at the sight of the wounded and derided figure of this mysterious defendant. He is counting on the compassion of those who see him.

"Ecce homo"—the expression spontaneously takes on a depth of meaning that reaches far beyond this moment in history. In Jesus, it is man himself that is manifested. In him is displayed the suffering of all who are subjected to violence, all the downtrodden. His suffering mirrors the inhumanity of worldly power, which so ruthlessly crushes the powerless. In him is reflected what we call "sin": this is what happens when man turns his back upon God and takes control over the world into his own hands.

There is another side to all this, though: Jesus' innermost dignity cannot be taken from him. The hidden God remains present within him. Even the man subjected to violence and vilification remains the image of God.

Ever since Jesus submitted to violence, it has been the
wounded, the victims of violence, who have been the
image of the God who chose to suffer for us. So Jesus in
the throes of his Passion is an image of hope: God is on
the side of those who suffer.

Finally, Pilate takes his place on the judgment seat. Once
again he says: "Here is your King!" (Jn 19:14). Then he
pronounces the death sentence.

Indeed the great "Truth" of which Jesus had spoken
was inaccessible to Pilate. Yet the concrete truth of this
particular case he knew very well. He knew that this
Jesus was not a political criminal and that the kingship he
claimed did not represent any political danger—that he
ought therefore to be acquitted.

As Prefect, Pilate represented Roman law, on which
the *Pax Romana* rested—the peace of the empire that
spanned the world. This peace was secured, on the one
hand, through Rome's military might. But military force
alone does not generate peace. Peace depends on justice.
Rome's real strength lay in its legal system, the juridical
order on which men could rely. Pilate—let us repeat—
knew the truth of this case, and hence he knew what
justice demanded of him.

Yet ultimately it was the pragmatic concept of law that
won the day with him: more important than the truth of
this case, he probably reasoned, is the peace-building role
of law, and in this way he doubtless justified his action
to himself. Releasing this innocent man could not only
cause him personal damage—and such fear was certainly

a decisive factor behind his action—it could also give rise to further disturbances and unrest, which had to be avoided at all costs, especially at the time of the Passover.

In this case peace counted for more than justice in Pilate's eyes. Not only the great, inaccessible Truth but also the concrete truth of Jesus' case had to recede into the background: in this way he believed he was fulfilling the real purpose of the law—its peace-building function. Perhaps this was how he eased his conscience. For the time being, all seemed to be going well. Jerusalem remained calm. At a later date, though, it would become clear that peace, in the final analysis, cannot be established at the expense of truth.

CHAPTER EIGHT

Crucifixion and Burial of Jesus

1. *Preliminary Reflection: Word and Event in the Passion Narrative*

All four Gospels tell of the hours that Jesus spent hanging on the Cross and of his death—they agree on the broad outlines of what happened, but there are differences of emphasis in the detail. What is remarkable about these accounts is the multitude of Old Testament allusions and quotations they contain: word of God and event are deeply interwoven. The facts are, so to speak, permeated with the word—with meaning; and the converse is also true: what previously had been merely word—often beyond our capacity to understand—now becomes reality, its meaning unlocked.

Underpinning this particular way of recounting events is the learning process that the infant Church had to undergo as she came into being. At first, Jesus' death on the Cross had simply been an inexplicable fact that placed his entire message and his whole figure in question. The story of the disciples on the road to Emmaus (Lk 24:13–35) presents this journeying, talking and searching together as the process by which the soul's darkness is gradually illumined by walking with Jesus (v. 15). It becomes clear that Moses and the Prophets—"all the Scriptures"—had spoken of the events of Christ's Passion (vv. 26–27): the "absurd" now yields its profound meaning. In the apparently senseless event, the real sense of human journeying is truly opened up: meaning triumphs over the power of destruction and evil.

What we find concisely expressed in Jesus' great dialogue with the two disciples is the process of searching and maturing that was to take place in the infant Church. In the light of the Resurrection, in the light of this new gift of journeying alongside the Lord, Christ's followers had to learn to read the Old Testament afresh: "No one had reckoned with the possibility of the Messiah dying on the Cross. Or had the relevant indications in sacred Scripture merely been overlooked?" (Reiser, *Bibelkritik*, p. 332). It was not the words of Scripture that prompted the narration of facts: rather, it was the facts themselves, at first unintelligible, that paved the way toward a fresh understanding of Scripture.

This discovery of the harmony between word and event not only determines the structure of the Passion narratives and the Gospels in general: it is constitutive of the Christian faith. Without it, the emergence of the Church could not be understood, the Church whose message acquired—and

continues to acquire—its credibility and historical importance precisely from this interplay of meaning and history:
where that connection is severed, the fundamental structure of Christian faith collapses.

A great many Old Testament allusions are woven into the
Passion narrative. Two of them are of fundamental significance, because they span, as it were, the whole of the Passion event and shed light upon it theologically: Psalm 22 and
Isaiah 53. So let us begin by briefly examining these two
texts, which are fundamental for the unity between Scripture (Old Testament) and Christ-event (New Testament).

Psalm 22 is Israel's great cry of anguish, in the midst of
its sufferings, addressed to the apparently silent God. The
word "cry", which is of central importance, especially in
Mark's account, for the story of Jesus' crucifixion, sets, as
it were, the tonality of this psalm. "Why are you so far ...
from the words of my groaning", we read in the opening
lines. In verses 2 and 5 this idea of calling out comes back.
Now we can hear the great anguish of the one suffering on account of God's seeming absence. Simply calling
out or pleading is not enough here. In extreme anguish,
prayer inevitably becomes a loud cry.

Verses 6–8 speak of the mockery directed at the psalmist. This mockery becomes a challenge to God and thus
an even sharper ridicule of the one who is suffering: "Let
[the Lord] rescue him, for he delights in him": helpless
suffering is cited as proof that God takes no delight in the
one being tortured. Verse 18 speaks of casting lots for his
garments, as actually happened at the foot of the Cross.

But then the cry of anguish changes into a profession of trust, for in the space of three verses a resounding answer to prayer is anticipated and celebrated. First: "From you comes my praise in the great congregation; my vows I will pay before those who fear [God]" (v. 25). The early Church recognized herself in that great assembly which celebrates the granting of the suppliant's prayer, his rescue—the Resurrection! Two further surprising elements now follow. Not only does salvation come to the psalmist, but it leads to the "afflicted [eating] and [being] satisfied" (v. 26). There is more: "All the ends of the earth shall ... turn to the LORD; and all the families of the nations shall worship before him" (v. 27).

In these last two verses, how could the early Church fail to recognize, in the first place, the "afflicted [eating] and [being] satisfied" as a sign of the mysterious new meal that the Lord had given them in the Eucharist? And secondly how could she fail to see there the unexpected development that the peoples of the earth were converted to the God of Israel, to the God of Jesus Christ—that the Church of Christ was gathered together from all peoples? Eucharist (praise and thanksgiving: v. 25; eating and being satisfied: v. 26) and universal salvation (v. 27) appear as God's great answer to prayer in response to Jesus' cry. It is important always to keep in mind the vast span of events portrayed in this psalm, if we are to understand why it occupies such a central place in the story of the crucifixion.

The second fundamental text—Isaiah 53—we have already considered in connection with Jesus' high-priestly prayer. In Marius Reiser's meticulous analysis of this mysterious passage, we can relive the early Christians' astonishment on seeing how one step after another of the path of Jesus Christ is foretold here. The Prophet—viewed through the lens of all the methods of modern critical textual analysis—speaks as an evangelist.

Let us now move on to a brief consideration of the essential elements of the crucifixion accounts.

2. Jesus on the Cross

The first of Jesus' words from the Cross: "Father, forgive them"

The first of Jesus' words from the Cross, spoken almost at the very moment when the act of crucifixion was being carried out, is a plea for the forgiveness of those who treat him thus: "Father, forgive them, for they know not what they do" (Lk 23:34). What the Lord had preached in the Sermon on the Mount, he now puts into practice. He knows no hatred. He does not call for revenge. He begs forgiveness for those who nail him to the Cross, and he justifies his plea by adding: "They know not what they do".

This theme of "not knowing" returns in Saint Peter's sermon in the Acts of the Apostles. He begins by reminding the crowd that had gathered after the healing of the lame man in the portico of Solomon that they had "denied the Holy and Righteous One, and asked for a murderer" to be granted to them (3:14). You "killed the

Author of life, whom God raised from the dead" (3:15). After this painful reminder, which forms part of his Pentecost sermon and which cut his hearers to the heart (cf. 2:37), he continues: "Now, brethren, I know that you acted in ignorance, as did also your rulers" (3:17).

Once again, the theme of "not knowing" appears in one of Saint Paul's autobiographical reflections. He recalls that he himself "formerly blasphemed and persecuted and insulted" Jesus; then he continues: "but I received mercy because I had acted ignorantly in unbelief" (1 Tim 1:13). In view of his earlier self-assurance as a perfect disciple of the Law who knew and lived by the Scriptures, these are strong words; he who had studied under the best masters and who might reasonably have considered himself a real expert on the Scriptures, has to acknowledge, in retrospect, that he was ignorant. Yet his very ignorance is what saved him and made him fit for conversion and forgiveness. This combination of expert knowledge and deep ignorance certainly causes us to ponder. It reveals the whole problem of knowledge that remains self-sufficient and so does not arrive at Truth itself, which ought to transform man.

In a different way again, we encounter this same combination of knowledge and failure to understand in the story of the wise men from the East. The chief priests and scribes know exactly where the Messiah is to be born. But they do not recognize him. Despite their knowledge, they remain blind (cf. Mt 2:4–6).

Clearly this mixture of knowledge and ignorance, of material expertise and deep incomprehension, occurs in every period of history. For this reason, what Jesus says about ignorance, and the examples that can be found in the various passages from Scripture, is bound to be unsettling for the supposedly learned today. Are we not blind precisely as people with knowledge? Is it not on account of our knowledge that we are incapable of recognizing Truth itself, which tries to reach us through what we know? Do we not recoil from the pain of that heartrending Truth of which Peter spoke in his Pentecost sermon? Ignorance diminishes guilt, and it leaves open the path to conversion. But it does not simply excuse, because at the same time it reveals a deadening of the heart that resists the call of Truth. All the more, then, it remains a source of comfort for all times and for all people that both in the case of those who genuinely did not know (his executioners) and in the case of those who did know (the people who condemned him), the Lord makes their ignorance the motive for his plea for forgiveness: he sees it as a door that can open us to conversion.

Jesus is mocked

Three groups of mockers are mentioned in the Gospel. The first are the passers-by. They remind the Lord of his words about the destruction of the Temple: "Aha, you who would destroy the temple and build it in three days, save yourself, and come down from the cross!" (Mk 15:29–30). By taunting the Lord in this way, they express their contempt for his powerless state; they bring home to him once more how powerless he is. At the same time they try to lead him into temptation, as the devil himself had done: "Save yourself!" Exercise your power! They do not realize that at this very moment the destruction of the Temple is being accomplished and that the new Temple is rising up before them.

At the end of the Passion, as Jesus dies, the veil of the Temple is torn in two—so the Synoptics tell us—from top to bottom (Mt 27:51; Mk 15:38; Lk 23:45). Probably it is the inner of the two Temple veils that is meant here, the one that seals off the Holy of Holies from human access. Only once a year is it permitted for the high priest to pass through the veil, to enter the presence of the Most High, and to utter the Holy Name.

This veil, at the very moment of Jesus' death, is torn in two from top to bottom. There are two things we learn from this: on the one hand, it becomes apparent that the era of the old Temple and its sacrifices is over. In place of symbols and rituals that point ahead to the future, the reality has now come, the crucified Jesus who reconciles us all with the Father. At the same time, though, the tearing of the Temple veil means that the pathway to God is now open. Previously God's face had been concealed. Only in a symbolic way could the high priest once a year enter his presence. Now God himself has removed the veil and revealed himself in the crucified Jesus as the one who loves to the point of death. The pathway to God is open.

The second group of mockers consists of members of the Sanhedrin. Matthew mentions all three elements: priests, scribes, and elders. They formulate their mockery using language drawn from the Book of Wisdom, the second chapter of which tells of the just man who stands in the way of the wicked life of the others, who calls himself a son of God and is handed over to suffering (Wis 2:10–20). The members of the Sanhedrin, taking their cue from these words, now say of Jesus, the Crucified One: "He is the King of Israel; let him come down now from the cross, and we will believe in him. He trusts in God; let God deliver him now, if he desires him; for he said, 'I am the Son of God'" (Mt 27:42–43; cf. Wis 2:18). Without realizing it, the mockers thereby acknowledge that Jesus is truly the one of whom the Book of Wisdom speaks. His situation of outward helplessness proves him to be the true Son of God.

We may add that the author of the Book of Wisdom could have been familiar with Plato's speculations from his work on statecraft, in which he asks what would become of a perfectly just person in this world, and he comes to the conclusion that such a person would be crucified (*The Republic* II, 361e–362a). The Book of Wisdom may have taken up this idea from the philosopher and introduced it into the Old Testament, so that it now points directly to Jesus. It is in the mockery that the mystery of Jesus Christ is proved true. Just as he refused to be induced by the devil to throw himself down from the parapet of the Temple (Mt 4:5–7; Lk 4:9–13), so now he refuses to yield to a similar temptation. He knows that God will indeed deliver him, but not in the way these people imagine. The Resurrection will be the moment when God raises him from death and accredits him as Son.

The third group of mockers consists of the two men crucified alongside Jesus, to whom Matthew and Mark refer using the same word—*lēstēs* (robber)—that John uses for Barabbas (cf. Mt 27:38; Mk 15:27; Jn 18:40). This clearly shows that they are regarded as resistance fighters, to whom the Romans, in order to criminalize them, simply attach the label "robber". They are crucified with Jesus because they have been found guilty of the same crime: resistance to Roman power.

The offense attributed to Jesus, though, is of a different kind from that of the two "robbers", who may have taken part in Barabbas' uprising. Pilate is well aware that Jesus had nothing like that in mind, and so he adopts a particular formulation of Jesus' "crime" in the charge that is placed above the Cross: "Jesus of Nazareth, King of the Jews" (Jn 19:19). Up to this point, Jesus had avoided the title Messiah or king, or else he had immediately linked it with his suffering (cf. Mk 8:27-31) in order to prevent false interpretations. Now the title "king" can appear quite openly. In the three great languages of that time, Jesus is publicly proclaimed king.

It is understandable that the members of the Sanhedrin object to this title, in which Pilate clearly wants to express his cynicism toward the Jewish authorities and to take his revenge on them *post factum*. But this inscription now stands before world history, and it amounts to a proclamation of kingship. Jesus is "exalted". The Cross is his throne, from which he draws the world to himself. From this place of total self-sacrifice, from this place of truly divine love, he reigns as the true king in his own way—a way that neither Pilate nor the members of the Sanhedrin had been able to comprehend.

Of the two men crucified with Jesus, only one joins in the mockery: the other grasps the mystery of Jesus. He knows and he sees that the nature of Jesus' "offense" was quite different—that Jesus was nonviolent. And now he sees that this man crucified beside him truly makes the face of God visible, he is truly God's Son. So he asks him: "Jesus, remember me when you come in your kingly power" (Lk 23:42). What exactly the good thief understood by Jesus' coming in his kingly power, and what he therefore meant by asking Jesus to remember him, we do not know. But clearly, while on the Cross, he realized that this power-less man was the true king—the one for whom Israel was waiting. Now he wanted to be at this man's side not only on the Cross, but also in glory.

Jesus' response goes beyond what is asked of him. Instead of an unspecified future, he speaks of that very day: "Today you will be with me in Paradise" (Lk 23:43). This too is a mysterious saying, but it shows us one thing for certain: Jesus knew he would enter directly into fel-lowship with the Father—that the promise of "Paradise" was something he could offer "today". He knew he was leading mankind back to the Paradise from which it had fallen: into fellowship with God as man's true salvation.

So in the history of Christian devotion, the good thief has become an image of hope—an image of the consoling certainty that God's mercy can reach us even in our final moments, that even after a misspent life, the plea for his gracious favor is not made in vain. So, for example, the *Dies Irae* prays: "Qui ... latronem exaudisti, mihi quoque spem dedisti" (just as you answered the prayer of the thief, so you have given me hope).

Jesus' cry of abandonment

Both Matthew and Mark recount that at the ninth hour Jesus called out in a loud voice: "My God, my God, why have you forsaken me?" (Mt 27:46; Mk 15:34). They give the text of Jesus' cry in a mixture of Hebrew and Aramaic and then translate it into Greek. This prayer of Jesus has prompted constant questioning and reflection among Christians: How could the Son of God be abandoned by God? What does this exclamation mean? Rudolf Bultmann, for example, comments as follows: Jesus was put to death "because his activity was misconstrued as a political activity. In that case it would have been—historically speaking— a meaningless fate. We cannot tell whether or how Jesus found meaning in it. We may not veil from ourselves the possibility that he suffered a collapse" (*The Primitive Christian Kerygma*, p. 24). What are we to reply to all this?

First of all, we must remember that, in each of these Passion narratives, the bystanders failed to understand Jesus' cry and took him to be calling upon Elijah. There have been scholarly attempts to reconstruct Jesus' exact words in such a way that they either could be construed as a call to Elijah or could have reproduced the cry of abandonment from Psalm 22 (cf. Pesch, *Markusevangelium* II, p. 495). Be that as it may: it was only the community of the faithful, with hindsight, who recognized Jesus' cry, misheard and misinterpreted by the bystanders, as the opening verse of Psalm 22, and on that basis they could understand it as a truly Messianic cry.

It is no ordinary cry of abandonment. Jesus is praying the great psalm of suffering Israel, and so he is taking upon himself all the tribulation, not just of Israel, but of all those in this world who suffer from God's concealment. He brings the world's anguished cry at God's absence before the heart of God himself. He identifies himself with suffering Israel, with all who suffer under "God's darkness"; he takes their cry, their anguish, all their help-lessness upon himself—and in so doing he transforms it.

As we have seen, Psalm 22 pervades the whole Passion story and points beyond it. The public humiliation, the mockery and shaking of heads by the scoffers, the pain, the terrible thirst, the piercing of Jesus' hands and feet, the cast-ing of lots for his garments—the whole Passion is, as it were, anticipated in the psalm. Yet when Jesus utters the opening words of the psalm, the whole of this great prayer is essen-tially already present—including the certainty of an answer to prayer, to be revealed in the Resurrection, in the gather-ing of the "great assembly", and in the poor having their fill (cf. vv. 24–26). The cry of extreme anguish is at the same time the certainty of an answer from God, the certainty of salvation—not only for Jesus himself, but for "many".

In recent theology, there have been many serious attempts, based on Jesus' cry of anguish, to gaze into the depths of his soul and to understand the mystery of his person in his final agony. Ultimately, all these efforts are hampered by too narrowly individualistic an approach.

I think that the Church Fathers' way of understanding Jesus' prayer was much closer to the truth. Even in the days of the Old Covenant, those who prayed the Psalms were not just individual subjects, closed in on themselves. To be sure, the Psalms are deeply personal prayers, formed while wrestling with God, yet at the same time they are uttered in union with all who suffer unjustly, with the whole of Israel, indeed with the whole of struggling humanity, and so these Psalms always span past, present, and future. They are prayed in the presence of suffering, and yet they already contain within themselves the gift of an answer to prayer, the gift of transformation.

On the basis of their belief in Christ, the Fathers took up and developed this fundamental theme, which modern scholarship calls "corporate personality": in the Psalms, so Augustine tells us, Christ prays both as head and as body (cf., for example, *En. in Ps.* 60: 1–2; 61:4; 85:1, 5). He prays as "head", as the one who unites us all into a single common subject and incorporates us all into himself. And he prays as "body", that is to say, all of our struggles, our voices, our anguish, and our hope are present in his praying. We ourselves are the ones praying this psalm, but now in a new way, in fellowship with Christ. And in him, past, present, and future are always united.

Again and again we find ourselves caught up in the unfathomable depths of suffering "here and now". Yet the Resurrection and the poor having their fill are also always "here and now". This perspective takes nothing away from the horror of Jesus' Passion. On the contrary: it increases it, because now it is not merely individual, but truly bears within itself the anguish of us all. Yet at the same time, Jesus' suffering is a Messianic Passion. It is suffering in fellowship with us and for us, in a solidarity—born of love— that already includes redemption, the victory of love.

The casting of lots for Jesus' garments

The evangelists tell us that the execution squad, consisting of four soldiers, divided Jesus' garments among them by casting lots. This was following Roman custom, according to which the clothing of those who had been executed fell to the executioners. John quotes Psalm 22:18 in this regard: "This was to fulfil the Scripture, 'They parted my garments among them, and for my clothing they cast lots'" (19:24).

In keeping with the parallelism typical of Hebrew poetry, by which a single idea is expressed in two ways, John presents two distinct elements: first the soldiers sorted Jesus' clothes into four bundles and distributed them among themselves. Then they also took his tunic, which "was without seam, woven from top to bottom; so they said to one another, 'Let us not tear it, but cast lots for it to see whose it shall be'" (19:23–24).

The reference to the seamless tunic (*chitōn*) is formulated in this precise way because John evidently wanted to highlight something more than a casual detail. Some exegetes make a connection here with a piece of information provided by Flavius Josephus, who points out that the high priest's garment (*chitōn*) was woven from a single thread (cf. *Antiquitates Judaicae* III, 7, 4). Thus we may detect in the evangelist's passing reference an allusion to Jesus' high-priestly dignity, which John had expounded theologically in the high-priestly prayer of chapter 17. Not only is this dying man Israel's true king: he is also the high priest who accomplishes his high-priestly ministry precisely in this hour of his most extreme dishonor.

The Church Fathers drew out a different aspect in their consideration of this passage: in the seamless garment, which even the soldiers were reluctant to tear, they saw an image of the indestructible unity of the Church. The seamless garment is an expression of the unity that Jesus the high priest implored for his followers on the evening before he suffered. Indeed, Jesus' priesthood and the unity of his followers are inseparably linked together in the high-priestly prayer. At the foot of the Cross we hear once more the poignant message that Jesus had held up before us and inscribed on our souls in the prayer that he uttered before setting out on that final journey.

"I thirst"

At the beginning of the crucifixion, Jesus was offered the customary anaesthetizing drink to deaden the unbearable pain. Jesus declined to drink it—he wanted to endure his suffering consciously (Mk 15:23). At the climax of the Passion under the burning midday sun, stretched out on the Cross, Jesus called out: "I thirst" (Jn 19:28). According to custom, he was offered sour wine, which was commonly found among the poor and could also be described as vinegar: it was considered thirst-quenching.

Here we find a further example of the interweaving of events and scriptural allusions on which we reflected at the beginning of this chapter. On the one hand, the account is quite factual—we have the thirst of the crucified Jesus and the sour drink that the soldiers customarily administered in such cases. On the other hand, we hear a direct echo of the "Passion Psalm" 69, in which the victim laments: "for my thirst they gave me vinegar to drink" (v. 21). Jesus is the just man exposed to suffering. The Passion of the just, as presented in Scripture through the great experiences of praying amid suffering, is fulfilled in him.

This scene can hardly fail to remind us also of the song of the vineyard in the fifth chapter of the Prophet Isaiah, which we considered in connection with the parable of the vine (cf. Part One, pp. 254–57). Here God brings his lament before Israel. He had planted a vineyard on a fruitful height and had taken every possible care over it. "He looked for it to yield grapes, but it yielded wild grapes" (Is 5:2). The vineyard of Israel fails to yield for God the noble fruit of justice, which is grounded in love. It yields the sour grapes of man, who is concerned only for himself. It yields vinegar instead of wine. God's lament, which we hear in the song of the Prophet, is brought to fulfillment as the vinegar is proffered to the thirsting Savior.

Just as Isaiah's song portrays God's suffering over his people in a way that far transcends the historical moment, so too the scene at the Cross far transcends the hour of

Jesus' death. It is not only Israel, but the Church, it is we ourselves who repeatedly respond to God's bountiful love with vinegar—with a sour heart that is unable to perceive God's love. "I thirst": this cry of Jesus is addressed to every single one of us.

The women at the foot of the Cross—the Mother of Jesus

All four evangelists, in their different ways, speak of the presence of women at the foot of the Cross. Mark puts it like this: "There were also women looking on from afar, among whom were Mary Magdalene, and Mary the mother of James the younger and of Joses, and Salome, who, when he was in Galilee, followed him, and ministered to him; and also many other women who came up with him to Jerusalem" (15:40–41). Even if the evangelists do not mention it explicitly, one can sense the shock and grief of these women over what had happened simply from the reference to their presence.

At the end of his crucifixion account, John quotes a line from the Prophet Zechariah: "They shall look on him whom they have pierced" (Jn 19:37; Zech 12:10). At the beginning of the Book of Revelation, he will return to this same expression, here referring to the crucifixion scene, and he will apply it prophetically to the end time, to the moment when the Lord comes again, when all will look upon the one coming on the clouds—the Pierced One—and beat their breasts (cf. Rev 1:7).

Now it is the women who look upon the Pierced One. We may also reflect on the words of the Prophet

Zechariah that follow immediately afterward: "They shall mourn for him, as one mourns for an only child, and weep bitterly over him, as one weeps over a first-born" (12:10). While up to the moment of Jesus' death, the suffering Lord had been surrounded by nothing but mockery and cruelty, the Passion narratives end on a conciliatory note, which leads into the burial and the Resurrection. The faithful women are there. Their compassion and their love are held out to the dead Savior.

We need not hesitate to add the concluding words of Zechariah's text: "On that day there shall be a fountain opened for the house of David and the inhabitants of Jerusalem to cleanse them from sin and uncleanness" (13:1). Gazing upon the Pierced One and suffering with him have now become a fount of purification. The transforming power of Jesus' Passion has begun.

John not only tells us that there were women at the foot of the Cross—"his mother, and his mother's sister, Mary the wife of Clopas, and Mary Magdalene" (19:25)—but he continues: "When Jesus saw his mother, and the disciple whom he loved standing near, he said to his mother, 'Woman, behold your son!' Then he said to the disciple, 'Behold your mother!' And from that hour the disciple took her to his own home" (19:26–27). This is one of Jesus' final acts, an adoption arrangement, as it were. He is the only son of his mother, who will be left alone in the world after his death. He now assigns the beloved disciple to accompany her and, as it were, makes him her son in his place; from that time onward, John is responsible for her—he takes her to himself. The literal translation is stronger still; it could be rendered like this: he took her into his own—received her into his inner life-setting. In the first instance, then, this is an entirely human gesture on the part of the dying Savior. He does not leave his mother alone; he places her in the custody of the disciple who was especially close to him. And so a new home is also given to the disciple—a mother to care for him, a mother for him to look after.

If John takes the trouble to record such human concerns, it is because he wants to set down what really happened. But his concern always goes deeper than mere facts of the past. The event points beyond itself to that which endures. What is he trying to say?

The first clue comes from his form of address to Mary: "Woman". Jesus had used this same form of address at the marriage feast of Cana (Jn 2:4). The two scenes are thus linked together. Cana had been an anticipation of the definitive marriage feast—of the new wine that the Lord wanted to bestow. What had then been merely a prophetic sign now becomes a reality.

The name "Woman" points back in the first instance to the account of creation, when the Creator presents the woman to Adam. In response to this new creation, Adam says: "This at last is bone of my bones and flesh of my flesh; she shall be called Woman ..." (Gen 2:23). Saint Paul in his letters interprets Jesus as the new Adam, with whom mankind begins afresh. In the figure of Mary, Saint John shows us "the Woman" who belongs now to this new Adam. In the Gospel the allusion is a hidden one, but it was gradually explored in the context of the Church's faith.

When the Book of Revelation speaks of the great sign of a Woman appearing in heaven, she is understood to represent all Israel, indeed, the whole Church. The Church must continually give birth to Christ in pain (cf. Rev 12:1–6). Another stage in the evolution of this idea is found in the Letter to the Ephesians, where the saying about the man who leaves his father and mother to become one flesh with his wife is applied to Christ and the Church (cf. 5:31–32). On the basis of the "corporate personality" model—in keeping with biblical thought—the early Church had no difficulty recognizing in the Woman, on the one hand, Mary herself and, on the other hand, transcending time, the Church, bride and mother, in which the mystery of Mary spreads out into history.

Just like Mary, the Woman, so too the beloved disciple is both a historical figure and a type for discipleship as it will always exist and must always exist. It is to the disciple, a true disciple in loving communion with the Lord, that the Woman is entrusted: Mary—the Church.

These words spoken by Jesus as he hung upon the Cross continue to be fulfilled in many concrete ways. They are constantly repeated to both mother and disciple, and each person is called to relive them in his own life, as the Lord has allotted. Again and again the disciple is asked to take Mary as an individual and as the Church into his own home and, thus, to carry out Jesus' final instruction.

Jesus dies on the Cross

According to the account of the evangelists, Jesus died, praying, at the ninth hour, that is to say, around 3:00 P.M. Luke gives his final prayer as a line from Psalm 31: "Father, into your hands I commit my spirit" (Lk 23:46; Ps 31:5). In John's account, Jesus' last words are: "It is finished!" (19:30). In the Greek text, this word (*tetélestai*) points back to the very beginning of the Passion narrative, to the episode of the washing of the feet, which the evangelist introduces by observing that Jesus loved his own "to the end (*télos*)" (13:1). This "end", this *ne plus ultra* of loving, is now attained in the moment of death. He has truly gone right to the end, to the very limit and even beyond that limit. He has accomplished the utter fullness of love—he has given himself.

In our reflection on Jesus' prayer on the Mount of Olives in chapter 6, we encountered a further meaning of this same word (*teleioūn*) in connection with Hebrews 5:9: in the Torah it means consecration, bestowal of priestly dignity, in other words, total dedication to God. I think we may detect this same meaning here, on the basis of Jesus' high-priestly prayer. Jesus has accomplished the act of consecration—the priestly handing-over of himself and the world to God—right to the end (cf. Jn 17:19). So in this final word, the great mystery of the Cross shines forth. The new cosmic liturgy is accomplished. The Cross of Jesus replaces all other acts of worship as the one true glorification of God, in which God glorifies himself through him in whom he grants us his love, thereby drawing us to himself.

The Synoptic Gospels explicitly portray Jesus' death on the Cross as a cosmic and liturgical event: the sun is darkened, the veil of the Temple is torn in two, the earth quakes, the dead rise again.

Even more important than the cosmic sign is an act of faith: the Roman centurion—the commander of the execution squad—in his consternation over all that he sees taking place, acknowledges Jesus as God's Son: "Truly, this man was the Son of God" (Mk 15:39). At the foot of the Cross, the Church of the Gentiles comes into being. Through the Cross, the Lord gathers people together to form the new community of the worldwide Church. Through the suffering Son, they recognize the true God.

While the Romans, as a deterrent, deliberately left victims of crucifixion hanging on the cross after they had died, Jewish law required them to be taken down on the same day (cf. Deut 21:22–23). Hence the execution squad had to hasten the victims' death by breaking their legs. This applied also in the case of the crucifixion on Golgotha. The legs of the two "thieves" are broken. But then the soldiers see that Jesus is already dead. So they do not break his legs. Instead, one of them pierces Jesus' right side—his heart—and "at once there came out blood and water" (Jn 19:34). It is the hour when the paschal lambs are being slaughtered. It was laid down that no bone of these lambs was to be broken (cf. Ex 12:46). Jesus appears here as the true Paschal Lamb, pure and whole.

So in this passage we may detect a tacit reference to the very beginning of Jesus' story—to the hour when John the

Baptist said: "Behold, the Lamb of God, who takes away the sin of the world!" (Jn 1:29). Those words, which were inevitably obscure at the time as a mysterious prophecy of things to come, are now a reality. Jesus is the Lamb chosen by God himself. On the Cross he takes upon himself the sins of the world, and he wipes them away.

Yet at the same time, there are echoes of Psalm 34, which says: "Many are the afflictions of the righteous, but the LORD delivers him out of them all. He keeps all his bones; not one of them is broken" (vv. 19–20). The Lord, the just man, has suffered much, he has suffered everything, and yet God has kept guard over him: no bone of his has been broken.

Blood and water flowed from the pierced heart of Jesus. True to Zechariah's prophecy, the Church in every century has looked upon this pierced heart and recognized therein the source of the blessings that are symbolized in blood and water. The prophecy prompts a search for a deeper understanding of what really happened there.

An initial step toward this understanding can be found in the First Letter of Saint John, which emphatically takes up the theme of the blood and water flowing from Jesus' side: "This is he who came by water and blood, Jesus Christ, not with the water only but with the water and the blood. And the Spirit is the witness, because the Spirit is the truth. There are three witnesses, the Spirit, the water, and the blood; and these three agree" (5:6–8).

What does the author mean by this insistence that Jesus came not with water only but also with blood? We may assume that he is alluding to a tendency to place all the emphasis on Jesus' baptism while setting the Cross aside. And this probably also meant that only the word, the doctrine, the message was held to be important, but not "the flesh", the living body of Christ that bled on the Cross; it probably meant an attempt to create a Christianity of thoughts and ideas, divorced from the reality of the flesh—sacrifice and sacrament.

In this double outpouring of blood and water, the Fathers saw an image of the two fundamental sacraments—Eucharist and Baptism—which spring forth from the Lord's pierced side, from his heart. This is the new outpouring that creates the Church and renews mankind. Moreover, the opened side of the Lord asleep on the Cross prompted the Fathers to point to the creation of Eve from the side of the sleeping Adam, and so in this outpouring of the sacraments they also recognized the birth of the Church: the creation of the new woman from the side of the new Adam.

Jesus' burial

All four evangelists recount that a wealthy member of the Sanhedrin, Joseph of Arimathea, asked Pilate for the body of Jesus. Mark (15:43) and Luke (23:51) add that Joseph was one "who was also himself looking for the kingdom of God", whereas John (19:38) speaks of him as a secret disciple of Jesus, who had hitherto kept quiet about this for fear of the ruling Jewish circles. John also mentions the involvement of Nicodemus (19:39), whose night con-versation with Jesus about being born and reborn John had reported in 3:1–8. After the drama of the trial, in which everything seemed to conspire against Jesus and there seemed to be no one left to speak up for him, we now encounter the other Israel: people who are waiting, people who trust God's promises and await their fulfill-ment, people who recognize in the words and deeds of Jesus the in-breaking of God's kingdom, the incipient fulfillment of the promises.

Up to this point in the Gospels, we have encountered such people mainly among simple folk: Mary and Joseph, Elizabeth and Zechariah, Simeon and Anna, and also the disciples, none of whom, while they came from a variety of cultural backgrounds and movements in Israel, actu-ally belonged to the leading circles. Now—after Jesus' death—we meet two highly regarded representatives of the educated class of Israel who had not yet dared to pro-fess their discipleship, but who nevertheless were blessed with the kind of simple heart that makes man capable of the truth (cf. Mt 10:25–26).

Whereas the Romans would leave the corpses of cruci-fixion victims to the vultures, the Jews were anxious that they should be buried, and suitable places were assigned for this purpose by the authorities. Joseph's request was therefore in keeping with normal Jewish practice. Mark says that Pilate was surprised to learn that Jesus was already dead and that he immediately inquired of the cen-turion whether it was true. Once Jesus' death had been confirmed, he handed over Jesus' body to Joseph.

Regarding the burial itself, the evangelists supply a number of important pieces of information. First, they emphasize that Joseph arranged for the Lord's body to be laid in a new tomb that belonged to him, a tomb in which no one had yet been buried (Mt 27:60; Lk 23:53; Jn 19:41). Here we see a mark of respect for this dead person. Just as on "Palm Sunday" Jesus availed himself of a donkey on which no one had yet ridden (Mk 11:2), so now he is laid to rest in a new tomb.

Equally important is the indication that Joseph bought a linen cloth in which he wrapped the corpse. Whereas the Synoptics speak simply of a linen sheet in the singular, John uses the plural "linen cloths" (cf. 19:40) in keeping with Jewish burial customs—the Resurrection account will return to this matter in greater detail. The question of matching this description to the Turin Shroud need not detain us here; in any case, the shape of that relic can in principle be harmonized with both accounts.

Finally, John tells us that Nicodemus brought a mixture of myrrh and aloes, "about a hundred pounds' weight". He continues: "They took the body of Jesus, and bound it in linen cloths with the spices, as is the burial custom of the Jews" (Jn 19:39–40). The quantity of balm is extraordinary and exceeds all normal proportions: this is a royal burial. If Jesus was manifested to us as high priest by the casting of lots for his robe, so now he is revealed to us as king by the manner of his burial: just when it seems that everything is finished, his glory mysteriously shines through.

The Synoptic Gospels tell us that some women observed the burial (Mt 27:61; Mk 15:47), and Luke reports that they were the ones "who had come with him from Galilee" (23:55). He adds: "then they returned, and prepared spices and ointments" (23:56). After the Sabbath rest, on the morning of the first day of the week, they would come to anoint the body of Jesus and thus to carry out the definitive burial. Anointing is an attempt to hold death at bay, to preserve the corpse from decomposition. And yet it is a vain effort: anointing can only maintain the dead person in death; it cannot restore him to life.

On the morning of the first day, the women will see that their concern for the dead body and its preservation was all too human a concern. They will see that Jesus is not to be held captive by death, but lives anew—now he is truly alive for the first time. They will see that God has preserved him from decomposition in a definitive way, possible only to God, and has thereby preserved him from the power of death. Nevertheless, in the loving care of these women, Easter morning—the Resurrection—is already proclaimed.

3. Jesus' Death as Reconciliation (Atonement) and Salvation

In this concluding section I shall attempt to show, in broad terms, how the early Church, under the guidance of the Holy Spirit, slowly penetrated more deeply into the truth of the Cross, in order to grasp at least remotely why and for what purpose it happened. One thing was astonishingly clear from the outset: with the Cross of Christ, the old Temple sacrifices were definitively surpassed. Something new had happened.

The expectations expressed in the Prophets' critique of Temple worship, and particularly in the Psalms, were now fulfilled: God did not want to be glorified through the sacrifices of bulls and goats, whose blood is powerless to purify and make atonement for men. The long-awaited but as yet undefined new worship had become a reality. In the Cross of Jesus, what the animal sacrifices had sought in vain to achieve actually occurred: atonement was made for the world. The "Lamb of God" took upon himself the sins of the world and wiped them away. God's relationship to the world, formerly distorted by sin, was now renewed. Reconciliation had been accomplished.

Paul provides a synthesis of the Christ-event, the new message of Jesus Christ, in these words: "In Christ God was reconciling the world to himself, not counting their trespasses against them, and entrusting to us the message of reconciliation. So we are ambassadors for Christ, God making his appeal through us. We beg you on behalf of Christ, be reconciled to God" (2 Cor 5:19–20). It is principally in Saint Paul's letters that we read of the sharp disagreements in the early Church over the question of the continuing validity of the Mosaic Law for Christians. This makes it all the more remarkable, then, that on one matter—as we have seen—there was agreement from the outset: the Temple sacrifices, the cultic heart of the Torah, were a thing of the past. Christ had taken their place. The Temple remained a venerable place of prayer and proclamation. Its sacrifices, though, were no longer relevant for Christians.

But how exactly is this to be understood? In the New Testament literature there are various attempts to explain Christ's Cross as the new worship, the true atonement and the true purification of this corrupted world.

We have spoken a number of times already of the fundamental text in Romans 3:25, where Paul, evidently drawing upon a tradition of the earliest Jewish Christian community in Jerusalem, refers to the crucified Jesus as "*hilastērion*". This, as we have seen, was the name given to the covering of the Ark of the Covenant, on which the expiatory blood was sprinkled on the great Day of Atonement during the expiatory sacrifice. Let us explain straightaway how the Christians now interpreted this archaic ritual: it is not through the blood of animals touching a holy object that God and man are reconciled. In Jesus' Passion, all the filth of the world touches the infinitely pure one, the soul of Jesus Christ and, hence, the Son of God himself. While it is usually the case that anything unclean touching something clean renders it unclean, here it is the other way around: when the world, with all the injustice and cruelty that make it unclean, comes into contact with the infinitely pure one—then he, the pure one, is the stronger. Through this contact, the filth of the world is truly absorbed, wiped out, and transformed in the pain of infinite love. Because infinite good is now at hand in the man Jesus, the counterweight to all wickedness is present and active within world history, and the good is always infinitely greater than the vast mass of evil, however terrible it may be.

If we reflect more deeply on this insight, we find the answer to an objection that is often raised against the idea of atonement. Again and again people say: It must be a cruel God who demands infinite atonement. Is this not a notion unworthy of God? Must we not give up the idea of atonement in order to maintain the purity of our image of God? In the use of the term "*hilastērion*" with reference to Jesus, it becomes evident that the real forgiveness accomplished on the Cross functions in exactly the opposite direction. The reality of evil and injustice that disfigures the world and at the same time distorts the image of God—this reality exists, through our sin. It cannot simply be ignored; it must be addressed. But here it is not a case of a cruel God demanding the infinite. It is exactly the opposite: God himself becomes the locus of reconciliation, and in the person of his Son takes the suffering upon himself. God himself grants his infinite purity to the world. God himself "drinks the cup" of every horror to the dregs and thereby restores justice through the greatness of his love, which, through suffering, transforms the darkness.

As it happens, these very ideas are explored in Saint John's Gospel (especially through the theology of the high-priestly prayer) and in the Letter to the Hebrews (through its interpretation of the Torah cult in terms of the theology of the Cross). At the same time, these texts explain how the inner meaning of the Old Testament is fulfilled on the Cross—not just the Prophets' critique of the cult, but also the positive content that had always been signified and intended in that cult.

From the great riches contained in the Letter to the Hebrews I would like to propose just one fundamental text for our reflection. The author describes Old Testament worship as a "shadow" (10:1) and gives this as his reason: "It is impossible that the blood of bulls and goats should take away sins" (10:4). He then quotes Psalm 40:6–8 and interprets these psalm verses as a dialogue between the Son and the Father in which the Incarnation is accomplished and at the same time the new worship of God is established: "Sacrifices and offerings you have not desired, but a body have you prepared for me; in burnt offerings and sin offerings you have taken no pleasure. Then I said, 'Behold, I have come to do your will, O God,' as it is written of me in the roll of the book" (Heb 10:5–7; cf. Ps 40:6–8).

In this brief psalm quotation, there is an important modification of the original text, which represents the conclusion of a threefold development in the theology of worship. Whereas in the Letter to the Hebrews we read; "a body have you prepared for me", the psalmist had said: "but you have given me an open ear." Obedience had already replaced the Temple sacrifices here: living within and on the basis of God's word had been recognized as the right way to worship God. In this respect, the psalm was reflecting a strand of Greek thought from the period immediately prior to the birth of Christ: the Greek world also sensed more and more acutely the inadequacy of animal sacrifices, which God does not require and in which man does not give God what he might expect from man. So here the idea of spiritual sacrifice, or "sacrifice in the manner of the word", was formulated: prayer, the self-opening of the human spirit to God, is true worship.

The more man becomes "word"—or rather: the more his whole existence is directed toward God—the more he accomplishes true worship.

In the Old Testament, from the early Books of Samuel to the late prophecy of Daniel, we find constantly new ways of wrestling with this idea, which becomes linked more and more closely with love for God's guiding word, the Torah. God is rightly venerated when we live in obedience to his word and are hence thoroughly shaped by his will, thoroughly godly.

Yet, on the other hand, a feeling of insufficiency still remains. Again and again our obedience proves patchy. Our own will imposes itself repeatedly. The deep sense of the inadequacy of all human obedience to God's word causes the urgent desire for atonement to break out again and again, yet it is not something we can accomplish by ourselves or on the basis of our "rendering of obedience". Repeatedly, therefore, alongside talk of the insufficiency of sacrifices and offerings, the longing for them to come back in a more perfect form breaks out anew (cf., for example, Ps 51:18–19).

The version given in the Letter to the Hebrews of these verses from Psalm 40 contains the answer to this longing: the longing that God will one day be given what we cannot give him, and yet that it should still be our gift, is now fulfilled. The psalmist had prayed: "Sacrifice and offering you do not desire; but you have given me an open ear." The true Logos, the Son, says to the Father: "Sacrifices and offerings you have not desired, but a body have you prepared for me." The Logos himself, the Son, becomes flesh; he takes on a human body. In this way a new obedience becomes possible, an obedience that surpasses all human fulfillment of the commandments. The Son becomes man and in his body bears the whole of humanity back to God. Only the incarnate Word, whose love is fulfilled on the Cross, is perfect obedience. In him not only does the critique of the Temple sacrifices become definitive, but whatever longing still remains is also fulfilled: his incarnate obedience is the new sacrifice, and in this obedience he draws us all with him and at the same time wipes away all our disobedience through his love.

To put it yet another way: our own morality is insufficient for the proper worship of God. This Saint Paul stated quite emphatically in the dispute over justification. Yet the Son, the Incarnate One, bears us all within himself, and in this way he gives what we ourselves would not be able to give. Central to the Christian life, then, are both the sacrament of Baptism, by which we are taken up into Christ's obedience, and also the Eucharist, in which the Lord's obedience on the Cross embraces us all, purifies us, and draws us into the perfect worship offered by Jesus Christ.

What the early Church is saying here about the Incarnation and the Cross as she reflects prayerfully upon the Old Testament and the path of Jesus must be seen against the background of the dramatic struggles of that period for a proper understanding of man's relationship with God. It answers not only the question "why the Cross?" but also the urgent questions, arising in both the Jewish and the

Gentile world, about how man can become just before God and, conversely, how he can understand God aright, the mysterious and hidden one, insofar as this is possible for man at all.

In all that we have said so far, it is clear that not only has a theological interpretation of the Cross been given, together with an interpretation, based on the Cross, of the fundamental Christian sacraments and Christian worship, but also that the existential dimension is involved: What does this mean for me? What does it mean for my path as a human being? The incarnate obedience of Christ is presented as an open space into which we are admitted and through which our own lives find a new context. The mystery of the Cross does not simply confront us; rather, it draws us in and gives a new value to our life.

This existential aspect of the new concept of worship and sacrifice appears with particular clarity in the twelfth chapter of the Letter to the Romans: "I appeal to you therefore, brethren, by the mercies of God, to present your bodies as a living sacrifice, holy and acceptable to God, which is your spiritual [word-like] worship" (v. 1). The idea of worshipping God in the manner of the word (*logikē latreía*) is taken up here, and it means the offering of one's whole existence to God, in which, so to speak, the whole person becomes "word-like", "god-like". In the process, the physical dimension is emphasized: it is our physical existence that must be penetrated by the word and must become a gift to God. Paul, who places so much emphasis on the impossibility of justification on the basis of one's own morality, is doubtless presupposing that this new form of Christian worship, in which Christians themselves are the "living and holy sacrifice", is possible only through sharing in the incarnate love of Jesus Christ, a love that conquers all our insufficiency through the power of his holiness.

If, on the one hand, we should acknowledge that Paul in no way yields to moralism in this exhortation or in any sense belies his doctrine of justification through faith and not through works, it is equally clear that this doctrine of justification does not condemn man to passivity—he does not become a purely passive recipient of a divine righteousness that always remains external to him. No, the greatness of Christ's love is revealed precisely in the fact that he takes us up into himself in all our wretchedness, into his living and holy sacrifice, so that we truly become "his body".

In the fifteenth chapter of the Letter to the Romans, Paul takes up the same idea quite emphatically once more when he interprets his apostolate in terms of priesthood and describes the Gentiles who have become believers as the living sacrifice that is pleasing to God: I have written to you "because of the grace given me by God to be a minister of Christ Jesus to the Gentiles in the priestly service of the gospel of God, so that the offering of the Gentiles may be acceptable, sanctified by the Holy Spirit" (vv. 15–16).

In more recent times, this way of speaking about priesthood and sacrifice has been dismissed as pure allegory. It has been claimed that the language of priesthood and sacrifice is meant only in a figurative, purely spiritual, not in a real, cultic sense. Paul himself and the whole early Church viewed this matter exactly the other way around. For them, the truth was that the material sacrifices were only figuratively sacrifices and worship—they were an attempt to reach out toward something that they themselves could not bring about. True worship is the living human being, who has become a total answer to God, shaped by God's healing and transforming word. And true priesthood is therefore the ministry of word and sacrament that transforms people into an offering to God and makes the cosmos into praise and thanksgiving to the Creator and Redeemer. Therefore Christ, who makes an offering of himself on the Cross, is the true high priest, anticipated symbolically by the Aaronic priesthood. Hence his self-giving—his obedience, which takes us all up and brings us back to God—is the true worship, the true sacrifice.

To this extent, entering into the mystery of the Cross must constitute the heart of the apostolic ministry, the heart of the proclamation of the Gospel designed to lead people to faith. If on this basis we may identify the central focus of Christian worship as the celebration of the Eucharist, the constantly renewed participation in the priestly mystery of Jesus Christ, at the same time the full scope of that worship must always be kept in mind: it is always a matter of drawing every individual person, indeed, the whole of the world, into Christ's love in such a way that everyone together with him becomes an offering that is "acceptable, sanctified by the Holy Spirit" (Rom 15:16).

Finally, on the basis of these ideas, a further dimension of Christian thought regarding worship and sacrifice is opened up to view. It comes across clearly in the following verse from the Letter to the Philippians, in which Paul anticipates his martyrdom and at the same time offers a theological interpretation of it: "Even if I am to be poured as a libation upon the sacrificial offering [literally: sacrifice and liturgy] of your faith, I am glad and rejoice with you all" (2:17; cf. 2 Tim 4:6). Paul views his expected martyrdom as liturgy and as sacrificial event. Once again, this is no mere allegory or figurative way of speaking. No, in martyrdom he is drawn fully into the obedience of Christ, into the liturgy of the Cross, and hence into true worship.

On the basis of this understanding, the early Church was able to grasp the true depth and nobility of martyrdom. Thus it has been handed down to us that Ignatius of Antioch, for example, described himself as the grain of wheat of Christ, ground through martyrdom in order to become the bread of Christ (cf. *Ad Rom* 4:1). In the account of the martyrdom of Saint Polycarp, it is reported that the flames in which he was to be burned formed themselves into the shape of a sail billowing in the wind; the fire "formed a wall round about the martyr's figure; and there was he in the center of it, not like burning flesh, but like a loaf baking in the oven", and it spread "a delicious fragrance, like the odor of incense" (*Martyrdom of Polycarp*, 15). The Christians of Rome also arrived at a similar interpretation of the martyrdom of Saint Lawrence, who was burned to death on the gridiron.

They saw it not only as Lawrence's perfect union with the mystery of Christ, who in martyrdom became bread for us, but also as an image of Christian life in general: in the trials of life we are slowly burned clean; we can, as it were, become bread, to the extent that the mystery of Christ is communicated through our life and our suffering, and to the extent that his love makes us an offering to God and to our fellowmen.

In living out the Gospel and in suffering for it, the Church, under the guidance of the apostolic preaching, has learned to understand the mystery of the Cross more and more, even though ultimately it is a mystery that defies analysis in terms of our rational formulae. The darkness and irrationality of sin and the holiness of God, too dazzling for our eyes, come together in the Cross, transcending our power of understanding. And yet in the message of the New Testament, and in the proof of that message in the lives of the saints, the great mystery has become radiant light.

The mystery of atonement is not to be sacrificed on the altar of overweening rationalism. The Lord's response to the request of the sons of Zebedee for seats at his right hand and at his left remains a key text for Christian faith in general: "The Son of man ... came not to be served but to serve, and to give his life as a ransom for many" (Mk 10:45).

CHAPTER NINE

Jesus' Resurrection from the Dead

1. What Is the Resurrection of Jesus?

"If Christ has not been raised, then our preaching is in vain and your faith is in vain. We are even found to be misrepresenting God, because we testified of God that he raised Christ" (1 Cor 15:14–15). With these words Saint Paul explains quite drastically what faith in the Resurrection of Jesus Christ means for the Christian message overall: it is its very foundation. The Christian faith stands or falls with the truth of the testimony that Christ is risen from the dead.

If this were taken away, it would still be possible to piece together from the Christian tradition a series of interesting ideas about God and men, about man's being and his obligations, a kind of religious world view: but the Christian faith itself would be dead. Jesus would be a failed religious leader, who despite his failure remains great and can cause us to reflect. But he would then remain purely human, and his authority would extend only so far as his message is of interest to us. He would no longer be a criterion; the only criterion left would be our own judgment in selecting from his heritage what strikes us as helpful. In other words, we would be alone. Our own judgment would be the highest instance.

Only if Jesus is risen has anything really new occurred that changes the world and the situation of mankind. Then he becomes the criterion on which we can rely. For then God has truly revealed himself.

To this extent, in our quest for the figure of Jesus, the Resurrection is the crucial point. Whether Jesus merely *was* or whether he also *is*—this depends on the Resurrection. In answering yes or no to this question, we are taking a stand not simply on one event among others, but on the figure of Jesus as such.

Therefore it is necessary to listen with particular attention as the New Testament bears witness to the Resurrection. Yet first we have to acknowledge that this testimony, considered from a historical point of view, is presented to us in a particularly complex form and gives rise to many questions.

What actually happened? Clearly, for the witnesses who encountered the risen Lord, it was not easy to say. They were confronted with what for them was an entirely new reality, far beyond the limits of their experience. Much as the reality of the event overwhelmed them and impelled them to bear witness, it was still utterly unlike anything they had previously known. Saint Mark tells us that the disciples on their way down from the mountain of the Transfiguration were puzzled by the saying of Jesus that the Son of Man would "rise from the dead". And they asked one another what "rising from the dead" could mean (9:9–10). And indeed, what does it mean? The disciples did not know, and they could find out only through encountering the reality itself.

Anyone approaching the Resurrection accounts in the belief that he knows what rising from the dead means will inevitably misunderstand those accounts and will then dismiss them as meaningless. Rudolf Bultmann raised an objection against Resurrection faith by arguing that even if Jesus had come back from the grave, we would have to say that "a miraculous natural event such as the resuscitation of a dead man" would not help us and would be existentially irrelevant (cf. *New Testament and Mythology*, p. 7).

Now it must be acknowledged that if in Jesus' Resurrection we were dealing simply with the miracle of a resuscitated corpse, it would ultimately be of no concern to us. For it would be no more important than the resuscitation of a clinically dead person through the art of doctors. For the world as such and for our human existence, nothing would have changed. The miracle of a resuscitated corpse would indicate that Jesus' Resurrection was equivalent to the raising of the son of the widow of Nain (Lk 7:11–17), the daughter of Jairus (Mk 5:22–24, 35–43 and parallel passages), and Lazarus (Jn 11:1–44). After a more or less short period, these individuals returned to their former lives, and then at a later point they died definitively.

The New Testament testimonies leave us in no doubt that what happened in the "Resurrection of the Son of Man" was utterly different. Jesus' Resurrection was about breaking out into an entirely new form of life, into a life that is no longer subject to the law of dying and becoming, but lies beyond it—a life that opens up a new dimension of human existence. Therefore the Resurrection of Jesus is not an isolated event that we could set aside as something limited to the past, but it constitutes an "evolutionary leap" (to draw an analogy, albeit one that is easily misunderstood). In Jesus' Resurrection a new possibility of human existence is attained that affects everyone and that opens up a future, a new kind of future, for mankind.

So Paul was absolutely right to link the resurrection of Christians and the Resurrection of Jesus inseparably together: "If the dead are not raised, then Christ has not been raised.... But in fact Christ has been raised from the dead, the first fruits of those who have fallen asleep" (1 Cor 15:16, 20). Christ's Resurrection is either a universal event, or it is nothing, Paul tells us. And only if we understand it as a universal event, as the opening up of a new dimension of human existence, are we on the way toward any kind of correct understanding of the New Testament Resurrection testimony.

On this basis we can understand the unique character of this New Testament testimony. Jesus has not returned to a normal human life in this world like Lazarus and the others whom Jesus raised from the dead. He has entered upon a different life, a new life—he has entered the vast breadth of God himself, and it is from there that he reveals himself to his followers.

For the disciples, too, this was something utterly unexpected, to which they were only slowly able to adjust. Jewish faith did indeed know of a resurrection of the dead at the end of time. New life was linked to the inbreaking of a new world and thus made complete sense. If there is a new world, then there is also a new mode of life there. But a resurrection into definitive otherness in the midst of the continuing old world was not foreseen and therefore at first made no sense. So the promise of resurrection remained initially unintelligible to the disciples.

The process of coming to Resurrection faith is analogous to what we saw in the case of the Cross. Nobody had thought of a crucified Messiah. Now the "fact" was there, and it was necessary, on the basis of that fact, to take a fresh look at Scripture. We saw in the previous chapter how Scripture yielded new insights in the light of the unexpected turn of events and how the "fact" then began to make sense. Admittedly, the new reading of Scripture could begin only after the Resurrection, because it was only through the Resurrection that Jesus was accredited as the one sent by God. Now people had to search Scripture for both Cross and Resurrection, so as to understand them in a new way and thereby come to believe in Jesus as the Son of God.

This also presupposes that for the disciples the Resurrection was just as real as the Cross. It presupposes that they were simply overwhelmed by the reality, that, after their initial hesitation and astonishment, they could no longer ignore that reality. It is truly he. He is alive; he has spoken to us; he has allowed us to touch him, even if he no longer belongs to the realm of the tangible in the normal way.

The paradox was indescribable. He was quite different, no mere resuscitated corpse, but one living anew and forever in the power of God. And yet at the same time, while no longer belonging to our world, he was truly present there, he himself. It was an utterly unique experience, which burst open the normal boundaries of experience and yet for the disciples was quite beyond doubt. This explains the unique character of the Resurrection accounts: they speak of something paradoxical, of something that surpasses all experience and yet is utterly real and present.

But could it really be true? Can we—as men of the modern world—put our faith in such testimony? "Enlightened" thinking would say no. For Gerd Lüdemann, for example, it seems clear that in consequence of the "revolution in the scientific image of the world ... the traditional concepts of Jesus' Resurrection are to be considered outdated" (quoted in Wilckens, *Theologie des Neun Testaments* I/2, pp. 119–20). But what exactly is this "scientific image of the world"? How far can it be considered normative? Hartmut Gese in his important article "Die Frage des Weltbildes", to which I should like to draw attention, has painstakingly described the limits of this normativity.

Naturally there can be no contradiction of clear scientific data. The Resurrection accounts certainly speak of something outside our world of experience. They speak of something new, something unprecedented—a new dimension of reality that is revealed. What already exists is not called into question. Rather we are told that there is a further dimension, beyond what was previously known. Does that contradict science? Can there really only ever be what there has always been? Can there not be something unexpected, something unimaginable, something new? If there really is a God, is he not able to create a new dimension of human existence, a new dimension of reality altogether? Is not creation actually waiting for this last and highest "evolutionary leap", for the union of the finite with the infinite, for the union of man and God, for the conquest of death?

Throughout the history of the living, the origins of anything new have always been small, practically invisible, and easily overlooked. The Lord himself has told us that "heaven" in this world is like a mustard seed, the smallest of all the seeds (Mt 13:31–32), yet contained within it are the infinite potentialities of God. In terms of world history, Jesus' Resurrection is improbable; it is the smallest mustard seed of history.

This reversal of proportions is one of God's mysteries. The great—the mighty—is ultimately the small. And the tiny mustard seed is something truly great. So it is that the Resurrection has entered the world only through certain mysterious appearances to the chosen few. And yet it was truly the new beginning for which the world was silently waiting. And for the few witnesses—precisely because they themselves could not fathom it—it was such

247

an overwhelmingly real happening, confronting them so powerfully, that every doubt was dispelled, and they stepped forth before the world with an utterly new fearlessness in order to bear witness: Christ is truly risen.

2. *The Two Different Types of Resurrection Testimony*

Let us turn now to the individual Resurrection accounts in the New Testament. As we consider them, the first thing we notice is that there are two different types of testimony, which we may label the "confessional tradition" and the "narrative tradition".

A. *The Confessional Tradition*

The confessional tradition crystallizes the essentials in short phrases that establish the kernel of what took place. They are an expression of Christian identity, a "confession" indeed, by which Christians recognize one another, by which they identify themselves before God and man. I would like to propose three examples.

At the end of the Emmaus story, the two disciples find the eleven Apostles assembled in Jerusalem and are greeted with these words: "The Lord has risen indeed, and has appeared to Simon!" (Lk 24:34). In its context, this functions as a brief narrative, but it also serves as a formula of acclamation and confession, in which the essential is proclaimed: the event itself and the witness who testifies to it.

We find a combination of two formulae in the tenth chapter of the Letter to the Romans: "If you confess with your lips that Jesus is Lord and believe in your heart that God raised him from the dead, you will be saved" (v. 9). In this example—as also in the account of Peter's confession at Caesarea Philippi (cf. Mt 16:13–16)—there are two elements to the confession: it is said that Jesus is "Lord", which in terms of the Old Testament meaning of the word refers to his divinity. Then comes the confession of the fundamental historical event: God raised him from the dead. This already makes clear what the significance of the confession is for Christians: it brings salvation. It leads us to the truth that is salvation. We have here a prototype of the confessional formulae used in Baptism, which always link Christ's lordship to the story of his life, death, and Resurrection. In Baptism man hands himself over to the new life of the Risen One. Confession becomes life.

By far the most important of the Easter confessions is found in the fifteenth chapter of the First Letter to the Corinthians. As with the account of the Last Supper (1 Cor 11:23–26), Paul emphasizes strongly that he is not speaking on his own initiative here: "I delivered to you as of first importance what I also received" (15:3). Paul deliberately takes his place within the chain of reception and transmission. Here, regarding the essential content on which everything depends, what is demanded above all is fidelity. And Paul, who characteristically places so much emphasis on his personal witness of the Risen One and on the apostolate that he received directly from the Lord, insists here with great emphasis on literal fidelity in

the transmission of what has been received, on the common tradition of the Church from her beginnings.

The Gospel of which Paul speaks is the foundation "in
which you stand, by which you are saved, if you hold it
[that is, the word, the literal formulation] fast" that "I
preached to you" (15:1–2). In this central message, what
matters is not only the content, but also the literal formulation, which must be preserved intact. This link with
the very earliest tradition is the source of both the unity
of the faith and its universally binding nature. "Whether
then it was I or they [the others who proclaimed it]: so
we preach and so you believed" (15:11). In its nucleus
the faith, even down to its literal formulation, is one—it
binds all Christians.

When exactly and from whom Paul received this confession has been the object of further inquiry, just as we saw in
the case of the Last Supper tradition. In any event, it forms
part of the primary catechesis that he as a convert would
have received while still in Damascus, but its essential content was doubtless formulated in Jerusalem and therefore
dates back to the 30s—a real testimony to the origins.

The text handed down in the First Letter to the Corinthians has been extended by Paul, inasmuch as he has
added, among others, his own encounter with the risen
Lord. For Saint Paul's self-understanding and for the faith
of the early Church I find it significant that Paul felt entitled to add on to the original confession, with equally
binding character, the risen Lord's appearance to him and
the apostolic mission that came with it. He was evidently
convinced that this revelation of the risen Lord to him

was still a central part of the emerging creedal formula, that it belonged to the faith of the universal Church as an essential element intended for all.

Let us listen now to the whole text, as Paul presents it:

"That Christ died for our sins in accordance with the Scriptures, that he was buried, that he was raised on the third day in accordance with the Scriptures, and that he appeared to Cephas, then to the Twelve. Then he appeared to more than five hundred brethren at one time, most of whom are still alive.... Then he appeared to James, then to all the apostles. Last of all, as to one untimely born, he appeared also to me" (1 Cor 15:3–8).

In the view of most exegetes, the original confession ends with verse 5, that is, with the appearance to Cephas and the Twelve. From further traditions, Paul added James, the group of over five hundred brethren, and "all" the Apostles—here he is evidently applying an understanding of "apostles" that extends beyond the circle of the Twelve. James is important because with him, Jesus' family, who had previously been decidedly ambivalent (cf. Mk 3:20–21, 31–35; Jn 7:5), enter the circle of believers and also because James is the one who assumed the leadership of the Mother Church in the Holy City after Peter's flight from Jerusalem.

Jesus' death

Let us turn now to the confession itself, which demands more detailed consideration. It begins with the phrase:

"Christ died for our sins in accordance with the Scriptures." The fact of his death is qualified by two additional expressions: "for our sins" and "in accordance with the Scriptures".

Let us begin with the second expression. It is important for the whole approach taken by the early Church toward the facts of Jesus' life. What the risen Lord taught the disciples on the road to Emmaus now becomes the basic method for understanding the figure of Jesus: everything that happened to him is fulfillment of the "Scriptures". Only on the basis of the "Scriptures", the Old Testament, can he be understood at all. With reference to Jesus' death on the Cross, this means that his death is no coincidence. It belongs in the context of God's ongoing relationship with his people, from which it receives its inner logic and its meaning. It is an event in which the words of Scripture are fulfilled; it bears within itself Logos, or logic; it proceeds from the word and returns to the word; it surrounds the word and fulfills it.

A pointer toward a deeper understanding of this fundamental relationship with the word is given by the earlier qualification: Christ died "for our sins". Because his death has to do with the word of God, it has to do with us, it is a dying "for". In the chapter on Jesus' death on the Cross, we saw what an enormous wealth of tradition in the form of scriptural allusions feeds into the background here, chief among them the fourth Suffering Servant Song (Is 53). Insofar as Jesus' death can be located within this context of God's word and God's love, it is differentiated from the kind of death resulting from man's original sin as a consequence of his presumption in seeking to be like God, a presumption that could only lead to man's plunge into wretchedness, into the destiny of death.

Jesus' death is of another kind: it is occasioned, not by the presumption of men, but by the humility of God. It is not the inevitable consequence of a false hubris, but the fulfillment of a love in which God himself comes down to us, so as to draw us back up to himself. Jesus' death is rooted, not in the sentence of expulsion from Paradise, but in the Suffering Servant Songs. It is a death in the context of his service of expiation—a death that achieves reconciliation and becomes a light for the nations. Thus it is that the twofold qualification that Paul adds, when handing on this creedal formula, to the expression "he died" opens up the path from the Cross to the Resurrection.

The question of the empty tomb

Next in the confession of faith, direct and without commentary, comes the statement "he was buried." This makes it clear that Jesus really was dead, that he fully participated in the human destiny of death. Jesus traveled the path of death right to the bitter and seemingly hopeless end in the tomb. Jesus' tomb was evidently known. And here the question naturally arises: Did he remain in the tomb? Or was it empty after he had risen?

In modern theology this question has been extensively debated. Most commentators come to the conclusion that an empty tomb would not be enough to prove the Resurrection. If the tomb were indeed empty, there could be some other explanation for it. On this basis, the commentators conclude that the question of the empty tomb is immaterial and can therefore be ignored, which tends also to mean that it probably was not empty anyway, so at least a dispute with modern science over the possibility of bodily resurrection can be avoided. But at the basis of all this lies a distorted way of posing the question.

Naturally, the empty tomb as such does not prove the Resurrection. Mary Magdalene, in John's account, found it empty and assumed that someone must have taken Jesus' body away. The empty tomb is no proof of the Resurrection, that much is undeniable. Conversely, though, one might ask: Is the Resurrection compatible with the body remaining in the tomb? Can Jesus be risen if he is still lying in the tomb? What kind of resurrection would that be? Today, notions of resurrection have been developed for which the fate of the corpse is inconsequential. Yet the content of the Resurrection becomes so vague in the process that one must ask with what kind of reality we are dealing in this form of Christianity.

Be that as it may: Thomas Söding, Ulrich Wilckens, and others rightly point out that in Jerusalem at the time, the proclamation of the Resurrection would have been completely impossible if anyone had been able to point to a body lying in the tomb. To this extent, for the sake of posing the question correctly, we have to say that the empty tomb as such, while it cannot prove the Resurrection, is nevertheless a necessary condition for Resurrection faith, which was specifically concerned with the body and, consequently, with the whole of the person.

In Saint Paul's confessional statement, it is not explicitly stated that the tomb was empty, but this is clearly presupposed. All four Gospels speak of it extensively in their Resurrection accounts.

For a theological understanding of the empty tomb, a passage from Saint Peter's Pentecost sermon strikes me as important, when Peter for the first time openly proclaims Jesus' Resurrection to the assembled crowds. He communicates it, not in his own words, but by quoting Psalm 16:8–10 as follows: "... my flesh will dwell in hope. For you will not abandon my soul to Hades, nor let your Holy One see corruption. You have made known to me the ways of life" (Acts 2:26–28). Peter quotes the psalm text using the version found in the Greek Bible. The Hebrew text is slightly different: "You do not give me up to Sheol, or let your godly one see the Pit. You show me the path of life" (Ps 16:10–11). In the Hebrew version the psalmist speaks in the certainty that God will protect him, even in the threatening situation in which he evidently finds himself, that God will shield him from death and that he may dwell securely: he will not see the grave. The version Peter quotes is different: here the psalmist is confident that he will not remain in the underworld, that he will not see corruption.

Peter takes it for granted that it was David who originally prayed this psalm, and he goes on to state that this hope was not fulfilled in David: "He both died and was buried, and his tomb is with us to this day" (Acts 2:29). The tomb containing his corpse is the proof of his not having risen. Yet the psalm text is still true: it applies to the definitive David. Indeed, Jesus is revealed here as the true David, precisely because in him this promise is fulfilled: "You will not let your Holy One see corruption."

We need not go into the question here of whether this address really goes back to Peter and, if not, who else may have redacted it and precisely when and where it originated. Whatever the answer may be, we are dealing here with a primitive form of Resurrection proclamation, whose high authority in the early Church is clear from the fact that it was attributed to Saint Peter himself and was regarded as the original proclamation of the Resurrection.

If in the early creedal formula from Jerusalem, transmitted by Saint Paul, it is stated that Jesus rose according to the Scriptures, then surely Psalm 16 must have been seen as key scriptural evidence for the early Church. Here they found a clear statement that Christ, the definitive David, will not see corruption—that he must truly have risen.

"Not to see corruption": this is virtually a definition of resurrection. Only with corruption was death regarded as definitive. Once the body had decomposed, once it had broken down into its elements—marking man's dissolution and return to dust—then death had conquered. From now on this man no longer exists as a man—only a shadow may remain in the underworld. From this point of view, it was fundamental for the early Church that Jesus' body did not decompose. Only then could it be maintained that he did not remain in death, that in him life truly conquered death.

What the early Church deduced from the Septuagint version of Psalm 16:10 also determined the viewpoint of the entire patristic period. Resurrection essentially implies that Jesus' body was not subject to corruption. In this sense, the empty tomb is a strongly scriptural element of the Resurrection proclamation. Theological speculations arguing that Jesus' decomposition and Resurrection could be mutually compatible belong to modern thinking and stand in clear contradiction of the biblical vision. On this basis, too, we have further confirmation that a Resurrection proclamation would have been impossible if Jesus' body had been lying in the grave.

The third day

Let us return to our creedal formula. The next article states: "He was raised on the third day in accordance with the Scriptures" (I Cor 15:4). "In accordance with the Scriptures" applies to the entire phrase, not specifically to the third day, although this is included. The essential point is that the Resurrection itself is in accordance with the Scriptures—that it forms part of the whole promise that in Jesus became, not just word, but reality. So for scriptural background we could certainly look to Psalm 16:10, but also to basic promise texts like Isaiah 53. There is no direct scriptural testimony pointing to the "third day".

The thesis that the third day may possibly have been derived from Hosea 6:1–2 cannot be sustained, as Hans Conzelmann and likewise Martin Hengel and Anna Maria Schwemer have shown. The text reads: "Come, let us return to the LORD; for he has torn, that he may heal us; he has stricken, and he will bind us up. After two days he will revive us; on the third day he will raise us up, that we may live before him." This text is a penitential prayer on the part of sinful Israel. There is no mention of resurrection from the dead, properly speaking. The text is not quoted in the New Testament or at any point during the second century (cf. Hengel and Schwemer, *Jesus und das Judentum*, p. 631). It could become an anticipatory pointer toward resurrection on the third day only once the event that took place on the Sunday after the Lord's crucifixion had given this day a special meaning.

The third day is not a "theological" date, but the day when an event took place that became the decisive turning point for the disciples after the calamity of the Cross. Josef Blank formulated it like this: "The expression 'on the third day' is a chronological indication in harmony with the earliest Christian tradition in the Gospels, and it relates to the discovery of the empty tomb" (*Paulus und Jesus*, p. 156).

I would add: it relates to the first encounter with the risen Lord. The first day of the week—the third after Friday—is attested in the New Testament from a very early stage as a day when the Christian community assembled for worship (cf. 1 Cor 16:2; Acts 20:7; Rev 1:10). Ignatius of Antioch (late first century, early second century), provides evidence, as we saw earlier, that for Christians Sunday had already supplanted the Jewish Sabbath culture: "We have seen how former adherents of the ancient customs have since attained to a new hope; so that they have given up keeping the Sabbath and now order their lives by the Lord's day instead (the day when life first dawned for us, thanks to him and his death)" (*Ad Magn.*, 9:1).

If we bear in mind the immense importance attached to the Sabbath in the Old Testament tradition on the basis of the Creation account and the Decalogue, then it is clear that only an event of extraordinary impact could have led to the abandonment of the Sabbath and its replacement by the first day of the week. Only an event that marked souls indelibly could bring about such a profound realignment in the religious culture of the week. Mere theological speculations could not have achieved this. For me, the celebration of the Lord's day, which was a characteristic part of the Christian community from the outset, is one of the most convincing proofs that something extraordinary happened that day—the discovery of the empty tomb and the encounter with the risen Lord.

The witnesses

While verse 4 of the Pauline confession expounds the fact of the Resurrection, verse 5 introduces the list of witnesses. "He appeared to Cephas, then to the Twelve", it states succinctly. If we regard this verse as the conclusion of the original Jerusalem formula, then this indication of names carries particular theological weight: it reveals the very foundation of the Church's faith.

On the one hand, "the Twelve" remain the actual foundation stone of the Church, the permanent point of reference. On the other hand, the special task given to

Peter is underlined here, the commission that was first assigned to him at Caesarea Philippi and then confirmed during the Last Supper (Lk 22:32), when Peter was, as it were, introduced into the Church's eucharistic structure. Now, after the Resurrection, the Lord appears first to him, before appearing to the Twelve, and thus once again renews Peter's particular mission.

If being a Christian essentially means believing in the risen Lord, then Peter's special witnessing role is a confirmation of his commission to be the rock on which the Church is built. John, in his account of the risen Lord's threefold question to Peter, "Do you love me?" and Peter's threefold commissioning to feed Christ's flock, clearly underlined once more Peter's continuing mission vis-à-vis the faith of the whole Church (Jn 21:15–17). So the Resurrection account flows naturally into ecclesiology; the encounter with the risen Lord is mission, and it shapes the nascent Church.

B. *The Narrative Tradition*

Let us now move on—having considered the most important element of the confessional tradition—to the narrative tradition. Whereas the former authoritatively condenses the shared faith of Christianity in fixed formulae and insists on their binding character, down to the letter, for the whole believing community, the narrative accounts of the Resurrection appearances reflect different traditions. They are linked to various bearers of tradition, and they can be divided geographically between

Jerusalem and Galilee. They are not binding in every detail in the same way as the confessions; but by virtue of being taken up into the Gospels, they are clearly to be regarded as valid testimony, giving content and shape to the faith. The confessions presuppose the narratives and grew out of them. They express in concentrated form the nucleus of the narrative content, and at the same time they point back toward the narratives.

Every reader will be struck immediately by the differences between the Resurrection accounts of the four Gospels. Matthew, apart from the risen Lord's appearance to the women at the empty tomb, gives only one other appearance—in Galilee to the Eleven. Luke gives only Jerusalem traditions. John tells of appearances in both Jerusalem and Galilee. None of the evangelists recounts Jesus' Resurrection itself. It is an event taking place within the mystery of God between Jesus and the Father, which for us defies description: by its very nature it lies outside human experience.

The ending of Mark poses a particular problem. According to authoritative manuscripts, the Gospel comes to a close with 16:8—"and they went out and fled from the tomb; for trembling and astonishment had come upon them; and they said nothing to any one, for they were afraid." The authentic text of the Gospel as it has come down to us ends with the fear and trembling of the women. Previously the text had spoken of the discovery of the empty tomb by the women who came to anoint the body and of the appearance of angels who announced Jesus' Resurrection to them and urged them to tell the disciples, "and Peter", that Jesus would go before them to Galilee as he had promised. It is impossible that the Gospel would have ended with the words that follow concerning the women's silence: it takes for granted that the news of their encounter was passed on. And it must obviously have known of the appearance to Peter and the Twelve, described in the essentially older account of the First Letter to the Corinthians. For what reason our text breaks off at this point, we do not know. In the second century, a concluding summary was added, bringing together the most important Resurrection traditions and the mission of the disciples to proclaim the Gospel to the whole world (Mk 16:9–20). Whatever the facts of the case, even the short ending of Mark presupposes the discovery of the empty tomb by the women, the message of the Resurrection, and knowledge of the appearances to Peter and to the Twelve. Its enigmatic interruption we must leave unexplained.

The narrative tradition tells of encounters with the risen Lord and the words spoken by him on those occasions; the confessional tradition merely establishes the key facts that serve to confirm the faith: this is another way of describing the essential difference between the two types of tradition. Specific differences ensue from this.

One initial difference is that in the confessional tradition only men are named as witnesses, whereas in the narrative tradition women play a key role, indeed they take precedence over the men. This may be linked to the fact that in the Jewish tradition only men could be admitted as witnesses in court—the testimony of women was considered unreliable. So the "official" tradition, which is, so to speak, addressing the court of Israel and the court of the world, has to observe this norm if it is to prevail in what we might describe as Jesus' ongoing trial.

The narratives, on the other hand, do not feel bound by this juridical structure, but they communicate the whole breadth of the Resurrection experience. Just as there were only women standing by the Cross—apart from the beloved disciple—so too the first encounter with the risen Lord was destined to be for them. The Church's juridical structure is founded on Peter and the Eleven, but in the day-to-day life of the Church it is the women who are constantly opening the door to the Lord and accompanying him to the Cross, and so it is they who come to experience the Risen One.

Jesus' appearances to Paul

A second important difference, by which the narrative tradition completes the creedal formulae, lies in the fact that the risen Lord's appearances are not only confessed but described in a certain amount of detail. How are we to picture to ourselves the appearances of the Risen One, who had not returned to normal human life, but had passed over into a new manner of human existence?

To begin with, there is a marked difference between, on the one hand, the appearance of the risen Jesus to Paul, described in the Acts of the Apostles, and, on the other hand, the Gospel narratives concerning the encounters of the Apostles and the women with the living Lord.

According to all three accounts of Saint Paul's conversion in the Acts of the Apostles, there were two elements to his encounter with the risen Christ: a light that shone "brighter than the sun" (26:13) together with a voice that spoke to Saul "in the Hebrew language" (26:14). Whereas the first account says that the people accompanying Saul could hear the voice but "[saw] no one" (9:7), the second account says, conversely, that they "saw the light but did not hear the voice of the one who was speaking to me" (22:9). The third account says of the people accompanying Saul only that they all fell to the ground with him (cf. 26:14).

This much is clear: there was a difference between what was perceived by the people accompanying Saul and what Saul himself perceived. Only he was the direct recipient of a message involving a mission, but the people with him were also in some sense witnesses of an extraordinary event.

For the one who actually received the message, Saul/Paul, the two elements belong together: first, the blinding light that recalls the Tabor story—the Risen One is simply light (cf. Part One, pp. 309–10), and second, the words by which Jesus identifies himself with the persecuted Church and entrusts Paul with a mission. While in the first and second accounts Paul is sent to Damascus, where he will receive more precise instructions for his mission, in the third account a detailed and quite specific mission statement is communicated directly: "Rise and stand upon your feet; for I have appeared to you for this purpose, to appoint you to serve and bear witness to the things in which you have seen me and to those in which

I will appear to you, delivering you from the people and from the Gentiles—to whom I send you to open their eyes, that they may turn from darkness to light and from the power of Satan to God, that they may receive forgiveness of sins and a place among those who are sanctified by faith in me" (Acts 26:16–18).

Despite all the differences between the three accounts, it is still clear that the apparition (light) and the word belong together. The risen Lord, whose essence is light, speaks as a man with Paul in Paul's own language. His words serve, on the one hand, as self-identification, and this includes his identification with the persecuted Church, and, on the other hand, they serve to communicate a mission, whose content will be further explained in what follows.

The appearances of Jesus in the Gospels

The appearances that we read of in the Gospels are manifestly different. On the one hand, the Lord appears as a man like other men: he walks alongside the Emmaus disciples; he invites Thomas to touch his wounds, and in Luke's account he even asks for a piece of fish to eat, in order to prove his real bodily presence. And yet these narratives do not present him simply as a man who has come back from death in the same condition as before.

One thing that strikes us straightaway is that the disciples do not recognize him at first. This is true not only of the two in the Emmaus story, but also of Mary Magdalene and then again at the Lake of Gennesaret: "Just as day was breaking, Jesus stood on the beach; yet the disciples did not know that it was Jesus" (Jn 21:4). Only after the Lord has instructed them to set out once again does the beloved disciple recognize him: "That disciple whom Jesus loved said to Peter, 'It is the Lord!'" (21:7). It is, as it were, an inward recognition, which nevertheless remains shrouded in mystery. For after the catch of fish, when Jesus invites them to eat, there is still a strange quality about him. "None of the disciples dared ask him, 'Who are you?' They knew it was the Lord" (21:12). They knew from within, not from observing the Lord's outward appearance.

This dialectic of recognition and non-recognition corresponds to the manner of the apparitions. Jesus comes through closed doors; he suddenly stands in their midst. And in the same way he suddenly withdraws again, as at the end of the Emmaus encounter. His presence is entirely physical, yet he is not bound by physical laws, by the laws of space and time. In this remarkable dialectic of identity and otherness, of real physicality and freedom from the constraints of the body, we see the special mysterious nature of the risen Lord's new existence. Both elements apply here: he is the same embodied man, and he is the new man, having entered upon a different manner of existence.

The dialectic, which pertains to the nature of the Risen One, is presented quite clumsily in the narratives, and it is this that manifests their veracity. Had it been necessary to invent the Resurrection, then all the emphasis would have been placed on full physicality, on immediate recognizability, and perhaps, too, some special power would have been thought up as a distinguishing feature of the risen Lord. But in the internal contradictions characteristic of all the accounts of what the disciples experienced, in the mysterious combination of otherness and identity, we see reflected a new form of encounter, one that from an apologetic standpoint may seem rather awkward but that is all the more credible as a record of the experience.

A help toward understanding the mysterious appearances of the risen Jesus can, I think, be provided by the theophanies of the Old Testament. I would like to mention briefly just three types of such theophanies.

First there is God's appearance to Abraham at the oak of Mamre (Gen 18:1–33). Three men present themselves at Abraham's home. And yet Abraham knows at once, from deep within, that it is "the Lord" who wishes to be his guest. In the Book of Joshua, we are told that, lifting up his eyes, Joshua suddenly sees standing before him a man with a drawn sword in his hand. Not recognizing him, Joshua asks: "Are you for us, or for our adversaries?" He receives this reply: "No, but as commander of the army of the LORD I have now come.... Put off your shoes from your feet; for the place where you stand is holy" (Josh 5:13–15). The stories of Gideon (Judg 6:11–24) and Samson (Judg 13) are also significant. In each case the "angel of the Lord" appearing in human form is recognized only at the moment of his mysterious withdrawal. Both times a flame consumes the food-offering as the "angel of the Lord" disappears. The mythological language expresses, on the one hand, the Lord's closeness, as he reveals himself in human form, and, on the other hand, his otherness, as he stands outside the laws of material existence.

Admittedly these are only analogies. What is radically new about the "theophany" of the risen Lord is that Jesus is truly man: he suffered and died as man and now lives anew in the dimension of the living God. He appears now as true man and yet as coming from God—as being God himself.

So two qualifications are important. On the one hand, Jesus has not returned to the empirical existence that is subject to the law of death, but he lives anew in fellowship with God, permanently beyond the reach of death. On the other hand, it is important that the encounters with the risen Lord are not just interior events or mystical experiences—they are real encounters with the living one who is now embodied in a new way and *remains* embodied. Luke emphasizes this very strongly: Jesus is not, as the disciples initially feared, a "ghost" or a "spirit": he has "flesh and bones" (Lk 24:36–43).

What a ghost is, what is meant by the apparition of a "spirit" as opposed to the apparition of the risen Lord, can best be seen in the biblical account of the medium at Endor, who at Saul's behest conjures up the spirit of Samuel from the underworld (cf. 1 Sam 28:7–19). The "spirit" that she calls forth is a dead man dwelling among the shadows in the underworld, who from time to time can be summoned forth, only to return to the realm of the dead.

Jesus, however, does not come from the realm of the dead, which he has definitively left behind: on the contrary, he comes from the realm of pure life, from God; he comes as the one who is truly alive, who is himself the source of life. Luke underlines quite dramatically how different the risen Lord is from a mere "spirit" by recounting that Jesus asked the still fearful disciples for something to eat and then ate a piece of grilled fish before their eyes.

Most exegetes take the view that Luke is exaggerating here in his apologetic zeal, that a statement of this kind seems to draw Jesus back into the empirical physicality that had been transcended by the Resurrection. Thus Luke ends up contradicting his own narrative, in which Jesus appears suddenly in the midst of the disciples in a physicality that is no longer subject to the laws of space and time.

I think it is helpful here to consider the other three passages in which the risen Jesus is presented participating in a meal.

Immediately before the text just mentioned is the Emmaus story. It ends with Jesus sitting down to table with the disciples, taking the bread, giving thanks and praise, breaking the bread, and giving it to the two of them. At this moment their eyes are opened, "and they recognized him; and he vanished out of their sight" (Lk 24:31). The Lord sits at table with his disciples as before, with thanks and praise and breaking of bread. Then he vanishes from their outward view, and through this vanishing their inner vision is opened up: they recognize him. It is real table fellowship, and yet it is new. In the breaking of the bread he manifests himself, yet only in vanishing does he become truly recognizable.

In terms of their inner structure, these two meal narratives are quite similar to the one in John 21:1–14: the disciples have spent a fruitless night, and not a single fish has been caught in their nets. In the morning, Jesus is standing on the shore, but they do not recognize him. He asks them: "Children, have you any fish?" When they respond in the negative, he instructs them to set out once again, and this time they come back with an abundant catch. Yet Jesus, who already has fish cooking on a charcoal fire, himself invites them: "Come and have breakfast." And now "they knew" that it was Jesus.

Particularly important and helpful for an understanding of the risen Jesus' participation in meals is the last account, found in the Acts of the Apostles. In most translations, admittedly, the singular significance of this text is not brought out. The Jerusalem Bible corresponds to the conventional type of translation when it says: "For forty days he had continued to appear to them and tell them about the kingdom of God. When he had been at table with them, he had told them not to leave Jerusalem" (1:3–4). Through the period after the word "God", which the sentence construction requires, an inner connection is concealed. Luke speaks of three elements that characterized the time spent by the risen Jesus in the company of his disciples: he appeared to them, he spoke to them, he sat at table with them. Appearing, speaking, and sharing meals: these three self-manifestations of the risen Lord belong together; they were his ways of proving that he was alive.

For a correct understanding of the third element, which like the first two extends over the "forty days", the word used by Luke—*synalizómenos*—is of great significance. Literally translated, it means "eating salt with them". Luke must have chosen this word quite deliberately. Yet what is it supposed to mean? In the Old Testament the shared enjoyment of bread and salt, or of salt alone, served to establish lasting covenants (cf. Num 18:19; 2 Chron 13:5; cf. Hauck, *TDNT* I, p. 228). Salt is regarded as a guarantee of durability. It is a remedy against putrefaction, against the corruption that pertains to the nature of death. To eat is always to hold death at bay—it is a way of preserving life. The "eating of salt" by Jesus after the Resurrection, which we therefore encounter as a sign of new and everlasting life, points to the risen Lord's new banquet with his followers. It is a covenant-event, and in this sense it has an inner association with the Last Supper, when the Lord established the New Covenant. So the mysterious cipher of eating salt expresses an inner bond between the meal on the eve of Jesus' Passion and the risen Lord's new table fellowship: he gives himself to his followers as food and thus makes them sharers in his life, in life itself.

Finally, it is helpful to recall here a saying of Jesus from Saint Mark's Gospel: "For every one will be salted with fire. Salt is good; but if the salt has lost its saltness, how will you season it? Have salt in yourselves, and be at peace with one another" (9:49–50). Some manuscripts add, with reference to Leviticus 2:13: "and every sacrifice will be salted with salt." The salting of sacrifices was similarly intended to add spice to the offering and preserve it from putrefaction. So different meanings come together here: covenant renewal, the gift of life, and purification of one's own being for self-offering to God.

When Luke summarizes the post-Resurrection events at the beginning of the Acts of the Apostles and makes reference to the risen Lord's table fellowship with his followers by means of the expression "eating salt with them" (1:4), on the one hand, the mystery of this new table fellowship remains. On the other hand, though, its essential meaning is made clear: the Lord is drawing the disciples into a new covenant-fellowship with him and with the living God; he is giving them a share in real life, making them truly alive and salting their lives through participation in his Passion, in the purifying power of his suffering.

What this table fellowship with the disciples actually looked like is beyond our powers of imagination. But we can recognize its inner nature, and we can see that in the worshipping community, in the celebration of the Eucharist, this table fellowship with the risen Lord continues, albeit in a different form.

3. *Summary: The Nature of Jesus' Resurrection and Its Historical Significance*

Let us ask once more, by way of summary, what it was like to encounter the risen Lord. The following distinctions are important:

— Jesus did not simply return to normal biological life as one who, by the laws of biology, would eventually have to die again.

— Jesus is not a ghost ("spirit"). In other words, he does not belong to the realm of the dead but is somehow able to reveal himself in the realm of the living.

— Nevertheless, the encounters with the risen Lord are not the same as mystical experiences, in which the human spirit is momentarily drawn aloft out of itself and perceives the realm of the divine and eternal, only to return then to the normal horizon of its existence. Mystical experience is a temporary removal of the soul's spatial and cognitive limitations. But it is not an encounter with a person coming toward me from without. Saint Paul clearly distinguished his mystical experiences, such as his elevation to the third heaven described in 2 Corinthians 12:1–4, from his encounter with the risen Lord on the road to Damascus, which was a historical event—an encounter with a living person.

On the basis of all this biblical evidence, what are we now in a position to say about the true nature of Christ's Resurrection?

It is a historical event that nevertheless bursts open the dimensions of history and transcends it. Perhaps we may draw upon analogical language here, inadequate in many ways, yet still able to open up a path toward understanding: as already anticipated in the first section of this chapter, we could regard the Resurrection as something akin to a radical "evolutionary leap", in which a new dimension of life emerges, a new dimension of human existence.

Indeed, matter itself is remolded into a new type of reality. The man Jesus, complete with his body, now belongs totally to the sphere of the divine and eternal. From now on, as Tertullian once said, "spirit and blood" have a place within God (cf. *De Resurrect. Mort.* 51:3, *CCSL* II, 994). Even if man by his nature is created for immortality, it is only now that the place exists in which his immortal soul can find its "space", its "bodiliness", in which immortality takes on its meaning as communion with God and with the whole of reconciled mankind. This is what is meant by those passages in Saint Paul's prison letters (cf. Col 1:12–23 and Eph 1:3–23) that speak of the cosmic body of Christ, indicating thereby that Christ's transformed body is also the place where men enter into communion with God and with one another and are thus able to live definitively in the fullness of indestructible life. Since we ourselves have no experience of such a renewed and transformed type of matter, or such a renewed and transformed kind of life, it is not surprising that it oversteps the boundaries of what we are able to conceive.

Essential, then, is the fact that Jesus' Resurrection was not just about some deceased individual coming back to life at a certain point, but that an ontological leap occurred, one that touches being as such, opening up a dimension that affects us all, creating for all of us a new space of life, a new space of being in union with God.

It is in these terms that the question of the historicity of the Resurrection should be addressed. On the one hand, we must acknowledge that it is of the essence of the Resurrection precisely to burst open history and usher in a new dimension commonly described as eschatological. The Resurrection opens up the new space that transcends history and creates the definitive. In this sense, it follows that Resurrection is not the same kind of historical event as the birth or crucifixion of Jesus. It is something new, a new type of event.

Yet at the same time it must be understood that the Resurrection does not simply stand outside or above history. As something that breaks out of history and transcends it, the Resurrection nevertheless has its origin within history and up to a certain point still belongs there. Perhaps we could put it this way: Jesus' Resurrection points beyond history but has left a footprint within history. Therefore it can be attested by witnesses as an event of an entirely new kind.

Indeed, the apostolic preaching with all its boldness and passion would be unthinkable unless the witnesses had experienced a real encounter, coming to them from outside, with something entirely new and unforeseen, namely, the self-revelation and verbal communication of the risen Christ. Only a real event of a radically new quality could possibly have given rise to the apostolic preaching, which cannot be explained on the basis of speculations or inner, mystical experiences. In all its boldness and originality, it draws life from the impact of an event that no one had invented, an event that surpassed all that could be imagined.

To conclude, all of us are constantly inclined to ask the question that Saint Jude Thaddaeus put to Jesus during the Last Supper: "Lord, how is it that you will manifest yourself to us, and not to the world?" (Jn 14:22). Why, indeed, did you not forcefully resist your enemies who brought you to the Cross?—we might well ask. Why did you not show them with incontrovertible power that you are the living one, the Lord of life and death? Why did you reveal yourself only to a small flock of disciples, upon whose testimony we must now rely?

The question applies not only to the Resurrection, but to the whole manner of God's revelation in the world. Why only to Abraham and not to the mighty of the world? Why only to Israel and not irrefutably to all the peoples of the earth?

It is part of the mystery of God that he acts so gently, that he only gradually builds up *his* history within the great history of mankind; that he becomes man and so can be overlooked by his contemporaries and by the decisive forces within history; that he suffers and dies and that, having risen again, he chooses to come to mankind only through the faith of the disciples to whom he reveals himself; that he continues to knock gently at the doors of our hearts and slowly opens our eyes if we open our doors to him.

And yet—is not this the truly divine way? Not to overwhelm with external power, but to give freedom, to offer and elicit love. And if we really think about it, is it not what seems so small that is truly great? Does not a ray of light issue from Jesus, growing brighter across the centuries, that could not come from any mere man and through which the light of God truly shines into the world? Could the apostolic preaching have found faith and built up a worldwide community unless the power of truth had been at work within it?

If we attend to the witnesses with listening hearts and open ourselves to the signs by which the Lord again and again authenticates both them and himself, then we know that he is truly risen. He is alive. Let us entrust ourselves to him, knowing that we are on the right path. With Thomas let us place our hands into Jesus' pierced side and confess: "My Lord and my God!" (Jn 20:28).

He Ascended into Heaven—He Is Seated at the Right Hand of the Father, and He Will Come Again in Glory

All four Gospels, as well as Saint Paul's Resurrection account in 1 Corinthians 15, presuppose that the period of the risen Lord's appearances was limited. Paul was conscious of being the last to whom an encounter with the risen Christ was granted. The meaning of the Resurrection appearances is also clear from the overall tradition. Above all, it was a matter of assembling a circle of disciples who would be able to testify that Jesus did not remain in the grave, that he lives on. Their testimony is essentially mission: they must proclaim to the world that Jesus is alive—that he is Life itself.

The first task they were given was to attempt once again to gather Israel around the risen Jesus. For Paul, too, the message begins with testimony to the Jews, the first to be destined for salvation. But the final command to those sent out by Jesus is universal: "All authority in heaven and on earth has been given to me. Go therefore and make disciples of all nations" (Mt 28:18–19). "You shall be my witnesses in Jerusalem and in all Judea and Samaria and to the end of the earth" (Acts 1:8). And as the risen Lord said to Paul: "Depart; for I will send you far away to the Gentiles" (Acts 22:21).

Included in the message of the witnesses is the proclamation that Jesus will come again to judge the living and the dead and to establish God's kingdom definitively in the world. There has been a substantial trend in recent theology to view this proclamation as the principal content, if not the very heart of the message. Thus it is claimed that Jesus himself was already thinking in exclusively eschatological categories. The "imminent expectation" of the kingdom was said to be the specific content of his message, while the original apostolic proclamation supposedly consisted of nothing else.

Had this been the case, one might ask how the Christian faith could have survived when that imminent expectation was not fulfilled. In fact, this theory goes against the texts as well as the reality of nascent Christianity, which experienced the faith as a force in the present and at the same time as hope.

The disciples undoubtedly spoke of Jesus' return, but first and foremost they bore witness to the fact that he is alive now, that he is Life itself, in whom we, too, come alive (cf. Jn 14:19). But how can this be? Where do we find him? Is he, the risen Lord now "exalted at the right hand of God" (Acts 2:33), not for that reason completely absent? Or is he somehow accessible? Can we penetrate "to the right hand of God"? Within his absence is there nonetheless at the same time a real presence? Is it not the case that he will come to us only on some unknown last day? Can he come today as well?

These questions have left their mark on John's Gospel, and Saint Paul's letters also attempt to answer them. Yet the essential content of this answer can be gleaned from the accounts of the "Ascension" at the end of Luke's Gospel and the beginning of the Acts of the Apostles.

Let us turn, then, to the end of Luke's Gospel. Here it is recounted that Jesus appears to the Apostles gathered in Jerusalem, who have just been joined by the two disciples from Emmaus. He eats with them and issues instructions. The closing lines of the Gospel are as follows: "Then he led them out as far as Bethany, and lifting up his hands he blessed them. While he blessed them, he parted from them, and was carried up into heaven. And they worshiped him, and returned to Jerusalem with great joy, and were continually in the temple blessing God" (24:50–53).

This conclusion surprises us. Luke says that the disciples were full of joy at the Lord's definitive departure. We would have expected the opposite. We would have expected them to be left perplexed and sad. The world was unchanged, and Jesus had gone definitively. They had received a commission that seemed impossible to carry out and lay well beyond their powers. How were they to present themselves to the people in Jerusalem, in Israel, in the whole world, saying: "This Jesus, who seemed to have failed, is actually the redeemer of us all"? Every parting causes sadness. Even if it was as one now living that Jesus had left them, how could his definitive separation from them not make them sad? And yet it is written that they returned to Jerusalem with great joy, blessing God. How are we to understand this?

In any case, it follows that the disciples do not feel abandoned. They do not consider Jesus to have disappeared far away into an inaccessible heaven. They are obviously convinced of a new presence of Jesus. They are certain (as the risen Lord said in Saint Matthew's account) that he is now present to them in a new and powerful way. They know that "the right hand of God" to which he "has been exalted" includes a new manner of his presence; they know that he is now permanently among them, in the way that only God can be close to us.

The joy of the disciples after the "Ascension" corrects our image of this event. "Ascension" does not mean departure into a remote region of the cosmos but, rather, the continuing closeness that the disciples experience so strongly that it becomes a source of lasting joy.

Thus the ending of Luke's Gospel helps us to understand better the beginning of the Acts of the Apostles, in which Jesus' "Ascension" is explicitly recounted. Before Jesus' departure, a conversation takes place in which the disciples—still trapped in their old ideas—ask whether the time has yet come for the kingdom of Israel to be established.

Jesus counters this notion of a restored Davidic kingdom with a promise and a commission. The promise is that they will be filled with the power of the Holy Spirit;

the commission is that they are to be his witnesses to the ends of the earth.

The questioning about times and seasons is explicitly rejected. Speculation over history, looking ahead into the unknown future—these are not fitting attitudes for a disciple. Christianity is the present: it is both gift and task, receiving the gift of God's inner closeness and—as a consequence—bearing witness to Jesus Christ.

In this context belongs the statement about the cloud that takes him up and withdraws him from their sight. The cloud reminds us of the hour of the Transfiguration, in which the bright cloud falls on Jesus and the disciples (cf. Mt 17:5; Mk 9:7; Lk 9:34–35). It reminds us of the hour of Mary's encounter with God's messenger, Gabriel, who announces to her the "overshadowing" with the power of the Most High (cf. Lk 1:35). It reminds us of the holy tent of God in the Old Covenant, where the cloud signified the Lord's presence (cf. Ex 40:34–35), the same Lord who, in the form of a cloud, led the people of Israel during their journey through the desert (cf. Ex 13:21–22). This reference to the cloud is unambiguously theological language. It presents Jesus' departure, not as a journey to the stars, but as his entry into the mystery of God. It evokes an entirely different order of magnitude, a different dimension of being.

The New Testament, from the Acts of the Apostles to the Letter to the Hebrews, describes the "place" to which the cloud took Jesus, using the language of Psalm 110:1, as sitting (or standing) at God's right hand. What does this mean? It does not refer to some distant cosmic space, where God has, as it were, set up his throne and given Jesus a place beside the throne. God is not in one space alongside other spaces. God is God—he is the premise and the ground of all the space there is, but he himself is not part of it. God stands in relation to all spaces as Lord and Creator. His presence is not spatial, but divine. "Sitting at God's right hand" means participating in this divine dominion over space.

In a dispute with the Pharisees, Jesus himself provides a new interpretation of Psalm 110, which points toward a Christian understanding. He contrasts the idea of the Messiah as a new David ushering in a new Davidic kingdom—the very idea that we have just encountered among the disciples—with a grander vision of the one who is to come: the true Messiah is not David's son, but David's Lord. He sits, not on David's throne, but on God's throne (cf. Mt 22:41–45).

The departing Jesus does not make his way to some distant star. He enters into communion of power and life with the living God, into God's dominion over space. Hence he has not "gone away", but now and forever by God's own power he is present with us and for us. In the farewell discourses of Saint John's Gospel, this is exactly what Jesus says to his disciples: "I go away, and I will come to you" (14:28). These words sum up beautifully what is so special about Jesus' "going away", which is also his "coming", and at the same time they explain the mystery of the Cross, the Resurrection, and the Ascension. His going away is in this sense a coming, a new form of closeness, of continuing presence, which for John, too, is linked with the "joy" that we saw in Luke's Gospel.

Because Jesus is with the Father, he has not gone away but remains close to us. Now he is no longer in one particular place in the world as he had been before the "Ascension": now, through his power over space, he is present and accessible to all—throughout history and in every place.

There is a very beautiful story in the Gospel (Mk 6:45–52 and parallel passages) where Jesus anticipates this kind of closeness during his earthly life and so makes it easier for us to understand.

After the multiplication of the loaves, the Lord makes the disciples get into the boat and go before him to Bethsaida on the opposite shore, while he himself dismisses the people. He then goes "up on the mountain" to pray. So the disciples are alone in the boat. There is a headwind, and the lake is turbulent. They are threatened by the power of the waves and the storm. The Lord seems to be far away in prayer on his mountain. But because he is with the Father, he sees them. And because he sees them, he comes to them across the water; he gets into the boat with them and makes it possible for them to continue to their destination.

This is an image for the time of the Church—intended also for us. The Lord is "on the mountain" of the Father. Therefore he sees us. Therefore he can get into the boat of our life at any moment. Therefore we can always call on him; we can always be certain that he sees and hears us. In our own day, too, the boat of the Church travels against the headwind of history through the turbulent ocean of time. Often it looks as if it is bound to sink. But the Lord is there, and he comes at the right moment. "I go away, and I will come to you"—that is the essence of Christian trust, the reason for our joy.

From a very different perspective, something similar emerges from a story that is extraordinarily rich in its theology and anthropology, namely, the risen Lord's first appearance to Mary Magdalene. For now, I shall concentrate on just one aspect.

After being addressed by the two angels in white garments, Mary turns around and sees Jesus, but she does not recognize him. Now he calls her by name: "Mary!" Once again she has to turn, and now she joyfully recognizes the risen Lord, whom she addresses as *Rabbuni*, meaning Teacher. She wants to touch him, to hold him, but the Lord says to her: "Do not hold me, for I have not yet ascended to the Father" (Jn 20:17). This surprises us. We would have thought that now, while he is standing before her, she can indeed touch him and hold him. When he has ascended to the Father, this will no longer be possible. But the Lord says the opposite: Now she cannot touch him or hold him. The earlier way of relating to the earthly Jesus is no longer possible.

It is the same phenomenon that Paul describes in 2 Corinthians 5:16-17: "Even though we once regarded Christ according to the flesh, we regard him thus no longer. Therefore, if any one is in Christ, he is a new creation."

The old manner of human companionship and encounter is over. From now on we can touch Jesus only "with the Father". Now we can touch him only by ascending. From the Father's perspective, in his communion with the Father, he is accessible and close to us in a new way.

This new accessibility presupposes a newness on our part as well. Through Baptism, our life is already hidden with Christ in God—in our current existence we are already "raised" with him at the Father's right hand (cf. Col 3:1–3). If we enter fully into the essence of our Christian life, then we really do touch the risen Lord, then we really do become fully ourselves. Touching Christ and ascending belong together. And let us not forget that for John the place of Christ's "exaltation" is his Cross and that our own ever-necessary "ascension", our "going up on high" in order to touch him, has to be traveled in company with the crucified Jesus.

Christ, at the Father's right hand, is not far away from us. At most we are far from him, but the path that joins us to one another is open. And this path is not a matter of space travel of a cosmic-geographical nature: it is the "space travel" of the heart, from the dimension of self-enclosed isolation to the new dimension of world-embracing divine love.

Let us return once more to the first chapter of the Acts of the Apostles. The content of the Christian life, we said, is not predicting the future, but it is, on the one hand, the gift of the Holy Spirit and, on the other hand, the disciples' worldwide testimony to Jesus, the crucified and risen Lord (Acts 1:6–8). And when Jesus was taken from their sight by the cloud, this does not mean that he was transported to another cosmic location, but that he was taken up into God's very being, participating in God's powerful presence in the world.

The text continues. As happened earlier at the tomb (Lk 24:4), so now there appear two men dressed in white, and they pronounce this message: "Men of Galilee, why do you stand looking into heaven? This Jesus, who was taken up from you into heaven, will come in the same way as you saw him go into heaven" (Acts 1:11). With these words, faith in Jesus' return is strengthened, but at the same time it is stressed once more that the disciples are not to gaze into heaven or to know times and seasons, which are concealed in the mystery of God. Their task at this moment is to proclaim to the ends of the earth their witness to Christ.

Faith in Christ's return is the second pillar of the Christian confession. He who took flesh and now retains his humanity forever, he who has eternally opened up within God a space for humanity, now calls the whole world into this open space in God, so that in the end God may be all in all and the Son may hand over to the Father the whole world that is gathered together in him (cf. 1 Cor 15:20–28). Herein is contained the certainty of hope that God will wipe away every tear, that nothing meaningless will remain, that every injustice will be remedied and justice restored. The triumph of love will be the last word of world history.

Vigilance is demanded of Christians as the basic attitude for the "interim time". This vigilance means, on the one hand, that man does not lock himself into the here and now and concern himself only with tangible things, but that he raises his eyes above the present moment and its immediate urgency. Keeping one's gaze freely fixed upon God in order to receive from him the criterion of right action and the capacity for it—that is what matters.

Vigilance means first of all openness to the good, to the truth, to God, in the midst of an often meaningless world and in the midst of the power of evil. It means that man tries with all his strength and with great sobriety to do what is right; it means that he lives, not according to his own wishes, but according to the signpost of faith. All this is presented in Jesus' eschatological parables, especially in the parable of the vigilant servant (Lk 12:42–48) and, in a different way, in the parable of the wise and foolish virgins (Mt 25:1–13).

But what is the position now in the Christian life regarding expectation of the Lord's return? Are we to expect him, or do we prefer not to? Even in his day, Cyprian of Carthage (d. 258) had to warn his readers not to neglect to pray for Christ's second coming through fear of great calamities or fear of death. Should this passing world be dearer to us than the Lord for whom we are actually waiting?

The Book of Revelation concludes with the promise of the Lord's return and with a prayer for it: "He who testifies to these things says, 'Surely I am coming soon.' Amen. Come, Lord Jesus!" (22:20). It is the prayer of one who loves, one who is surrounded in the besieged city by all the dangers and terrors of destruction and can only wait for the arrival of the beloved who has the power to end the siege and to bring salvation. It is the hope-filled cry for Jesus to draw near in a situation of danger where he alone can help.

At the end of the First Letter to the Corinthians, Saint Paul quotes the same prayer in an Aramaic version, which as it happens can be divided differently and is therefore open to different interpretations: *Marana tha* (Lord, come!), or *Maran atha* (the Lord has come). This two-fold reading brings out clearly the peculiar nature of the Christian expectation of Jesus' coming. It is the invocation "Come!" and at the same time the grateful certainty that "he has come".

From the *Teaching of the Twelve Apostles* (*Didachē*, ca. 100), we know that this invocation formed part of the liturgical prayers of the eucharistic celebrations of the earliest Christian communities, and here too we find a concrete illustration of the unity of the two readings. Christians pray for Jesus' definitive coming, and at the same time they experience with joy and thankfulness that he has already anticipated this coming and has entered into our midst here and now.

Christian prayer for the Lord's return always includes the experience of his presence. It is never purely focused on the future. The words of the risen Lord make the point: "I am with you always, to the close of the age" (Mt 28:20). He is with us *now*, and especially close in the eucharistic presence. Yet, conversely, the Christian experience of the Lord's presence does include a certain tension toward the future, toward the moment when that presence will be definitively fulfilled: the presence is not yet complete. It pushes beyond itself. It sets us in motion toward the definitive.

This inherent tension in Christian expectation of the Lord's return, which must leave its mark on Christian life and prayer, may be helpfully clarified by two contrasting theological approaches. On the First Sunday of Advent, the Roman breviary presents us with a catechesis by Cyril of Jerusalem (*Cat.* XV, 1–3; *PG* 33, 870–874), which begins with the words: "We preach not one coming only of Christ, but a second also ... Generally speaking, everything that concerns our Lord Jesus Christ is twofold. His birth is twofold: one, of God before time began; the other, of the Virgin in the fullness of time. His descent is twofold: one, unperceived ... the other, before the eyes of all, is yet to happen." This language of the twofold coming of Christ has left its mark on Christianity, and it is an essential element of the Advent proclamation. It is correct, but incomplete.

A few days later, on Wednesday of the First Week of Advent, the breviary offers a reflection from the Advent sermons of Saint Bernard of Clairvaux, which fills out the picture somewhat. There we read: "We have come to know a threefold coming of the Lord. The third coming takes place between the other two [*adventus medius*] ... his first coming was in the flesh and in weakness, this intermediary coming is in the spirit and in power, the last coming will be in glory and majesty" (*In Adventu Domini*, serm. III, 4; V, 1; *PL* 183, 45 A; 50 C-D). Bernard bases his thesis on John 14:23: "If a man loves me, he will keep my word, and my Father will love him, and we will come to him and make our home with him."

Specific reference is made to a "coming" of the Father and the Son: it is an eschatology of the present that John has developed. It does not abandon the expectation of a definitive coming that will change the world, but it shows that the interim time is not empty: it is marked by the *adventus medius*, the middle coming, of which Bernard speaks. This anticipatory presence is an essential element in Christian eschatology, in Christian life.

Even if the term *adventus medius* was unknown before Bernard, the idea has nevertheless been present in different forms throughout the whole of Christian tradition from the outset. Let us recall, for example, that Saint Augustine sees the clouds on which the Judge of the world is to arrive as the word of proclamation. The words of the message, handed on by the witnesses, are the cloud that brings Christ into the world—here and now. And in this way the world is prepared for his definitive coming. The "middle coming" takes place in a great variety of ways. The Lord comes through his word; he comes in the sacraments, especially in the most Holy Eucharist; he comes into my life through words or events.

Yet he also comes in ways that change the world. The ministry of the two great figures Francis and Dominic in the twelfth and thirteenth centuries was one way in which Christ entered anew into history, communicating his word and his love with fresh vigor. It was one way in which he renewed his Church and drew history toward himself. We could say much the same of the saints of the sixteenth century. Teresa of Avila, John of the Cross, Ignatius Loyola, and Francis Xavier all opened up new ways for the Lord to enter into the confused history of their century as it was pulling away from him. His mystery, his figure enters anew—and most importantly, his power to transform men's lives and to refashion history becomes present in a new way.

Can we pray, therefore, for the coming of Jesus? Can we sincerely say: "*Marana tha!* Come, Lord Jesus!"? Yes, we can. And not only that: we must! We pray for anticipations of his world-changing presence. We pray to him in moments of personal tribulation: Come, Lord Jesus, and draw my life into the presence of your kindly power. We ask him to be close to those we love or for whom we are anxious. We ask him to be present and effective in his Church.

Why not ask him to send us new witnesses of his presence today, in whom he himself will come to us? And this prayer, while it is not directly focused on the end of the world, is nevertheless a real prayer for his coming; it contains the full breadth of the prayer that he himself taught us: "Your kingdom come!" Come, Lord Jesus!

Let us return once more to the ending of Luke's Gospel. Jesus led his followers into the vicinity of Bethany, we are told. "Lifting up his hands he blessed them. While he blessed them, he parted from them, and was carried up into heaven" (24:50–51). Jesus departs in the act of blessing. He goes while blessing, and he remains in that gesture of blessing. His hands remain stretched out over this world. The blessing hands of Christ are like a roof that protects us. But at the same time, they are a gesture of opening up, tearing the world open so that heaven may enter in, may become "present" within it.

The gesture of hands outstretched in blessing expresses Jesus' continuing relationship to his disciples, to the world. In departing, he comes to us, in order to raise us up above ourselves and to open up the world to God. That is why the disciples could return home from Bethany rejoicing. In faith we know that Jesus holds his hands stretched out in blessing over us. That is the lasting motive of Christian joy.

General Bibliography for Part One (cf. Part One, pp. 365–66)

As explained in the foreword to Part One, this book presupposes historical-critical exegesis and makes use of its findings, but it seeks to transcend this method and to arrive at a genuinely theological interpretation of the scriptural texts. It is not the aim here to enter into the debates of historical-critical research. I have therefore made no attempt to compile a comprehensive bibliography, which would in any case be impossible. The titles of works cited in the book are briefly indicated in the text in parentheses; full bibliographical details are given below.

First of all, the following texts figure among the more important recent books on Jesus.

Joachim Gnilka. *Jesus of Nazareth: Message and History.* Translated by Siegfried S. Schatzmann. Peabody, Mass.: Hendrickson Publishers, 1997.

Klaus Berger. *Jesus.* Munich: Pattloch, 2004. On the basis of thorough exegetical knowledge, the author presents the figure and the message of Jesus in dialogue with the questions of the present time.

Heinz Schürmann. *Jesus: Gestalt und Geheimnis.* Edited by Klaus Scholtissek. Paderborn: Bonifatius, 1994. A collection of essays.

John P. Meier. *A Marginal Jew: Rethinking the Historical Jesus.* New York: Doubleday, 1991–2009. This four-volume work by an American priest is in many respects a model of historical-critical exegesis, in which the significance and the limits of the method emerge clearly. It is worth reading the review by Jacob Neusner of volume 1, *Who Needs the Historical Jesus?* in *Chronicles,* July 1993, pp. 32–34.

Thomas Söding. *Der Gottessohn aus Nazareth: Das Menschsein Jesu im Neuen Testament.* Freiburg: Herder, 2006. The book does not attempt to reconstruct the historical Jesus, but it presents the faith testimony of the various New Testament writings.

Rudolf Schnackenburg. *Jesus in the Gospels: A Biblical Christology.* Translated by O. C. Dean, Jr. Louisville: Westminster John Knox Press, 1995. Schnackenburg followed this work, which is quoted in the foreword of Part One of the present book, with a final, small, and very personal publication: *The Friend We Have in Jesus,* trans. Mark A. Christian (Louisville: Westminster John Knox Press, 1997), in which he "places the subjective (for instance, the effects that Jesus produces in the hearts and souls of men) before intellectual considerations" (p. vii).

In the exegesis of the Gospels, I rely principally on the individual volumes of *Herders Theologischer Kommentar zum Neuen Testament,* which unfortunately remains incomplete.

Extensive material on the Jesus story can be found in the six-volume work *La storia di Gesù.* Milan: Rizzoli, 1983–1985.

General Bibliography for Part Two

The general bibliography for Part One, which also applies to Part Two, may now be supplemented by some further titles that relate to the entire work.

The six-volume *Theologie des Neuen Testaments* (I/1–4; II/1–2) by Ulrich Wilckens is now complete (Neukirchener Verlag,

2002–2009). Of particular importance for Part Two of the present work is vol. I/2: *Jesu Tod und Auferstehung und die Entstehung der Kirche aus Juden und Heiden* (2003).

A second edition is now available of: Ferdinand Hahn, *Theologie des Neuen Testaments*, vol. 1, *Die Vielfalt des Neuen Testaments*, and vol. 2, *Die Einheit des Neuen Testaments*. Tübingen: Mohr Siebeck, 2002; 2nd ed., 2005.

In 2007, Martin Hengel published jointly with Anna Maria Schwemer a volume of some importance for the present book, namely: *Jesus und das Judentum* (Tübingen, Mohr Siebeck). It is the first of a projected four-volume work: *Geschichte des frühen Christentums*.

Of the numerous studies by Franz Mussner that are relevant for the present book, I should here like to mention especially: *Jesus von Nazareth im Umfeld Israels und der Urkirche: Gesammelte Aufsätze*. Edited by Michael Theobald. Tübingen: Mohr Siebeck, 1999.

I should like to make particular mention of the work by Joachim Ringleben to which I referred in the foreword to Part Two: *Jesus: Ein Versuch zu begreifen*. Tübingen: Mohr Siebeck, 2008.

In the foreword to Part Two, I also referred to a book that is essential for the question of methodology, namely: Marius Reiser. *Bibelkritik und Auslegung der Heiligen Schrift: Beiträge zur Geschichte der biblischen Exegese und Hermeneutik*. Tübingen: Mohr Siebeck, 2007.

Another helpful work on the same topic is: *Geist im Buchstaben? Neue Ansätze in der Exegese*. Edited by Thomas Söding. Quaestiones disputatae, vol. 225. Freiburg: Herder, 2007.

Also informative is: François Dreyfus. *Exégèse en Sorbonne, exégèse en Église: Esquisse d'une théologie de la Parole de Dieu*. Les-Plans-sur-Bex: Parole et Silence, 2006.

In the area of systematic theology, to the great Christologies of Wolfhart Pannenberg, Walter Kasper, and Christoph Schönborn may now be added: Karl-Heinz Menke. *Jesus ist Gott der Sohn: Denkformen und Brennpunkte der Christologie.* Regensburg: Pustet, 2008.

Angelo Amato. *Gesù, identità del cristianesimo: Conoscenza ed esperienza.* Vatican City: Libreria Editrice Vaticana, 2008.

Chapter One: The Entrance into Jerusalem and the Cleansing of the Temple

Issue 1/2009 of the *Internationale katholische Zeitschrift Communio* (vol. 38, pp. 1–43) is dedicated to Jesus' entrance into Jerusalem. I refer especially to the article by Harald Buchinger, " 'Hosanna dem Sohne Davids!' Zur Liturgie des Palmsonntags", pp. 35–43. Chapter 1 of the present book was written before the article was published.

Rudolf Pesch. *Das Markusevangelium: Zweiter Teil.* Herders theologischer Kommentar zum Neuen Testament II/2. Freiburg: Herder, 1977.

Eduard Lohse, article *"hōsanna"*, in *Theological Dictionary of the New Testament.* Edited by Gerhard Friedrich. Translated by Geoffrey W. Bromiley. Vol. 9. Grand Rapids: Eerdmans, 1974 (pp. 682ff.).

Concerning the cleansing of the Temple, in addition to the commentaries:

Vittorio Messori. *Patì sotto Ponzio Pilato.* Turin: SEI, 1992 (pp. 190–99).

Martin Hengel. *The Zealots: Investigations into the Jewish Freedom Movement in the Period from Herod I until 70 A.D.* Translated by David Smith. Edinburgh: T & T Clark, 1989.

—. *Was Jesus a Revolutionist?* Translated by William Klassen. Philadelphia: Fortress Press, 1971. Further bibliography is indicated there.

Ulrich Wilckens. *Theologie des Neuen Testaments.* 6 vols. Neukirchener Verlag, 2002–2009 (vol. I/2, pp. 59–65).

Chapter Two: Jesus' Eschatological Discourse

In these thoughts on Jesus' eschatological discourse, I attempt to continue, to explore in greater depth, and where necessary to correct the analysis that I originally put forward in my 1977 book: *Eschatology: Death and Eternal Life*, trans. Michael Waldstein, 2nd ed. (Washington, D.C.: CUA Press, 2007).

Flavius Josephus. *The Jewish War.* Translated by G. A. Williamson. Revised edition by E. Mary Smallwood. Harmondsworth: Penguin Books, 1981; the passage quoted corresponds to VI, 299–300, of the original text, and the reference to the death toll of 1,100,000 is found at VI , 420 of the original (*Bellum Judaicum*).

Alexander Mittelstaedt. *Lukas als Historiker: Zur Datierung des lukanischen Doppelwerkes.* Tübingen: Francke, 2006 (pp. 49–164).

Joachim Gnilka. *Die Nazarener und der Koran: Eine Spurensuche.* Freiburg: Herder, 2007.

Faith Gives Fullness to Reasoning: The Five Theological Orations of Gregory Nazianzen. Introduction and commentary by Frederick W. Norris. Translated by Lionel Wickham and Frederick Williams. Leiden: Brill, 1991. The passage quoted appears on p. 293.

On Romans 3:23: Ulrich Wilckens. *Theologie des Neuen Testaments.* 6 vols. Neukirchener Verlag, 2002–2009. Vols. I/3 and II/1.

Saint Bernard of Clairvaux. *Five Books on Consideration: Advice to a Pope.* Translated by John D. Anderson and Elizabeth T. Kennan. Cistercian Fathers Series no. 37. Kalamazoo: Cistercian Publications, 1976. (Original title: *De Consideratione ad Eugenium Papam Tertiam libri quinque*).

Hildegard Brem's comments on the above text that are quoted in the present chapter are found in: Bernhard von Clairvaux. *Sämtliche Werke.* Latin/German. Edited by Gerhard B. Winkler. Innsbruck: Tyrolia, 1990–99 (vol. 1 [1990], pp. 829–41).

For the significance of post-biblical Judaism, see: Franz Mußner. *Dieses Geschlecht wird nicht vergehen:Judentum und Kirche.* Freiburg: Herder, 1991.

Chapter Three: The Washing of the Feet

For the theme of purity and purification, I refer the reader to the important article "Reinheit/Reinigung", in *Historisches Wörterbuch der Philosophie*, ed. Joachim Ritter and Karlfried Gründer, vol. 8 (Basel: Schwabe, 1992), cols. 531–53, esp. II/1 *Griechische Antike* (Martin Arndt), II/2 *Judentum* (Maren Niehoff), III/1 *Neues Testament* (Martin Arndt), III/2 *Patristik* (Rita Sturlese).

For Plotinus, I refer the reader to Giovanni Reale. *Storia della filosofia greca e romana.* Vol. 8, *Plotino e il neoplatonismo pagano.* Milan: Bompiani, 2004 (pp. 19–186).

Rudolf Schnackenburg. *The Gospel according to St. John.* Vol. 3. Translated by David Smith and G. A. Kon. New York: Crossroad, 1982.

Charles K. Barrett. *The Gospel according to St. John.* 2nd ed. London: SPCK, 1978.

Franz Mußner. *Der Jakobusbrief.* Freiburg: Herder, 1964 (pp. 225–30).

Chapter Four: Jesus' High-Priestly Prayer

André Feuillet. *The Priesthood of Christ and His Ministers.* Translated by Matthew J. O'Connell. New York: Doubleday, 1975.

Der Hebräerbrief. Übersetzt und erklärt von Knut Backhaus. Regensburger Neues Testament. Regensburg: Pustet, 2009. This commentary was unfortunately not available when this chapter was written.

Rudolf Bultmann. *The Gospel of John: A Commentary.* Translated by G. R. Beasley-Murray. Oxford: Blackwell, 1971.

Rudolf Schnackenburg. *The Gospel according to St. John.* Vol. 3. Translated by David Smith and G. A. Kon. New York: Crossroad, 1982.

For the topic "name" in the Old Testament, see the article "*šem*" by Friedrich V. Reiterer and Heinz-Josef Fabry, trans. David Green, in *Theological Dictionary of the Old Testament,* ed. Heinz-Josef Fabry and Helmer Ringgren, vol. 15 (Grand Rapids: Eerdmans, 2006), pp. 128–76; also article "*ónoma*" by Hans Bietenhard, trans. Geoffrey W. Bromiley, in *Theological Dictionary of the New Testament,* ed. Gerhard Friedrich, vol. 5 (Grand Rapids: Eerdmans, 1967), pp. 242–83.

Basil Studer, *Gott und unsere Erlösung im Glauben der Alten Kirche.* Patmos: Düsseldorf 1985.

Chapter Five: The Last Supper

Annie Jaubert. "La Date de la dernière Cène". *Revue de l'histoire des religions* 146 (1954): 140–73.

—. *The Date of the Last Supper.* Translated by Isaac Rafferty. New York: Alba House, 1965.

Alberto Giglioli. "Il giorno dell'ultima Cena e l'anno della morte di Gesù". *Rivista Biblica* 10 (1962): 156–81.

From the immense quantity of literature on the dating of the Last Supper and of Jesus' death, I would like to single out the treatment of the subject, outstanding both in its thoroughness and its accuracy, found in the first volume of John P. Meier's book *A Marginal Jew: Rethinking the Historical Jesus*. Vol. 1, *The Roots of the Problem and the Person*. New York: Doubleday, 1991 (pp. 372–433).

For the content of the Last Supper tradition, I have found particularly helpful the various relevant studies by Rudolf Pesch. In addition to his commentary *Das Markusevangelium: Zweiter Teil* (Freiburg: Herder, 1977), I would also mention: *Das Abendmahl und Jesu Todesverständnis*, Quaestiones disputatae, vol. 80 (Freiburg: Herder, 1978); "Das Evangelium in Jerusalem", in *Das Evangelium und die Evangelien: Vorträge vom Tübinger Symposium 1982*, ed. Peter Stuhlmacher (Tübingen: Mohr Siebeck, 1983), pp. 113–55.

Another study of lasting importance is Joachim Jeremias. *The Eucharistic Words of Jesus*. Translated by Norman Perrin. London: SCM Press, 1966.

Erik Peterson. "Die Kirche". In *Theologische Traktakte: Ausgewählte Schriften*. Vol. 1, edited by Barbara Nichtweiß. Würzburg: Echter, 1994 (pp. 245–57).

Louis Bouyer. *Eucharist: Theology and Spirituality of the Eucharistic Prayer*. Translated by Charles Underhill Quinn. Notre Dame, Ind.: University of Notre Dame Press, 1968.

Peter Fiedler. "Sünde und Vergebung im Christentum". *Internationale Zeitschrift für Theologie Concilium* 10 (1974): 568–71.

Dietrich Bonhoeffer. *The Cost of Discipleship*. Translated by R. H. Fuller. Revised by Irmgard Booth. 2nd, rev. ed. New York: Macmillan, 1959 (chap. 1).

Ulrich Wilckens. *Theologie des Neuen Testaments*. 6 vols. Neukirchener Verlag, 2002–2009 (vol. I/2, pp. 77–85).

Norbert Baumert and Maria-Irma Seewann. "Eucharistie 'für alle' oder 'für viele'?" *Gregorianum* 89 (2008): 501–32.

Ferdinand Kattenbusch. "Der Quellort der Kirchenidee". In *Harnack-Ehrung: Beiträge zur Kirchengeschichte, ihrem Lehrer Adolf von Harnack zu seinem siebzigsten Geburtstage dargebracht von einer Reihe seiner Schüler.* Leipzig: J.C. Hinrichs, 1921 (pp. 143–72).

Willy Rordorf. *Sabbat und Sonntag in der Alten Kirche.* Zürich: Theologischer Verlag, 1972.

—. *Lex orandi—lex credenda: Gesammelte Aufsätze zum 60. Geburtstag.* Freiburg (Switzerland): Universitätsverlag, 1993 (esp. pp. 1–51).

Josef Andreas Jungmann, S.J., *Messe im Gottesvolk: Ein nach-konziliarer Durchblick durch Missarum Sollemnia.* Freiburg: Herder, 1970.

This chapter had just been completed when Manfred Hauke published a short and thorough study: *"Für viele vergossen": Studie zur sinngetreuen Wiedergabe des pro multis in den Wandlungsworten.* Augsburg: Dominus-Verlag, 2008.

Chapter Six: Gethsemane

For the topography of Gethsemane, see: Gerhard Kroll. *Auf den Spuren Jesu.* 5th ed. Leipzig: St. Benno, 1975.

Alois Stöger. *The Gospel according to Saint Luke.* Translated by Benen Fahy. 2 vols. London: Burns & Oates, 1969.

Rudolf Bultmann. *The Gospel of John: A Commentary,* Translated by G.R. Beasley-Murray. Oxford: Blackwell, 1971.

For the Council of Chalcedon, see Aloys Grillmeier, *Christ in Christian Tradition,* vol. 1, *From the Apostolic Age to Chalcedon*

(451), trans. John Bowden, 2nd rev. ed. (Atlanta: John Knox Press, 1987); for the Council's subsequent history, see vol. 2, esp. pt. 1, *Reception and Contradiction: The Development of the Discussion about Chalcedon from 451 to the Beginning of the Reign of Justinian,* trans. Pauline Allen and John Cawte (Atlanta: John Knox Press, 1987).

The troubled history of the reception of the Council of Chalcedon is thoroughly and accurately presented in: Hans-Georg Beck. "The Early Byzantine Church". In *History of the Church.* Edited by Hubert Jedin. Vol. 2, pt. 4. London: Burns & Oates, 1980 (pp. 421–514).

For Maximus the Confessor, see: Christoph Schönborn. *God's Human Face: The Christ-Icon.* Translated by Lothar Krauth. San Francisco: Ignatius Press, 1994 (pp. 102–33). Also : François-Marie Léthel. *Théologie de l'agonie du Christ: La Liberté humaine du Fils de Dieu et son importance sotériologique mise en lumière par saint Maxime le Confesseur.* Paris: Beauchesne, 1979.

Joachim Jeremias. "Abba": *The Prayers of Jesus.* London: SCM Press, 1967 (pp. 11–65).

An important text on the theology of the Mount of Olives is: François Dreyfus. *Did Jesus Know He Was God?* Translated by Michael J. Wrenn. Chicago: Franciscan Herald Press, 1989.

Albert Vanhoye. *Let Us Confidently Welcome Christ Our High Priest.* Translated by Joel Wallace. Leominster: Gracewing, 2010.

Adolf von Harnack. "Zwei alte dogmatische Korrekturen im Hebräerbrief". In *Sitzungsberichte der Preußischen Akademie der Wissenschaften.* Berlin, 1929 (pp. 69–73, esp. 71). See also the in-depth exegesis of the text of Hebrews 5:7–10 in *Der Hebräerbrief.* Übersetzt und erklärt von Knut Backhaus.

Regensburger Neues Testament. Regensburg: Pustet, 2009 (pp. 206–11).

Chapter Seven: The Trial of Jesus

The classic study of the trial of Jesus is still: Josef Blinzler. *Der Prozess Jesu*. 4th ed. Regensburg: Pustet, 1969. Translated into English by Isabel and Florence McHugh as *The Trial of Jesus*, 2nd rev. ed. (Westminster, Md.: Newman Press, 1959).

On historical questions, I am essentially following: Martin Hengel and Anna Maria Schwemer. *Jesus und das Judentum*. Tübingen: Mohr Siebeck, 2007 (pp. 587–611).

Important insights can be gleaned from: Franz Mußner. *Die Kraft der Wurzel: Judentum—Jesus—Kirche*. Freiburg: Herder, 1987 (esp. pp. 125–36).

For John's presentation of the trial and for the question of truth, I have drawn upon: Thomas Söding. "Die Macht der Wahrheit und das Reich der Freiheit: Zur johanneischen Deutung des Pilatus-Prozesses". *Zeitschrift für Theologie und Kirche* 93 (1996): 35–58.

Gerhard von Rad. *Old Testament Theology*. Vol. 1, *The Theology of Israel's Historical Traditions*. Translated by D. M. G. Stalker. Edinburgh and London: Oliver and Boyd, 1962.

Charles K. Barrett. *The Gospel according to St. John*. 2nd ed. London: SPCK, 1978.

Rudolf Pesch. *Das Markusevangelium: Zweiter Teil*. Freiburg: Herder, 1977 (pp. 461–67).

Joachim Gnilka. *Das Matthäusevangelium: Zweiter Teil*. Freiburg: Herder, 1988.

Francis S. Collins. *The Language of God: A Scientist Presents Evidence for Belief*. New York: Free Press, 2006.

Chapter Eight: Crucifixion and Burial of Jesus

There is an impressive analysis of Isaiah 53 in: Marius Reiser. *Bibelkritik und Auslegung der Heiligen Schrift: Beiträge zur Geschichte der biblischen Exegese und Hermeneutik.* Tübingen: Mohr Siebeck, 2007 (pp. 337–46).

Likewise, for Plato and the Book of Wisdom, see Reiser, *Bibelkritik*, pp. 347–53.

For the inscription over the Cross, see: Ferdinand Hahn. *Christologische Hoheitstitel: Ihre Geschichte im frühen Christentum.* 3rd ed. Göttingen: Vandenhoeck & Ruprecht, 1966 (pp. 195–96). Translated into English by Harold Knight and George Ogg as *The Titles of Jesus in Christology: Their History in Early Christianity* (New York: World Publishing, 1969).

For modern theologies of God's pain and Jesus' suffering at God's absence, I refer the reader to: Jürgen Moltmann, *The Crucified God: The Cross of Christ as the Foundation and Criticism of Christian Theology*, trans. R. A. Wilson and John Bowden (New York: Harper, 1974), and Hans Urs von Balthasar, *Theo-Drama*, vol. 5: *The Last Act,* trans. Graham Harrison (San Francisco: Ignatius Press, 1998).

Rudolf Bultmann. "The Primitive Christian Kerygma and the Historical Jesus". In *The Historical Jesus and the Kerygmatic Christ: Essays on the New Quest of the Historical Jesus.* Translated and edited by Carl E. Braaten and Roy A. Harrisville. New York: Abingdon Press, 1964 (pp. 15–42).

Rudolf Pesch. *Das Markusevangelium: Zweiter Teil.* Freiburg: Herder, 1977 (pp. 468–503).

Rudolf Schnackenburg. *The Gospel according to St. John.* Vol. 3. Translated by David Smith and G. A. Kon. New York: Crossroad, 1982 (pp. 268–99).

On the Marian question: *Storia della mariologia*. Vol. 1, *Dal modello biblico al modello letterario*. Edited by Enrico dal Covolo and Aristide Serra. Rome: Città Nuova and Marianum, 2009 (pp. 105–27).

For the final section, see vol. 11 of my collected writings: *Theologie der Liturgie*. Edited by Gerhard Ludwig Müller. Freiburg: Herder, 2008. An English translation of this volume is forthcoming (San Francisco: Ignatius Press, 2012).

Chapter Nine: Jesus' Resurrection from the Dead

Fundamental for exegetical questions (confessional tradition, appearances, and so on) is: Béda Rigaux. *Dieu l'a ressuscité: Exégèse et théologie biblique*. Gembloux: Duculot, 1973.

Also important is: Franz Mußner. *Die Auferstehung Jesu*. Munich: Kösel, 1969.

Helpful insights are provided in: Thomas Söding. *Der Tod ist tot, das Leben lebt: Ostern zwischen Skepsis und Hoffnung*. Ostfildern: Matthias Grünewald, 2008.

An earlier analysis of 1 Corinthians 15, which I am broadly following here, is contained in my small book: *The God of Jesus Christ: Meditations on the Triune God*. Translated by Brian McNeil. San Francisco: Ignatius Press, 2008 (pp. 92–101).

Josef Blank. *Paulus und Jesus: Eine theologische Grundlegung*. Munich: Kösel, 1968.

Rudolf Bultmann. *New Testament and Mythology*. Translated by Schubert M. Ogden. London: SCM Press, 1985.

Hartmut Gese. "Die Frage des Weltbildes". In *Zur biblischen Theologie: Alttestamentliche Vorträge*. Beiträge zur evangelischen Theologie, vol. 78. Munich: Kaiser, 1977 (pp. 202–22). Translated into English by Keith Crim as *Essays on Biblical Theology*

(Minneapolis: Augsburg Publishing House, 1981).

Hans Conzelmann. "Zur Analyse der Bekenntnisformel I. Kor. 15, 3–5". *Evangelische Theologie* 25 (1965): 1–11, esp. 7–8. Also found in: Conzelmann. *Theologie als Schriftauslegung: Aufsätze zum Neuen Testament.* Beiträge zur evangelischen Theologie, vol. 65. Munich: Kaiser, 1974 (pp. 131–41, esp. 137–38).

Martin Hengel and Anna Maria Schwemer. *Jesus und das Judentum.* Tübingen: Mohr Siebeck, 2007.

Friedrich Hauck. Article *"alas"*. In *Theological Dictionary of the New Testament.* Vol. 1. Edited by Gerhard Kittel. Translated by Geoffrey W. Bromiley. Grand Rapids: Eerdmans, 1965 (pp. 228–29).

In addition, the reader is referred to commentaries, especially to Ulrich Wilckens. *Theologie des Neuen Testaments.* 6 vols. Neukirchener Verlag, 2002–2009. Vol. I/2, pp. 107–60.

Abba: Aramaic word for "father". The word was used by Jesus to address God (Mk 14:36). It reflects God's unique relationship to Jesus. Paul also uses it as a way Christians address God in prayer (Rom 8:15; Gal 4:6). Some scholars hold that the word reflects an intimate form of address a small child would use for his father.

Abomination that makes desolate: An act of sacrilege that profaned the sacrificial cult of the Jerusalem Temple (see Dan 9:27; 11:31; 12:11). In the Book of Daniel, it refers to the seizure and profanation of the sanctuary by Antiochus Epiphanes in 167 B.C. Jesus used the expression in his eschatological discourse (Mt 24:15; Mk 13:14; translated "desolating sacrilege" in the RSV) to refer to a future sign for people to flee Jerusalem. Many commentators understand the sign to have been the Roman desecration of the Temple in A.D. 70. Pope Benedict does not reject this view, but he mentions another theory—that the "abomination that makes desolate" was taken to be the appointment of the former high priest Annas II, in A.D. 66, as a Jewish military leader against the Romans. In A.D. 62, Annas decreed the death of James, "the brother of the Lord" and leader of Jewish Christians. According to Benedict, Christians may have seen Annas' military appointment as the sign to flee Jerusalem.

Antiochus IV: Ruler of the Seleucid Empire (Syria) from 175 B.C. until his death in 163 B.C. Also known as Antiochus

Epiphanes (Greek, "manifest divine one"). He invaded Jerusalem in 167 B.C., set up an altar to Zeus Olympios in the Temple (2 Mac 6.2), and there sacrificed swine. The Book of Daniel (9:27; 11:31; 12:11) and 1 Maccabees 1:54 refer to this incident.

Augustine: Bishop, theologian, and Doctor of the Church (A.D. 354–430), sometimes called the "Second Founder of the Faith" because of his vast theological, pastoral, and literary contribution to Christianity.

Bar Kochba: Simon Bar-Kochba (meaning "son of the star" in Aramaic); led a revolt against Roman occupation of Judea in A.D. 132. He succeeded in his initial attempt and for three years ruled Judea as an independent country, after which time the Romans took back Judea and Bar Kochba was defeated. He consciously presented himself as a Messianic figure.

Barabbas: Political revolutionary whose agitations the Romans put down. The crowds intimidated Pontius Pilate into releasing Barabbas, a political Messianic figure, instead of Jesus (Mt 27:15–21; Mk 15:6–11; Lk 23:13–18; Jn 18:39–40). "Barabbas" is Aramaic for "son of the father".

Barrett, Charles K.: New Testament scholar (b. 1917). Emeritus professor of divinity at the University of Durham.

Baumert, S.J., Norbert: Jesuit and professor emeritus of New Testament theology at the Sankt Georgen Graduate School of Philosophy and Theology in Germany. He is coauthor, with Maria-Irma Seewann, of an important article on the meaning of Jesus' words "for many" used at the Last Supper.

Berakah: The Hebrew term for "blessing". It often refers to a Jewish prayer formula used for praise and thanksgiving. Examples can be found in the Old Testament (1 Chron 29:10–13; Ps 135:21; Dan 3:3–68) as well as the New Testament (Lk 1:68–79; Eph 1:3–10).

Bonhoeffer, Dietrich: German Lutheran theologian and pastor (1906–1945) executed for his anti-Nazi activities. He was critical of the idea of "cheap grace", too-easy forgiveness. His book *The Cost of Discipleship* stressed the demands of being a follower of Christ in the difficulties of "real life".

Book of Jubilees: A Jewish religious text from the second century B.C. It retells the biblical story from Creation to the Exodus, embellishing it with traditional elements said to have been revealed to Moses. Distinctive of the book is its conception of time: it divides history into forty-nine-year Jubilee cycles and follows a 364-day solar calendar (instead of the 354-day liturgical calendar used in the Temple of Jerusalem).

Bouyer, Louis: Prolific French theologian and former Lutheran minister (1913–2004) who entered the Catholic Church in 1939. He was a leading twentieth-century figure in the Catholic biblical and liturgical movements, and he influenced the Second Vatican Council. Pope Benedict refers to Father Bouyer's efforts to trace the development of the Christian eucharistic liturgy from the Jewish *berakah*.

Brandon, S. G. F.: British Anglican religious scholar and minister (1907–1971) best known for his work on comparative religion and for his thesis that Jesus was a political revolutionary shaped by the Zealots.

Bultmann, Rudolf: German Protestant biblical scholar and theologian (1884–1976) who attempted to "de-mythologize" Christianity—to separate what he considered the essence of Christianity from the world view of the scriptural authors, which he regarded as mythological. Bultmann was also among the leading proponents of "form criticism". He also maintained that the Gospels were not historical narratives but theology reshaped into the form of a story. He believed that Christianity needed to be understood in terms of the early philosophy of

Martin Heidegger rather than what he regarded as the mythical world view of the biblical writers.

Caiaphas: The Jewish high priest from A.D. 18 to 36. During this time he also presided over the Jewish high court, the Sanhedrin. The Gospels remember Caiaphas as the one who counseled the Jerusalem leadership that Jesus should die instead of the people (Jn 11:49–52) and who eventually declared him guilty of blasphemy (Mt 27:62; Mk 14:61). He was the son-in-law of the former high priest Annas, who also examined Jesus on the night of his arrest (Jn 18:13, 19–24).

Christ-event: A shorthand expression for the redemptive actions of Jesus in history. As used by scholars, it typically includes the full sweep of his Incarnation and public ministry as well as his death, Resurrection, and Ascension.

Christology: The branch of theology concerned with the person, nature, and activity of Christ.

Christology from above: An approach to the study of Christ that begins with the facts of his divinity and preexistence and draws conclusions about how these realities affected his historical experience as a man—as one person having a human as well as a divine nature.

Christology from below: An approach to the study of Christ that begins with a historical investigation of what can be known about the words and deeds of Jesus and the early Church's understanding of them.

Church Fathers: Saintly Christian writers who lived in the early centuries of the Church and whose writings have a special place in the understanding of normative Christian beliefs and practices. Also known as "the Fathers of the Church".

Chytraeus, David: Moderate German Lutheran theologian (1531–1600). He taught at the University of Rostock, was a pupil of Philip Melanchthon, and was one of the coauthors of the Lutheran statement of faith, the Formula of Concord (1577). He coined the expression "high-priestly prayer" for Jesus' prayer to the Father in John 17.

Collins, Francis S.: Contemporary American geneticist (b. 1950) and current director of the National Institutes of Health. In 2009 Pope Benedict XVI appointed him to the Pontifical Academy of Sciences. He is author of *The Language of God*, in which he argues for a compatibility of science and religion.

Corporate personality: The theological idea, based on Old Testament notions, that a group is represented by an individual, who "personifies" some aspect of the group's nature or by whom the group as a whole acts.

Council of Chalcedon: The Fourth Ecumenical Council of the Church (A.D. 451). It is famous for its Christological definition that Jesus Christ is one person in two natures, one human and one divine, without the two natures being confused or separated.

Council of Nicea: An assembly of Catholic bishops that met in 325. It rejected Arianism, which claimed that Jesus was not fully divine. Instead, it taught that Jesus was "begotten", not created. The Council of Nicea is the First Ecumenical Council of the Church.

Cult-etiology: A traditional story that explains the origin and founding of a particular form of worship and serves to legitimize it.

Day of Atonement: One of the principal liturgical feasts of Israel, held annually on the tenth day of the seventh month (Lev 16:1–34). It is known today in Hebrew as *Yom Kippur.* In ancient Israel, its purpose was twofold: to cleanse the sanctuary from ritual impurity and to atone for the sins of the priests and people accumulated throughout the preceding year. The latter is linked with the rite of the scapegoat, by which the sins of Israel were "offloaded" onto a goat that symbolically bore them away into the wilderness (Lev 16:20–22). Christians see in Jesus' death the accomplishment for mankind of what the Day of Atonement represents.

Day of preparation: The day before the Jewish Passover (Jn 19:14). The Passover lambs were slaughtered on this day so they could be consumed in the evening Passover meal. Pope Benedict follows most scholars in identifying the afternoon of Good Friday as the vigil of the Passover. Thus, Jesus was crucified as "the Lamb of God" on the afternoon when Passover lambs were being slaughtered in the Temple.

Didascalia Apostolorum: A Christian treatise the title of which means the "teaching of the apostles", dating from the third century and preserved mainly in Syriac. The document places the Last Supper and arrest of Jesus on Tuesday evening of Holy Week rather than on the traditional Thursday evening.

Dodd, Charles H.: British Protestant New Testament scholar (1884–1973) who espoused a "realized eschatology", the idea that the kingdom of God is a present reality. Dodd's best-known work is *The Interpretation of the Fourth Gospel* (1953). Pope Benedict agrees with Dodd's support for the historic authenticity of Jesus' exchange with Pilate regarding Jesus' kingly identity.

Ecce homo: Latin form of the words meaning "Behold the Man!" spoken by Pontius Pilate (Jn 19:5). Pilate's declaration came as he displayed the scourged Christ before the hostile mob.

Ecclesiology: The branch of theology concerned with the nature of the Church.

Ecumenical council: A special assembly of the bishops of the universal Church, together with the bishop of Rome (the Pope), to address doctrinal and pastoral matters. There have been twenty-one ecumenical councils, according to the reckoning generally accepted in the Catholic Church.

Ecumenism: The effort to promote unity among Christians.

Eschatological discourse: Name given to Jesus' discourse recorded in Matthew 24:3–24; Mark 13:3–37; and Luke 21:5–36. It is called "eschatological" because it refers to the divine judgment to come upon a disobedient Jerusalem (which came with the destruction of the Temple in A.D. 70) and because it anticipates the final judgment at the end of the world. Pope Benedict stresses three key elements of Jesus' discourse: the destruction of the Temple, the times of the Gentiles, and prophecy and apocalyptic teaching.

Eschatology: The branch of theology concerned with the "last things" (Greek, *eschatos*, "last [things]") or the final destiny of man and the world.

Epiphanius of Salamis: Fourth-century Church Father and bishop known for his staunch defense of orthodox Christian belief against various heresies. Pope Benedict quotes Epiphanius' explanation for the Christians' flight to Pella beyond the Jordan before the siege of Jerusalem in A.D. 70. According to Epiphanius, Christians fled because they recalled Jesus' warning to abandon the city before its destruction.

Essenes: A Jewish ascetical sect that existed in Palestine from the second century B.C. to the first Jewish revolt and fall of Jerusalem, ca. A.D. 66–70. Essenes probably made up the community at Qumran, with which the Dead Sea Scrolls are associated, although the sect also had members who lived elsewhere. The Essenes were critical of the religious establishment in Jerusalem, and they regarded the worship at the Temple as corrupt. They also anticipated an eschatological "showdown" between "the sons of light" (themselves) and "the sons of darkness", the enemies of God's righteous people.

Eternal life: Term used by Jesus to refer to the kind of life man may graciously come to possess in relationship with God, who is life. Eternal life begins in this life through a person's knowing God and entering into communion with him through Jesus Christ.

Evangelist: An author of one of the four Gospels of Matthew, Mark, Luke, and John.

Exegesis: The process of interpreting what a text means.

Exegete: An expert who interprets the meaning of a text.

Exemplum: Latin term meaning "example". It appears in the Vulgate translation of John 13:15, where Jesus, having washed the feet of his disciples, urges them to follow his example of humble service to others.

Exitus–Reditus: Latin terms meaning "departure" and "return". Originally *exitus-reditus* referred to a construct of the Neoplatonist philosopher Plotinus (ca. 205–270), who envisioned man's emanation (or creation) from the divine as a fall into the bondage of the material order and his return as a struggle to free himself from matter. Pope Benedict contrasts this scheme with the evangelist's remark that Jesus "had come from God and was going to God" (Jn 13:3). Christ's descent in the Incarnation affirms the goodness of material creation, just as his bodily ascension indicates that matter is destined for the presence of God.

Factum est: Part of a phrase used in the Latin translation of John 1:14. The whole passage runs: "Verbum caro factum est et habitavit in nobis", meaning: "The Word was made flesh and dwelt among us."

Feast of Tabernacles: Also called the Feast of Booths, a biblical pilgrimage feast lasting seven days. Participants built temporary dwellings to recall the temporary dwellings the Israelites used in their forty-year sojourn in the desert after the Exodus (see Lev 23:33–36; Deut 16:13–15). Jesus gave his "rivers of living water" discourse (Jn 7:38) in the context of this feast (Jn 7:2, 37). Pope Benedict also connects the shout of "Hosanna", used by the priests at the feast, with the exclamation of the pilgrims accompanying Jesus into Jerusalem (Mt 21:9; Mk 11:9–10; Jn 12:13).

Feast of Unleavened Bread: A week-long Jewish festival celebrated in conjunction with the springtime Passover (Lev 23:4–8; Ezek 45:21). It commemorates the haste with which Israel escaped from Egypt, and no leavened bread was to be eaten throughout the seven days of the feast (Ex 12:14–20). Preparation was made on the eve of Passover by a ritual removal of leaven from every Israelite home (cf. 1 Cor 5:7). The Feast of Unleavened Bread forms part of the historical backdrop for the Last Supper (Mt 26:17; Mk 14:12; Lk 22:7–8).

Feuillet, André: Prominent French biblical scholar (1909–1998) whose work *The Priesthood of Christ and His Ministers* deeply informs Pope Benedict's interpretation of John 17: 1–26. In particular, Feuillet's thesis that the high-priestly prayer of Jesus is modeled on the Day of Atonement liturgy generates rich theological reflections for the Pope that underscore the sacrificial dimensions of the Lord's Passion.

Fourth Gospel: The Gospel of John.

Gnilka, Joachim: Contemporary Scripture scholar writing in German (b. 1928).

Hallel Psalms: Psalms 113–118 and 136, which Jewish tradition prescribed for recitation at the yearly Passover. Pope Benedict suggests these may be the hymns sung by Jesus and the Apostles at the conclusion of the Last Supper (Mk 14:26). Insofar as these are psalms of thanksgiving for Israel's deliverance from Egypt, they also anticipate the new Passover deliverance that Jesus accomplishes through his death and Resurrection.

Heidegger, Martin: German philosopher (1889–1976) who focused on the meaning of being. Heidegger greatly influenced major thinkers such as Jacques Derrida, Hans-Georg Gadamer, Leo Strauss, Jean-Paul Sartre, Hannah Arendt, and Karl Rahner, among many others. Bultmann assimilated Heidegger's philosophy in his eschatology, which allowed Bultmann to try to explain Christian faith in an eschatological context of standing ready for the challenge of the Gospel.

Hellenists: Mentioned in Acts 6:1 as a community of Jewish believers from the Diaspora who had resettled in Jerusalem. Their name is an indication that Greek was their first language rather than Hebrew or Aramaic. The first Christian martyr, Saint Stephen, is the best known of the Hellenists (Acts 6:5; 7:54–60).

Hengel, Martin: German scholar of religion (1926–2009) who focused on Christian and Jewish religions from 200 B.C. to A.D. 200. His scholarship undermines the influential position of Rudolf Bultmann that the sources of the Gospel of John are Gnostic rather than Jewish.

Hermeneutics: The branch of study concerned with principles of interpretation. Originally, the term was applied to interpreting the Bible. Later it came to apply in general to methods of interpretation.

High priest: The chief religious representative of biblical Israel. He served as the primary mediator between God, to whom he interceded for the people with prayers and sacrifices, and the Israelite community, for whom he acquired blessings. In the New Testament period, the high priest was also the acting head of the Jewish Sanhedrin. The Gospels refer by name to two high priests: Caiaphas, who occupied the office from A.D. 18 to 36 (Mt 26:57; Jn 11:49), and Annas, who had formerly held the position but was deposed by the Romans in A.D. 15 (Jn 18:13, 24).

High-priestly prayer: Traditional designation for Jesus' impassioned prayer to the Father in John 17:1–26. Pope Benedict draws attention to four of its themes: the nature of eternal life, the sanctification of disciples in truth, the revelation of the Father's name, and the unity of believers.

Historical-critical method: Broad term for a modern method of understanding biblical texts by drawing exclusively on the findings of the human sciences, including history, linguistics, philology, comparative literature, textual criticism, and archaeology. The method seeks primarily to know the meaning of a text as originally written and received. It does not presuppose the divine inspiration of the Bible or the truth of theology. Pope Benedict affirms the value of this method but cautions against its exclusive use or the unqualified acceptance of certain presuppositions of some of its users.

Historical Jesus: Either Jesus insofar as historians have been able to reconstruct him or Jesus as he really was in history. The distinction between the two senses of the term is based on the idea that historical scholarship cannot discover everything about a person. Often the term "Jesus of history" is used to refer to "Jesus as he really was in history". In this case, there would be a difference between the historical Jesus and the Jesus of history. Some scholars posit an opposition between "the historical Jesus", understood as "Jesus as he really existed", and the Christ of faith—Jesus as proclaimed by the Bible and the Church. Pope Benedict rejects the idea that "Jesus as he really was" is different from the Christ of faith. At the same time, Benedict acknowledges the limits of what historical methods alone can tell us about Jesus.

Historicity: Historical reality. That is, the degree to which something really happened as reported. Benedict insists on the historicity of the key Gospel events.

Hosanna: Hebrew term meaning "Save, we ask". Originally, it invoked the God of Israel's aid (Ps 118:25), and the Jewish liturgy of the Feast of Tabernacles used the term. "Hosanna" came to be used as an acclamation of praise as well as a supplication for God's saving help through the Messiah. The crowd used it to greet Jesus as he solemnly entered Jerusalem during the final week of his earthly life (Mt 21:9; Mk 11:9–10; Jn 12:13). The expression revealed the crowd's hope in Jesus as the Messiah. After Jesus' cleansing of the Temple, children in the Temple use the word to express their homage of Jesus as the Messiah (Mt 21:15).

Hour of Jesus: Term used in the Gospels, especially in John's Gospel, to refer to the time identified with Jesus' suffering, death, and Resurrection. Jesus refers to his "hour" as the time in which he, the Son of Man, is exalted and glorified (Jn 12:23; 17:1). He associates it with his departure from earthly existence to be with the Father (Jn 13:1), which entails Jesus' gift of himself out of love. Since Jesus' suffering and death are brought about by the forces of evil, Jesus' "hour" is also the time or "hour" of his enemies (Mt 26:45; Mk 14:41; Lk 22:53), who unwittingly contribute to Jesus' triumph.

Immanence: God's presence in creation, including his presence among his people. The fullness of God's immanence is found in Jesus Christ, who is "God-with-us". By the Incarnation, death, and Resurrection of the God-man, Jesus Christ, believers are united with God in the Holy Spirit to form the Church. The mission of the Church involves the transformation of the whole of creation through Jesus Christ. In this way, divine immanence is complemented by divine transcendence, which means that God transcends or exists outside of or beyond his creation.

***Ipsissima verba* of Jesus:** Latin phrase meaning "the very words of Jesus". It refers to words Jesus himself spoke. The complementary expression is *ipsissima vox* of Jesus, which means "the very voice of Jesus". The latter refers to words that express Jesus' ideas or meaning, rather than his exact words.

Jaubert, Annie: French scholar (1912–1980) best known for a theory accounting for the apparent discrepancies between the Synoptic Gospels (Matthew, Mark, and Luke) and the Gospel of John regarding whether the Last Supper took place on the evening of the Passover sacrifices or before it. According to Jaubert's theory, two different liturgical calendars were followed, one associated with the Essenes and the Qumran community, which placed the first day of Passover on Wednesday, and one recognized by the Jewish authorities, which placed the first day of Passover on Friday. Jesus and his disciples, on this view, participated in the Passover meal at the Last Supper according to the first calendar, on Tuesday night; while the Jewish authorities observed the Passover according to the second calendar, on Friday. Pope Benedict sympathetically summarizes Jaubert's theory without embracing it.

Jeremias, Joachim: German Lutheran Scripture scholar (1900–1979). He took a positive view of scholarship's ability to know the historical truth about Jesus. Jeremias taught the significance of Jesus' understanding of God as his Father, expressed by Jesus' use of the term "Abba". Jeremias also authored an important study of the eucharistic words of Jesus spoken during the Last Supper.

Jewish War: Sometimes also called the Jewish-Roman War or the First Jewish-Roman War, the term refers to the conflict between Jewish nationalists and the Roman authority in Palestine (ca. A.D. 66–70). The Roman legions under the general Titus crushed the rebellion and destroyed Jerusalem, its Temple, and the remaining rebel strongholds. The Jewish historian Flavius Josephus recounted the story of the conflict in *The Jewish War*. Jesus prophesied the Temple's destruction (Lk 20:5–6) and Jerusalem's conquest (Lk 20:21).

Josephus, Flavius: Jewish historian (A.D. 37–ca. A.D. 100) who recorded the events of the Jewish War and the destruction of Jerusalem by the Roman armies.

Jungmann, J. A.: Austrian theologian (1889–1975) best known for his work in liturgy and catechetics. He was a theological expert at the Second Vatican Council (1962–1965) and one of the architects of its Constitution on the Sacred Liturgy. Pope Benedict refers to Jungmann's view that the Mass is the sacramental memorial of Jesus' sacrificial death, not a celebration of the Last Supper as such.

Kattenbusch, Ferdinand: German Protestant theologian (1851–1935) perhaps best known for his book on the Apostles' Creed. Pope Benedict refers sympathetically to Kattenbusch's thesis that Jesus' words of institution at the Last Supper constitute the act of founding the Church.

Maranatha: An Aramaic expression meaning "Our Lord, come!" or possibly "Our Lord has come." It is found transliterated into Greek in 1 Corinthians 16:22. The early Christians used the expression in the Eucharistic liturgy, to emphasis Jesus' presence with his people. They also used it in supplication for, or in anticipation of, the second coming of Jesus.

Maximus the Confessor: Church Father and Byzantine theologian (A.D. 580–662) known best for his outspoken opposition to monothelitism, a heresy that claimed Christ had a divine will but not a human will. According to Maximus, Jesus' agony in Gethsemane is inexplicable unless he possessed a human will that could yield itself to the Father's will. Though exiled and tortured for his insistence on this point, Maximus was eventually vindicated by the Sixth Ecumenical Council (Constantinople III, 680), which defined that the incarnate Son had two wills, one human and one divine. Pope Benedict draws upon the insights of Maximus in his treatment of Jesus' prayer in Gethsemane.

Meier, John P.: A biblical scholar and Catholic priest. He is perhaps best known for his historical-critical multivolume work on the historical Jesus called *A Marginal Jew*. The premise of his critical work is that he proceeds using a critical method the results of which he maintains might produce agreement about Jesus of Nazareth's identity and intentions among critical Catholic, Protestant, Jewish, and agnostic scholars.

Melchisedek: The king of Salem identified in Genesis 14:18 as "priest of God Most High" to whom Abram offers a tithe. The Letter to the Hebrews, citing Psalm 110:4, speaks of Christ as belonging to the priesthood according to "the order of Melchizedek" (Heb 7:17). Pope Benedict, following the Jesuit biblical scholar Albert Cardinal Vanhoye, stresses Jesus' obedient "yes" in the Garden of Gethsemane to the Father's will as "consecrating" Jesus as a priest "according to the order of Melchisedek", as opposed to the priesthood possessed by descendants of Aaron.

Messori, Vittorio: Contemporary Italian journalist and author of a book on the Passion and death of Jesus Christ called *Patì sotto Ponzio Pilato?* (He suffered under Pontius Pilate?). Pope Benedict refers to Messori's thesis that Jesus acted according to the Law when he cleansed the Jerusalem Temple.

Mittelstaedt, Alexander: Author of an important study in German, *Lukas als Historiker*, that maintains that both the Gospel of Luke and the Acts of the Apostles were written before the fall of Jerusalem in A.D. 70.

Monothelitism: The view that Christ had only one will. Catholic, Orthodox, and traditional Protestant Christianity affirm that Christ possessed both a human and a divine will. The term monothelitism comes from two Greek terms, "mono" meaning "one", and "thelelis" meaning "will".

Monophysitism: The view that Christ had only one nature, in which his humanity had been absorbed into his divinity.

Catholic, Orthodox, and traditional Protestant Christianity maintains that Christ possessed a fully human and a fully divine nature. The term monophysitism comes from two Greek terms, "mono" meaning "one" and "physis" meaning "nature".

Mount of Olives: Mount that rises directly east of Jerusalem and is separated from the city by the Kidron Valley. Gethsemane, the garden where Jesus prayed in agony after the Last Supper, was part of an ancient farmstead on the lower slopes of the mount where olives were harvested and pressed into oil (Mt 26:30, 36). The Gospels indicate that Jesus often spent time there with his disciples (Lk 22:39; Jn 18:1–2).

Nestorians: Advocates of the view of Nestorius, a fifth-century bishop who taught that in Christ there were two distinct persons, one human and one divine, who were united only by the perfect agreement of their wills. Nestorianism was rejected by the Council of Ephesus in 431.

Ochlos: Greek word meaning "crowd" or "mob". Pope Benedict discusses the term's meaning in relation to the crowd who sought the death of Jesus.

Ontological: Having to do with the *being* of a thing or a person.

Passover: Jewish feast commemorating the Exodus of the Israelites from Egypt (see Ex 12:1–20; Lev 23:5; Deut 16:1–8, 12). Jesus' bread of life discourse (Jn 6:1–51), the Last Supper (Jn 12:1; 13:1–2, 21–28), and Jesus' death occur during or near the time of the Passover. Scholars debate whether Jesus died on the Passover or on the day of preparation, before the Passover. Pope Benedict seems to favor the latter view, which is the position presented in the Gospel of John.

Pesch, Rudolf: German biblical scholar whose scholarship points to the Jewish sources of John's Gospel.

Pharisees: Jewish movement, founded after the Babylonian exile, known for its strict adherence to the laws and regulations of the Torah. In Jesus' time and before, the Pharisees strongly resisted the Hellenistic and Roman influence on Jewish life. The Pharisees often opposed the Sadducees, another group within Judaism. After the destruction of the Second Temple in A.D. 70, Pharisaic theology became the basis for rabbinic Judaism. Jesus frequently disputed with the Pharisees.

Pilate, Pontius: Prefect of the Roman province of Judea between A.D. 26 and A.D. 36, Pilate was the Roman official in charge of the execution of Jesus. At the end of his reign, Pilate was removed for his brutality by the Roman emperor. Pilate is present in all four Gospel accounts (Mt 27:1–26; Mk 15:1–15; Lk 23:1–15; Jn 18:28—19:16).

Plotinus: Ancient philosopher (ca. 205–270) generally regarded as the founder of Neoplatonism, a development of the system of philosophy based on the ideas of the Greek philosopher Plato. He taught a form of the doctrine of *exitus* and *reditus*.

Qumran: Site of the discovery of the Dead Sea Scrolls. Located near the northwest corner of the Dead Sea, it was the dwelling place of the Essenes, a Jewish sect opposed to worship in the Herodean Temple in Jerusalem. There are some indications that John the Baptist and perhaps Jesus and his family may have had some association with this community, though the teaching of John and of Jesus differed significantly from that of the Qumran community.

Redaction criticism: A method of studying texts that seeks to understand how authors or editors have selected or shaped the material they have put into their texts.

Resurrection of Jesus: The entrance by Jesus, following his death on the Cross, into an entirely new form of life that lies beyond the order of natural biological generation (Mt 22:30), resuscitation, and dying (I Cor 15:42–44) and that includes a transformed bodily dimension of existence (I Cor 15:50–54), possessing physical (Lk 24:39; Jn 20:24–27) and spiritual (Lk 24:31; Jn 20:19) aspects. The Resurrection is the Father's vindication of Jesus' divine sonship (Acts 2:24; Rom 1:4) and validation of the believer's faith in Jesus' redemption of sinful humanity (I Cor 15:14, 17). It is also the pledge or "first fruits" of a general resurrection of the righteous (I Cor 15:23), the beginning of a new kind of humanity to be realized in the age to come. The Resurrection of Jesus is not the mere passing of a spirit into the next life or a miraculous resuscitation to mortal existence, as with Lazarus. It is an entirely new mode of bodily existence.

Regula fidei: Latin phrase meaning "rule of faith". The term refers to a short summary of the essential content of the Christian faith, which was linked to confessions of faith used in Baptism. Benedict XVI, along with many other scholars, sees such a rule of faith as the key to unlocking the interpretation of Scripture, according to Scripture's own spirit.

Reiser, Marius: Catholic theologian and philologist (b. 1954) to whose work Pope Benedict refers as an important contribution to new ways of interpreting the Bible.

Sacramentum: Latin term for "sacrament", which Catholic teaching defines as an outward sign and instrument of grace. Ordinarily it refers to one of the seven sacraments of the Church. However, the term is sometimes used more broadly with reference to the Church herself as the sacrament of salvation for the world (e.g., Vatican II, *Lumen Gentium* 1) or more generally to the mysteries of the life of Jesus. In his study Pope Benedict uses *sacramentum* in the last sense.

Sadducees: Jewish sect founded in the second century B.C., known for its denial of the afterlife, including the resurrection from the dead. The Sadducees at the time of Jesus were committed to the integration of Hellenism and Judaism, and they attempted to make the best of Roman rule. They often opposed the Pharisees, but were generally united with them in opposition to Jesus.

Saint Thomas Aquinas: Italian saint and Dominican theologian and philosopher (1225–1274). He is called the Angelic Doctor and is highly regarded in the Catholic theological tradition. Two of his major works are the *Summa Theologiae* and the *Summa Contra Gentiles.* Pope Benedict draws on the *Summa Theologiae*'s meditation on the mysteries of Christ's life for his own approach to the subject.

Sanhedrin: The assembly (Greek, *synēdrion*, "assembly") of Jewish leaders. In this context, it refers to the Council of Jewish leaders in Jerusalem who condemned Jesus to death for blasphemy and who turned him over to the Romans for execution for sedition.

Scapegoat: One of two male goats that featured in the ancient Day of Atonement liturgy. One goat, chosen by lot, was sacrificed to the Lord as a sin offering; the other, which came to be known as the scapegoat, was designated to bear the sins of Israel into the wilderness (Lev 16:7–10). According to the rite, the high priest confessed the iniquities of the people over the animal and symbolically placed their transgressions upon its head before banishing it to a barren land (Lev 16:20–22).

Schnackenburg, Rudolf: German Catholic biblical exegete (1914–2002) who attempted to correct some of what he saw as the imbalances of historical-critical scholarship in order to support the Catholic faithful. Pope Benedict agrees with his basic goal but not with particular elements of his interpretations.

Schönborn, Christoph Cardinal: Catholic Dominican theologian and archbishop of Vienna, Austria (b. 1945); primary editor of the *Catechism of the Catholic Church.* Pope Benedict refers to Cardinal Schönborn's Christological work.

Seewann, Maria-Irma: Contemporary German scholar and coauthor with Norbert Baumert, S.J., of an important article on the meaning of Jesus' words at the Last Supper (*Gregorianum* 89 [2008]).

Servant Songs: The name given to four poems in the Book of Isaiah that describe the "servant" of Yahweh (Is 42:1–9; 49:1–7; 50:4–11; 52:13—53:12). This mysterious figure is closely identified with Israel (Is 49:3), yet his mission is to bring salvation to Israel and the nations alike (Is 42:1; 49:6). Most striking is the revelation that redemption will come through the servant's bitter experience of suffering and death (Is 50:6; 53:3–12). Christian tradition from earliest times sees the fulfillment of these visions in Jesus as the suffering and saving Messiah.

Son of Man: Title used by Jesus for himself and only rarely by others with respect to Jesus (e.g., Acts 7:56). It has strong roots in the Old Testament, especially in the Book of Daniel (7:13–14). The figure of the Son of Man in Daniel shares in the authority of God, the Ancient of Days. Jesus uses the expression in this way to indicate his divine authority, not merely his human nature.

Stuhlmacher, Peter: German Protestant theologian and New Testament scholar (b. 1926).

Suffering Servant: A tragic figure whose rejection and violent abuse are graphically depicted in two of Isaiah's poems, called the third and fourth Servant Songs (Is 50:4–11; 52:13—53:12). Because his suffering and demise are portrayed by the Prophet as acts of redemption for sinners, Christian interpretation going back to New Testament times identified the Suffering Servant with Jesus Christ (e.g., Mt 8:17; Lk 22:37; Acts 8:32–35).

Synoptics (Synoptic Gospels): The Gospels of Matthew, Mark, and Luke. They are called "synoptic" Gospels because of their similar structures and use of much of the same material to narrate Christ's works and teachings. "Synoptic" means "same view" or "view together".

Torah: Refers generally to the Law of Moses and specifically to the Pentateuch, the first five books of the Hebrew Scriptures, or Old Testament: Genesis, Exodus, Leviticus, Numbers, and Deuteronomy.

Twelve, The: A special group of disciples chosen by Jesus and given special authority in the community of his disciples. They are sometimes called the twelve Apostles (Lk 6:13), although the term "apostle" can extend to a wider category of leaders who witnessed the Resurrection of Jesus (1 Cor 15:8). The Twelve represent the spiritual foundation of the new Israel of the Church as the old Israel was made up of the biological foundation of the twelve tribes.

Vanhoye, Albert Cardinal: Jesuit biblical scholar and leading expert on the interpretation of the Letter to the Hebrews (b. 1923). He was a longtime professor at the Pontifical Biblical Institute in Rome until his retirement in 1998. Vanhoye was made a cardinal by Pope Benedict in 2006.

Wilckens, Ulrich: Contemporary German Lutheran bishop and New Testament scholar (b. 1928) who has argued that the beloved disciple in John's Gospel was not a historical figure but a symbol. Pope Benedict rejects his view as incompatible with the Gospel of John's presentation of the beloved disciple as an eyewitness of the events it describes.

Yom Kippur: Hebrew expression meaning "day of atonement", which is the English term for the corresponding Jewish feast.

Zealots: A militantly anti-Roman Jewish sect that lived and agitated in Palestine from at least the mid-first century B.C. until it was annihilated during the Roman destruction of the Jewish rebellion, ca. A.D. 70. At least one of the Twelve, Simon, called the Zealot, seems at some point to have been a Zealot sympathizer (Lk 6:15).

Luke

Acts

Romans

I *Corinthians*